The Innovator's Sourcebook

The Innovator's Sourcebook

A guide to creating compelling business ideas

Dan Roberts

WEST FULTON MEDIA
CHICAGO, IL

The Innovator's Sourcebook
by Dan Roberts

Published by West Fulton Media, P.O. Box 3981, Chicago, IL 60654.

West Fulton books may be purchased for educational, business or sales promotional use. Electronic editions are also available for most titles. For more information, please contact West Fulton Media, P.O. Box 3981, Chicago, IL 60654.

Cover Photo: © Kevin L. Kitchens, www.Fotolia.com

Printing History:

> January 2010:   First Edition

ISBN-10: 0-9844164-0-4
ISBN-13: 978-0-9844164-0-0

To my parents, Terri and Ron, who have instilled in me the value of an entrepreneurial mindset and to my wife, Ali, who patiently listens to and encourages each of my many ideas.

Contents

Choose Your Own Ending

The Sources

New Market Strategies

New Process Strategies

New Product Strategies

Consumer Based Strategies

New Inputs and New Knowledge

Recurring Techniques

Preface

I never set out to write a book. This might seem like an odd way to start a preface, but let me explain. What I did set out to do was to become an entrepreneur. However, somewhere between starting down that path and starting a business venture, I got hung up. In fact, I got caught up right out of the gates, in the idea stage. I couldn't figure out what business I should start. It wasn't that I couldn't have chosen a random business to start and ran with it, I could have. But I wanted to create a business that I was passionate about. I wanted to create something new, something innovative that people hadn't seen before. So, I began looking for information on the topic of business idea generation. However, when I went searching for that information, it was nowhere to be found. Information on business ideas and how to generate them barely exists. I continued to search. I wanted to know everything about ideas and how to create them. Throughout my entire college career I searched. It is from the frustration and let down of that search that I became motivated to write this book. Nothing that I could find in my research resembled anything close to what I had been hoping for, so I decided to create it. I decided to piece together the fragments of what does exist and turn it into a logical whole. Not because I wanted to be an author, but for more self-serving reasons. I wanted a complete picture of how innovation happens and how to generate great business ideas. I wanted this information so that I could exploit it for the future.

The information that follows began as an exploration of my personal interest in entrepreneurship and business idea generation. It began as a set of notes. That is why in this book you will not find extensive research. You will find few charts, graphs or data. I did not spend years documenting and collecting data. The following information is simply a collection of observations, conversations, readings and general research I have done over the past seven odd years. If you find the information as useful as I have to wrap your mind around innovation, then this book will have accomplished its goal. The important thing to remember is that I do not purport any of this as absolute fact. The goal is for this information to be a foundation for myself and others on a topic that is so widely misunderstood.

The problem, and possibly the source of the confusion, is that most lessons in entrepreneurship start with a statement to the effect

of… "OK you have an idea, now this is how to start your business."
I have always thought that the idea stage has been brushed over.
Maybe I find it most unfortunate because I think the idea phase is
the most interesting phase of business. Few people get excited about
standard operating procedures or manufacturing process control. To
me the exciting part of business is strategizing and thinking of market
changing ideas. Unfortunately, the idea phase of entrepreneurship
has been passed off as a "fuzzy art." Attempts to harness creativity
have had lackluster results. People don't know how it happens, why
it happens or under what circumstances. It has been left to a flash-in-
the-pan, lighting strike or AHA! moment in the shower. Soon after
realizing that this was the prevailing mindset, I decided to start out on
my own.

    The real tipping point to figuring out where I was headed
came while I was reading Innovation and Entrepreneurship by
Peter Drucker. In the book, Drucker set out to identify the sources
of innovation and he believed they could be identified. He also
believed that you could uncover the sources of innovation using a
systematic approach. He was one of the first to propose this and
many businessmen were critical of his efforts. I realized that what he
was doing was setting the stage for what I wanted to understand. I
wanted to better understand the source of ideas and the sources of
innovation. Where do they come from? Why? How? I wanted to
understand the framework of innovation and start finding ways to
make it systematic. I believe the information in this book is a solid
start to understanding these things. While there will never be a "how-
to" for innovation, I think you can get closer to a "how-to" approach
than Drucker offered. The resulting body of knowledge is something
I wish I had available to refer to over the past few years.

    As you begin to read this book, please feel free to skip around,
mix and match ideas and make the best sense of the information in
your own way. I have found that most of the information in this book
came together for myself in such a way. Each topic or source that I
discuss draws from many influences that I subsequently mixed and
matched. Some of the things mentioned are common and referred
to over and over again in many business disciplines. Other things in
the book are more subtle observations. The setup grabs one nugget
of an idea from an individual combined with another fragment of
an idea from a random conversation. The point is that you could
aggregate this same knowledge just like I have, but it wouldn't all
be found in one spot. I could pinpoint most of the original sources

and how I came across them. However, to get to this point where I could build a substantial body of knowledge about ideas, articulate it and differentiate between the sources has taken seven years. I don't think it should be that way. I would like to see the idea side of entrepreneurship get much more attention. I wrote the book for people to have a convenient whole as a starting point. Then I hope the next six or seven years of their lives can be spent diving deeper and building on that foundation.

Anyway, that is the driving purpose behind this book. Take the information for what it is worth, and I hope that it may serve as a foundation for your future entrepreneurial undertakings.

- Dan Roberts

Chapter 1:
The Most Basic Answer

"The lessons taught in great books are misleading. The commerce in life is rarely so simple and never so just."

- Anita Brookner

The drive to become an entrepreneur these days is as strong as it has ever been. Most of you probably feel overdue to take the plunge. However it probably isn't the motivation that is stopping you. The more likely roadblock is; what business should I start? or, how do I find a great idea for a business? At first, this doesn't seem like too difficult of a barrier to overcome. In fact, it shouldn't take long to come across the standard "how-to" answer. You've likely already encountered this answer if you have explored the topic before. The obligatory response is that you simply "solve a problem." You may also get the same answer with slightly different phrasing such as, "fulfill an unmet market need." However, they are essentially saying the same thing. I truly wonder if anyone has ever encountered these responses and been satisfied with the advice. Where should you look for this "problem?" It doesn't say. How do I create novel solutions? It doesn't say. In fact it doesn't give you any direction at all. What is sad is that this response might be the only answer that most people encounter in their lifetime. It might be all of the face time that the origin of business ideas gets as you continue your search. Most classes, most books and most discussions do not branch beyond this simple answer. Why? Because expanding on that answer directs you down a road of fuzzy concepts and hard to conceptualize notions. The answers to those questions do not fit into a process or an easy to explain theorem for innovation. I do not claim that this basic answer is incorrect, but it is a cliché and extremely vague. This chapter examines the basic answer and then the rest of the book requires that you go beyond it to get a full understanding of how to create truly great business ideas.

Entrepreneurial books and teachings consistently glaze over the idea creation stage of business. They would say something to the effect of "Ok, you have a business idea, now this is how you start the business." In my mind the second phase of business building after the idea is the most concrete. It is more of a process. As a marketing and logistics major, I am fully aware of how to manipulate marketing principles, logistical problems and the like once something exists. I know the concepts and I know how to put them in motion. The thing that bothers me is that the foundation of all those things we study so in depth gets the least attention, meaning the idea. So the rest of this chapter is the basic understanding of the origin of business ideas. It is a foundation for future discussions and needed to be mentioned. At the same time, do not let it be the only concept that forms your mindset on the sources of innovation. You need to dive deeper.

We begin with the premise that you need to find a problem or fulfill an unmet market need in order to form a business. Albeit vague, this is generally a true statement. So what are these problems and unmet needs? How do you characterize them? Even when probing beyond the first generalized answer, you would most likely get another such generalization. You might find something to the effect of "problems and unmet needs are where a gap exists between what the consumer demands (or should demand) and what they are actually getting from the market." Essentially, consumer demands or ideal states of being are not being met. A gap exists that needs filling. That is where entrepreneurs come in. Entrepreneurs fill, or at least close, the gap between what consumers want and what they actually are getting. How do they do that? Most simply, they achieve this by employing innovation and starting innovative ventures. They take the inputs that are available in the market and combine them in new ways to create value. That increase in value is what closes the gap for the consumer and gets them closer to their ideal solution. This second level of generalization is not much more helpful than the original answer. In fact, it barely elaborates on it. Sources that give you these type of answers will keep generalizing until you go away. Committing to a "how-to" statement is not in their best interest.

Another caveat to the most basic answer is that it does not differentiate between different levels of problems. When it instructs you to find a problem to solve, it does not say whether you should be looking to create an entirely new market or whether you should uncover a problem with a specific machine in a manufacturing plant. I guess this is purposeful so that you consider all problems, but this also creates a problem of its own. There are different levels of problems. Finding out that machine A has only 67% efficiency when it could have 72% efficiency is a minor consideration in the overall scheme of the business world. However, figuring out that the attitudes of 37 million people are shifting and are going to change an industry's landscape in the next five years is a much more interesting problem. In this book we are going to show you the different levels of where problems occur. It has to first start with consumers and their changing needs. Then you can get incrementally more specific in the business world to consider problems at the industry level, the firm level and finally individual products and processes. Not all problems are created equal and the most basic answer fails to distinguish that for the entrepreneur.

Somewhere between the basic sources of ideas (problems / unmet needs) and the end product of an innovative idea, a venture, is the process of actually formulating one. Many people aspire to be entrepreneurs and yet so few take the plunge. Even of those few who do, only a fraction of them succeed. Is it that entrepreneurs have great ideas and fail at the more concrete skills such as marketing and financing? Or is it the case that all of their more concrete practices such as marketing and financing are based on a poor idea? It is hard to say and obviously a bit of both. The one thing that is apparent is that one of these downfalls is much easier to avoid. You can read volumes of textbooks and readings on the major topics in business such as finance, marketing and economics. College business students probably read in excess of 30 such texts. However, the most course reading I ever had in college on the topic of idea creation and formulating ideas amounted to seven pages of a 560 page entrepreneurship text. Even then, those seven pages were encountered in an elective course, and weren't required. Those seven pages produced no new insights but did harp on the "most basic answer" that I keep referring to. The point here is that among all of the teachings available to aspiring entrepreneurs, few go beyond the most basic answer to creating business ideas, even in a scholarly business setting.

Think about it this way. Every business in the world was founded on an entrepreneur's desire to bring an idea to life. The intensity with which we study everything that happens after the idea is set in motion is incredible, yet the idea which was a tipping point to becoming entrepreneurial is rarely given a second glance. Of all the interesting ideas in the world and the "why didn't I think of that" type moments, the best we can come up with is that formulating business ideas is about "fulfilling an unmet need." The best tactic for formulating these unmet needs is something I learned in second grade; brainstorming. Literally, it is the best that all of the great business thinkers of the world could come up with since brainstorming was first articulated over six decades ago. Innovation has been left to AHA! random connection of neurons. Creativity and ideation are seen as a "fuzzy arts" and the best way we can articulate what happens is that entrepreneurs envision ways to "fulfill an unmet need." What it truly boils down to is that they simply do not care to go further. Why should they? Business schools and business teachings are more interested in making you successful as an employee as opposed to teaching you how to become an employer.

Enough ranting. Lucky for me, I've had a few professors and friends over the course of the years who pointed me in the right direction. As I will strive to do in this book, they gave me my starting point, somewhere to start looking. A book was recommended to me by my Professor of Marketing, Roger Blackwell. That book was Innovation and Entrepreneurship by Peter Drucker. That book is what started me down the path to writing this book. Drucker believed that the sources of innovation were identifiable and knowable. He believed that you could systematically identify and manage for innovation. He was also the first to assert that innovation should not be left to randomness. Drucker believed in a proactive and systematic search for ideas. That core theme will guide the remainder of this book.

As I mentioned, there is not a lot of good material on the subject of creating great business ideas, but in the same breath I said that Peter Drucker has a book on it. Let's add a little bit to the most basic answer. Let's briefly take a look at the first people who have attempted to characterize these "problems" and "unmet needs." We'll look at some of the first attempts to expand beyond these base statements. Granted, there is more material and ideas than I could put into this chapter, but I do want to touch on two of the main thinkers who are mentioned when we speak of innovation. These are usually the first two people you would encounter if you did any serious searching for answers to your innovation questions. Their ideas and theories changed the way we categorize innovation and think about it. Their ideas are the next steps beyond the most basic answer. The first individual is economist Joseph Schumpeter.

Joseph Schumpeter's name is mentioned quite often in the entrepreneurship realm. His work in the area bears his namesake, Schumpeterian Economics. Schumpeter is well known for examining the entrepreneur's role in the economy and describing how entrepreneurs affect markets. Basically, Schumpeter said that the entrepreneur was a disruptive force in the marketplace. They are the agents of change. His view was that entrepreneurs employ "creative destruction" to overthrow established industries and players.1 Schumpeter looked at how individuals had the power to affect entire industries with their ideas. The title of creative destruction comes from the idea that the new and novel business ideas that entrepreneurs employ have the power to change the way things are done. They destroy the industry by creating new rules and bases of competition. Months or years down the road when the original entrepreneur becomes the incumbent firm, they are also susceptible to being on the other end of the equation. The point of this is that Schumpeter's thinking in economics began to bring to light how entrepreneurs accomplish what they do. His ideas started to give us a basis beyond "solve a problem."

The second thing that Schumpeter described was a categorization of what new innovations are. He described for us what the end products are that entrepreneurs bring about. Although his initial purpose was categorization for the sake of economic thought, we, as innovators of the present can use his theories to figure out the "how" of innovation. We do this by taking his end categories and reasoning backwards. Schumpeter said that innovation came from new products, new processes, new knowledge, new markets and new business models.2 While he doesn't go on to tell you how to create them, it does form a good base of where innovation comes from in a general sense. His ideas start to put meat on the bones of our proposed structure. We went from an original nugget of where to start thinking about business ventures, to his theories about the end results of innovation. It is up to us to fill in the gaps. It is up to this book to figure out how to get you from point A to point B. Eventually we should have a relatively clear picture of what innovation is and how we can capture it. Our objective is going to be the "how" instead of the "what" that Schumpeter has contributed.

The second person that was influential in building on the most basic answer is Peter Drucker. While Drucker is probably best known for his ideas and writings on management, he also penned a book that shed some light on the origins of innovation. Drucker took a lot of criticism for the book, Innovation and Entrepreneurship, in which he attempts to identify the sources of innovation and how to recognize them. I think the most crucial thing that Drucker accomplished with

---

1 Baretto, H., "The Entrepreneur Throughout the History of Economic Thought," pp. 4-44.

2 Schumpeter, Joseph. The Theory of Economic Development. Cambridge, MA: Harvard Business School Press, 1934.

the book was instilling the thought that sources of innovation could be known and that humans could actively pursue innovation. His ideas were the first attempt to fill in the gaps that Schumpeter left us with. Drucker said that innovation comes from seven places that can be systematically identified and managed. Those places are: The Unexpected (random occurrences), Incongruities (unmet consumer needs), Process Needs, Industry and Market Structure Changes, Shifting Demographics, Changes in Perception and New Knowledge.3 Drucker expanded on some of Schumpeter's thoughts and also added some of his own. In chapter 34 I will elaborate on each of these seven sources and how they fit into the overall picture of innovation, but for now just realize his efforts to fill in the gap of innovation knowledge. Drucker's ideas are about being able to recognize chances to innovate. His focus was to prepare managers to see opportunities in the constantly changing business landscape. He was the first to make such a bold assertion that innovation could be systematically identified and managed. For that reason, Drucker was an inspiration for this book. However, Drucker stopped well short of producing a comprehensive text on the topic of innovation and entrepreneurship. While influential, his ideas lock practitioners into a waiting mode, waiting to identify change. His work doesn't focus on the creation of ideas or the creation of new markets. This book is going to expand on Drucker and try to take it from recognizing opportunity to creating opportunities.

In this chapter I have presented to you the most basic answer for the sources of innovation and some supplemental thinking around the most basic answer. Don't expect much more from any other source. The most basic answer is what a majority of the business population understands as the way to create business ideas. I would guess that most business people actually have less depth of knowledge on the subject than I just presented you. The goal of this book is to go way beyond this. The goal is to get specific and tread the same controversial waters that Drucker did. It will follow the theme that sources of innovation are identifiable and knowable. The rest of the book is designed to fill in the rest of gaps for you. Knowing about point A and point B is relatively worthless unless you have the means to get from one to the other.

---

3 Drucker, Peter. Innovation and Entrepreneurship. New York, NY: HarperCollins Publishers Inc., 1993 pp.35

Chapter 2:
Problem Finding

"The mere formulation of a problem is often far more essential than its solution, which may be merely a matter of mathematical or experimental skill. To raise new questions, new possibilities, to regard old problems from a new angle requires creative imagination and marks real advances in science."

- Albert Einstein

Find and solve a problem. Fulfill an unmet need. This is the equivalent of telling an art student to paint something culturally relevant and then walking away without further direction. Without the knowledge of color theory, composition, drawing techniques, cultural values, et cetera that person would be at a loss trying to figure out how to achieve success in the art world. But this happens in the world of entrepreneurship. Potential entrepreneurs are given these brief tips for success and then left to fend for themselves. What I want to do with the second chapter of this book is to give you something actionable right now. I want you to have something that, if you walked away from the book after this chapter, would be worth the price of admission. This chapter is a systematic approach to finding problems to solve. It is a process that you can use to find unmet needs in the marketplace. It is the answer to "how" we find problems and unmet needs that seems to trip up so many would-be entrepreneurs. You can use this technique from square one without any specific focus or idea of where you are headed. I do not claim to be the originator of this process. I owe this entire chapter to the late Richard M. White and his process titled "market gap analysis."[4] Having to pull this information from a chapter in his obscure book from 1977 titled The Entrepreneur's Manual is a sign of just how fragmented the idea market is. Without further ado, let's take a look at the process, the idea behind it and how we can use it.

To preface White's method of market gap analysis, we should be aware of what it is that he sought to accomplish and why it works. A great quote from Gilbert K. Chesterton comes to mind that illustrates the problem White was trying to diminish. Chesterton said,

---

4 White, Richard M. The Entrepreneur's Manual. Radnor, PA: Chilton Book Company, 1977, pp. 52 – 59.

"the perplexity of life arises from there being too many interesting
things in it for us to be interested properly in any of them." When
we are given the insight that in order to innovate we must find and
solve problems, we are left with a vast sea of possibilities. There are
too many interesting avenues we could take, which leaves us at a loss
about where to start. Essentially we need to focus in. White presents
a concrete method for identifying problems or "market gaps" as he
calls them. The process works because it allows us to start with no
previous conception of where you are headed and systematically
forces you to focus in and hone your thought stream. In the process
you break down a sea of potential markets into a smaller, more
manageable subset of ideas. When we are able to break it down in
this manner, our mind is able to wrap itself around the task at hand.
We are now able to have relevant, specific thought streams that
address innovation and allow us to identify potential problems. By
the last step we have concrete avenues and issues to research. Let's
now look at the process and see how White accomplishes all of these
things.

Step 1: Choose an Industry

While White didn't specifically state this as his first step, this
is a helpful precursor to his process. This is the first and only time
in this book that I will advise that you pick any industry, even at
random if you so choose. It can be however broad or narrow as you
choose. Call it travel or leisure or entertainment, it doesn't matter.
This process inherently has you focus in by the end, so feel free to
choose any industry that interests you at the outset. The process
is also relatively quick, so if you have lackluster results with one
industry, it doesn't take much to start all over. By the way, this isn't
just a read and remember chapter. Get out your pen and actually try
this. Without doing so, you will never appreciate the value.

Step 2: Lay out Objectives

For the second step, White says that we need to lay out our
objectives for the potential idea or venture. What he means by this
is that we need to define what type of opportunity we are willing to
pursue and what types we are not. Throughout the process White has
us continually coming back and comparing potential ideas with our
objectives. Any potential avenues or problems that we uncover that
do not match with the objectives of the venture can then be eliminated

so we can focus on problems that will meet the criteria we want in an idea. Some examples of criteria might be;

1. Must have a potential market of at least 1 million units
2. Must be a physical product, not a service
3. Total market potential must be $500 million plus
4. Must be able to attain at least 10% of that industry
5. Must be an electrical device

He also adds that you must address personal objectives and the type of industry when you lay this out. For instance;

6. Want to pursue a long term growth industry
7. Founders are visible in the public eye
8. Ability to attract top talent from other firms with the idea.

By incorporating your personal goals along with the objectives of the product, you get a clearer picture of the type of venture you want to start. By doing this you eliminate a lot of avenues that would never provide you with the opportunity you were searching for. It is the first level of focusing your efforts. Also, White mentions that numerous objectives might seem too restrictive to produce anything viable. You will quickly see that this is not the case. Ten to twelve objectives is considered low demands by White. Hashing out all your objectives is key to finding the right match for your venture. At this point, you want to write down your objectives for a venture. Putting the goals and necessities of your venture on paper now will eliminate a lot of the clutter for the future. Do this now on your own.

Step 3: Segment Your Industry into Major Components
For the purpose of examples, I am going to use the "Entertainment" industry as my industry of focus. The third step involves breaking down your industry of focus into its major components. This means you want to break it down into the types of entertainment you could possibly explore and also the potential consumers. Most of these examples are taken directly from White.

1. Senior Citizen, Adult, Children, Family
2. Male, Female, Both
3. Active, Passive or Combination

4. Indoor, Outdoor
5. Spring, Fall, Winter, Summer
6. Lower Class, Middle Class, Upper Class
7. Black, White, Hispanic, Combination or All

You can come up with any method for segmenting a market. These are just a few examples. As we proceed we are going to choose one of these major segments. Say, for instance, we choose Adult Entertainment (not in the pornography sense). This is another level of focusing in. By choosing this we are ignoring senior citizen entertainment, children's entertainment, family entertainment, et cetera. White has us follow only one leg of one of the major category breakdowns. You can always come back to this step and choose a different leg, but in order to focus, you only choose one at a time. Do this now with your pen and paper.

Step 4: Segment Again into Major Categories

The next step is to take the avenue we selected in step 3, adult entertainment, and segment it further into its major categories. Some good examples of how to segment might be the times adults have available for entertainment or the types of entertainment. Let's look at some of those breakdowns.

1. Weekday, Weekend, Vacation, Holiday, Retirement
2. Movies, Music, Art, Reading

Since I do not want to just blindly copy White's book, I am going to take a slightly different direction than he did with our example. However, I thought it was interesting that when he segmented the categories by time available to pursue them, it made it extremely easy to identify problems. For instance, if he chose weekday as his category, in the next step he would break it down into all the major time categories available in a day. Pre-breakfast, Breakfast, After Breakfast/ Before Lunch, Coffee breaks, et cetera. Segmentation is about getting specific. For some reason, "time" segmentation makes it easy to identify with in your mind.

Step 5: Segment Again into Major Categories

For my example I chose movies. So now we are at Adult-Entertainment-Movies. Again we break this down into its major categories.

1. DVDs, VHS, Internet Downloads
2. Pay per View, Movie Rentals, TV Movies, Theater Visits
3. Independent Movies, Major Motion Pictures

White says "You'll note that so far, all that we have done is focus, magnify, refocus, remagnify, refocus again, remagnify again until the large growth industry is divided into handleable portions. An industry like the [entertainment] industry is so large that you cannot begin to see it until you segment it down to its sub-sections. We are now just beginning to see the trees in the forest. The more complex an industry, the more you have to divide, redivide and reredivide."

Step 6: Elimination Based on Objectives

In this step you now take the breakdown of step 5 and eliminate any categories that do not mesh with the objectives you stated at the outset of this process. You may be able to keep them all intact or you may eliminate 75% of the subsets. Results will vary widely depending on the individual and their goals. Take a moment to briefly compare whether you think any of your segmented categories can be eliminated at this point based on your objectives.

Step 7: Identify Problems with the Subset You Select

For this step I am going to choose "theater visits" as my category to continue with. So now we are at Adult-Entertainment-Movies-Theater Visits. It should now be much easier to concentrate on identifying problems. If you hadn't been given some substance and a process to follow, trying to identify a "problem" out in the vast seas of possibilities might have lead you down a completely irrelevant path. You may have never even started thinking, you might have just given up and gone to mow the lawn or watch television. But with a specific stream of thought, you are now at a place that is much more specific. You are now faced with identifying problems when adults seek entertainment by making a trip to the movie theater. This is something we can all identify with and a specific situation on which we can focus our minds. Now let's explore some of the problems with this activity. I will limit my list to fifteen because I think you will get the point.

1. Going to the movies is expensive at $9.50 a ticket, $3.00 a gallon for gas, $5.00 for drink and $4.00 for candy, I can't afford to go see the movies I want to
2. Theaters are noisy, I have to hope that my fellow moviegoers do not include the teenage population, babies, cell phones, et cetera
3. Seats are uncomfortable
4. The floor is somehow always sticky
5. The person in front of me is blocking 1/8th of the screen and I have to crane my neck
6. The best seats are always taken. I end up in the front row or way in the back
7. I can't find more than one seat open and I have two people with me
8. Having to leave for the restroom or snacks, I miss part of the movie
9. My show is sold out and the next movie isn't for another hour and a half
10. The noise level is too loud
11. The theater is always cold
12. I feel cramped by the leg room
13. Only the theater built in 1978 is showing the movie I want to see so the picture quality is outdated
14. The closest movie theater is a 20 minute drive
15. Dinner finished early and I have an hour to kill before the movie starts

You could continue on and identify a plethora of other problems that exist with theater visits. When you actually perform a market gap analysis, please do exhaust the list with your ideas as it will give you the most opportunity to take advantage of this type of analysis.

Step 8: Eliminate Problems That Do Not Mesh

Step eight is the second round of elimination of those things that do not mesh well with the objectives we set out at the beginning of the exercise. Let's say for instance that I have no real interest in solving the problem that "theaters are too cold." I would eliminate this from my list and focus on those areas where I feel I have the skills to solve the problems at hand. Continue to eliminate problems until you are satisfied that the problems left have the capability to match the objectives of the venture.

Step 9: Matrix Analysis (White's title)

A "matrix analysis" sounds more complicated than it actually is. In this step you want to list out all of the problems you are moving forward with along the left hand side of a piece of paper. Then across the top of the paper from left to right you are going to make a column for each of the objectives you laid out at the outset of the process. After you have done that, go through each problem and place a check mark under each objective column that you feel the solution to that problem would mesh with. Once you have thought through this process and have a final tally, you want to move forward in this analysis with those problems you feel best match your objectives and capabilities.

Step 10: Listing Ideas for Solutions

At this point we have accomplished the goal of this chapter. Instead of aimlessly trying to locate problems, we have shown you a process to systematically identify where they might lie. The key part of the understanding of this chapter was to develop a way to add substance to the common mantra of "find a problem to solve." We have done that. This advice isn't as vague or obscure now that we have a substantive process with which to find those problems. From here we are going to proceed in two ways. First, I will tell you how White finishes his process and how he talks about solving problems. Secondly, we can diverge from White's process and talk about how this book and its chapters can aide you in solving the problems you have located. First for White.

Moving Forward with step 10, White recommends that you start listing out all of the possible solutions to each of the problems you have identified. This is pretty much a think tank/ brainstorming session. You can now start to theorize and explore ways in which to solve the problems you have uncovered. White suggests that you list as many possible solution avenues as you can come up with. Taking different angles and theorizing different solutions will allow you to get the whole picture.

Step 11: Select the Best Opportunities and Test Them

This step is mostly self explanatory. After you have exhausted your list of problems with all the possible solutions you can come up with, it is time to start testing the validity of some of those solution avenues. This is where the leg work of innovation begins to come in and branches out beyond the scope of this book. In this stage you want to start testing whether your ideas could actually solve the problem. This step is mostly about research and exploration. It is also about testing some of the assumptions you have made up until this point. For instance, you might discover that a solution you thought would have a 1 million unit market in fact is only a 200,000 unit market and, by your standards, not worth pursuing. Many books and texts will show you methods to test market viability and research methods to test the validity of your ideas. That is beyond the scope of what we are doing here, but I trust you will have no problem locating numerous sources that have some concrete methods for your analysis.

At this point White ends his process. He has given you the means necessary to identify problems and cuts you loose to research, test and compare solutions that you might employ. What White has given us is the great start. I keep reiterating that most books on entrepreneurship and new venture creation start by saying "OK, you have an idea...now here is how to build a business." White gets us closer to that point. Now we actually do have an idea or at least a problem to wrestle with. We have direction and can start working with more concrete processes. After identifying the problems you want to solve, the rest is leg work. It is about perseverance and a determination to find a solution. It is about research, testing, prototypes, et cetera. Once you have a direction, the rest is up to you. If you don't like the direction you have, White has given you a process to uncover a million more directions to start with. For me, having that starting point is the most reassuring part. I know that once I have a direction I am passionate about, I will do the leg work, the research and continue to push for solutions. The hard part was getting that first inkling of where to go, seeing where the problems lie. More importantly we have relevant problems to solve, not just-plucked-out-of-a-hat problems that we might have found given little initial direction. Now that we have that start, we can move forward with the concrete areas of work and getting closer to launching a venture.

As I mentioned before, we also need to look at how we can use the chapters of this book as well as White's "now solve it" ending to his process. I think what is unique about this book is that many of the chapters are essentially solution techniques that produce novel results. I think when White said to "think of all the possible solutions," what he was basically telling you to do was

use brainstorming to finish out the process. While brainstorming
is a good method, this ending to such a great process is somewhat
lackluster. We all know how to brainstorm. I think employing
some of the chapters of the book as solution methods can be much
more innovative. What I mean by this is that when you look at the
problems you have identified, you can start to run down all of the
innovative ways in which people create ventures to see what might
be applicable to the problems you have identified. The chapters
of the book are some of the areas and solution methods that the
entrepreneurial community have identified as methods that produce
novel results and consistently innovative solutions. Utilizing their
power can make the efforts of "market gap analysis" that much more
meaningful. Instead of just brainstorming, you can employ tactics
that, often, inherently create novel solutions to problems. So my
advice to you is that if you choose to use White's market gap analysis,
take his ending one step further by employing some of the updated
methods for solving problems innovatively. This greatly increases the
chances that you will be able to find novel business ideas and avenues
of success to further pursue.

I want to start wrapping up this chapter with some final
insights that Richard White laid out for his market gap analysis. The
first thing that I wanted to mention is a process White talks about
for choosing your industry of focus. White mentions that in order
to sustain and grow a firm, we need to pick industries that have the
potential for growth. Identifying a growth industry at the outset of
the market gap analysis will help ensure that any solutions you start
to come up with will not be lost efforts in a mature market space.
White said that in order to find the industries that people are calling
"growth" industries, you had to look no further than some of the
investment people and firms out there making decisions. Banks,
mutual funds, venture capitalists and other sources of funding for
ventures are a good way to see where smart people are putting
their money. These groups will generally have defined the growth
industries they believe will propel their investments for the future.
If you want to identify growth markets, start targeting your market
gap analysis around those industries that these people are investing
in. Ask around. Many magazines, websites and blogs will give you a
pretty clear picture of where growth industries may lie for the future.

Another caveat to market gap analysis that White talks about
is being able to classify the opportunities and solutions that you come
up with. Not all of the areas of opportunity are going to be right to

pursue. Part of this is common sense and part of it is investigatory
work. White put his opportunities into three main categories; long
term growth market, short term growth or mirages. Short term
growth markets were those markets where opportunity existed but
the chance to take advantage of it would be fleeting and short lived.
He also identified mirages where at first glimpse it might seem as
though there is a chance for growth, but in actuality the solution may
not be viable. An instance of this would be that there is a problem,
we have a solution, people would like it but they wouldn't be willing
to pay for the solution. Mirages are typically problems that exist but
consumers are not willing to pursue solutions because they are so
minor or maybe the solution is too complex to warrant a purchase.
Therefore, White recommends sticking to only opportunities that
you believe your research shows are going to be long term growth
industries. These are industries characterized by long term needs and
willingness of consumers to pay. Long term growth industries are
measured in years or decades whereas short term growth industries
might be measured in months. Know the difference between these
areas of opportunity and be conscious as you move forward that the
best venture ideas are founded in long term growth industries.

The final point is this, do not simply read this chapter. This
chapter is meant to show you the process. Only by actually doing
the process yourself on paper and putting in the time will you get
anything out of this. The more you practice something, the better you
can become at it. This chapter is no different. Start practicing now
and start putting in the effort it takes to uncover truly great sources
of business ideas. Just understanding the chapter is not enough. The
ideas aren't going to fall in your lap, so start doing a proactive search
for them. The more searching you do, the better your odds of success
will become.

It took me seven years to find this obscure, out of print method
that Richard White put to paper in 1977. Although this process is
not mind-blowing and is intuitive once someone shows it to you, I
think that it hits on a point that is often lost in innovation teachings.
Innovation is about breaking things down, taking one small step at
a time. Only later can you piece together the total picture. The nice
thing about White's method is that it can give you a kick-start if you
are spinning your wheels trying to locate a venture to start. It is
reassuring to know that you can start to define a direction and start
right now versus wandering aimlessly, wondering when intuitive
thought might hit. White's method gives us a way to break down

"finding problems" into manageable pieces and a definable direction. Utilize this as often as possible and I am sure that you will start seeing the world and its problems in a new light. In combination with the solution chapters of this book, you will be well on your way to creating great business ideas.

Chapter 3:
The Mindset

"Take charge, if no one knows what the future holds, your vision to navigate it is as good as anyone's. The future may as well belong to you."

- The Entrepreneurial Mindset

Even before you read the last chapter, I am sure that you have had at least a couple of ideas for businesses that you have not acted on. You've most likely had some ideas that weren't half bad, but not enough to tip you over the edge to starting your own venture. In this chapter I want to examine why this is the case with so many people in our society. What is it that keeps a majority of the population tied down as an employee, even when they have the motivation not to be? I want to look at why that one great business idea hasn't popped in to the minds of so many people who are searching for it. They say that ideas are a dime a dozen. If that is true, I would have never written this book and you would have never bought it. Let's take a look at the prevailing mindset and then see how we can change it to increase our odds of success for the future.

My viewpoint on this issue was forever changed by my professor of entrepreneurship, Michael Camp. What he talked about and what I came to figure out, is that the iconic status of the entrepreneur in America is at least part of the problem with the mindset of most would-be innovators in our society. What happens is that a mindset is formed that stems from the image of the successful entrepreneur in American culture. The entrepreneur is looked on as a wildly creative, constantly innovating individual. The entrepreneur has the stereotype of being a daring risk taker and a disruptive force in the marketplace. Notable Entrepreneurs usually have turbulent histories where they have risked everything on a business venture. They usually have fought back from the brink of financial disaster to be successful. They are viewed as having special personal qualities and that they are willing to sacrifice all else above work. Over time the original entrepreneur turns from a man with an idea into a myth and eventually a legend. Almost immediately the thought of replicating the successes of other "entrepreneurs" and their ideas is daunting.

With such a stereotype prevailing, a mindset is cast in the

minds of would be entrepreneurs. Potential entrepreneurs tend
to only see the end accomplishments of these iconic individuals.
What happens is that we start to believe that their entrepreneurial
accomplishments were envisioned from the outset. We seem to think
that the great innovators of our time were capable of dreaming up
new and daring markets and then subsequently went to work to make
them a reality. However, it is interesting to learn that this is certainly
not the case. In most cases wildly innovative entrepreneurs had little
clue as to what they were creating at the outset. In most cases they
were simply individuals who pursued what they loved to do with
tenacity. They pursued what they loved and solved the problems at
hand. At some point thereafter the world dubbed them innovative
and gave their innovation a catchy name. But, the entrepreneurs at
the time would not have been able to articulate their end situation.

Amadeo Giannini, the founder of the American Bank of
Italy, later merged with Bank of America, had no idea that he was
in the process of developing "branch banking" when he began to
expand his bank into multiple locations. His goal of expansion was
simply to have access to more money from a larger pool of Italian
immigrants. Giannini's idea to open multiple locations was also the
result of the 1906 San Francisco earthquake and the ensuing fires. He
almost lost all of his client's savings when his only location burned
to the ground. "Branch Banking" as it is known today was partially
created to distribute the risk of having one single location.[5] Likewise,
Ted Turner would not have told you in 1970 that his purchase of a
bankrupt television station was the first step to creating a 24 hour a
day new source that he would dub "CNN".[6] There are many stories
of great innovators that did not start out as great innovators. These
entrepreneurs did go on to create incredibly innovative concepts.
However, the initial entrepreneurial thrust was not conceived of in
this way. America gave the complex set of solved problems a name
and blanketed it into a convenient entity. These individuals could
not have envisioned their final outcomes from the start. This is what
I believe too many entrepreneurs attempt to do from the outset.
Would-be entrepreneurs too often try and develop the entire roadmap
from the beginning. They are trying to envision their "grand
innovation" from the first moment they try to think of ideas. They do
this without realizing that the successful innovators before them did

---

5 "Democratizers." They Made America. PBS Broadcasting. WBGH, Boston. (AP Gianinni)

6 "Pioneers." They Made America. PBS Broadcasting. WBGH, Boston. (Ted Turner)

not, and could not have sat down and brainstormed everything at one time. However, America's love of entrepreneurs and the aura of myth that surrounds them contributes to society's belief that this could be the case. Consequently, novice entrepreneurs are often doomed from the starting block.

The mindset that is created concretes the dilemma that is most damaging to new entrepreneurs. If potential entrepreneurs are under the impression that market disrupting ideas are planned from the beginning, they will start their search looking for these grand innovations. The whole process of duplicating such success is made highly unlikely. Novice entrepreneurs that buy into this are destined to be thinking through potential ideas on too grand of a scale. Potential ideas for businesses are being looked at through the wrong lens. If entrepreneurs are thinking on a scale where everything can be planned, then there is little chance for any viable business ideas to come forth. Chances are if the course could be envisioned by you, then it could be envisioned by another person. It is the first step to what makes the formulation of new business ideas so difficult in the first place.

So now what? The would-be entrepreneur has failed to conceive of the next big idea, the next innovation or the next big money generating business. What will they do? It has been my experience that when they take the entrepreneurial plunge they will revert back to very small ideas. They revert back to a comfort zone. They go back to ideas that already exist or put a small spin on existing ideas. They will start the next consulting business or the next spin on the day spa. They will start the next pet pampering business or eBay small business. They have failed to generate the wildly innovative idea that makes entrepreneurs into the myth they are today. They will revert back to smaller ideas. In the process they have lost what is inherently exciting about entrepreneurship. They have lost any room for real innovation to grow. Even though they may not be able to start out as incredibly innovative, they have pushed themselves back into a realm where they have left little overhead room for any innovation to come through. Many people have their favorite entrepreneurial stories and I doubt very many of them involve consulting or spa ownership. The point is, you may not be able to picture how you would ramp up to the next Bill Gates at the outset of your idea creation sessions, but at least do not back into a space that will prevent the possibility of such accomplishments.

Would be entrepreneurs who have reverted back to smaller

ideas are on the right track, however they fail to recognize any middle ground. They are trying to conceive of the grand innovation or they are not innovating whatsoever. When discussing this middle ground of ideas, a quote from The Entrepreneurial Mindset comes into mind. "…We ask aspiring entrepreneurs to go out and look only for business opportunities with the potential to generate twice as much income for themselves [at maturity] as they would earn if they continued to work in their present position." "Then we insist that they design a business that will get them there in two to three years."7 That is the middle ground. You wouldn't propose to have someone fund your trip to Mount Everest without having scaled a peak half of its size. Do not go through the ideation process thinking that it would be any different in a business setting. Focus your thinking on this middle ground. Focus your ideation sessions to get your salary to this level and then go from there. Shape your business ideas so that this is the case.

If potential entrepreneurs can grasp this concept and be conscious during the idea generation stage that this is the case, then we have already made progress in new venture idea formulation. A would be entrepreneur can now begin to establish this as a mindset. A mindset that is no different than any other area of life. People think through daily decisions in the context of their religious readings or in the context of their values. This is no different. If this mindset can be adopted, then many hours of time and effort could be saved and refocused onto creating viable business ideas that focus on the achievable middle ground of innovation. It would also be a relief to the entrepreneur. Coming up with ideas in the middle ground is substantially easier than envisioning the next Wal-Mart and subsequently drawing up the roadmap on how to get there.

---

7 MacMillan, Ian and McGrath, Rita G. The Entrepreneurial Mindset. Boston, MA: Harvard Business School Press, 2000, pp. 10.

Chapter 4:
Flash in the Pan Innovation

"Creativity is the ability to introduce order into the randomness of nature."

- Eric Hoffer

What we discovered over the past few chapters is that the mindset we have when we approach innovation plays a large role in our success or failure when we attempt to harness it. A misguided mindset about innovation tends to breed misguided techniques for producing innovative ideas. Thus the contents of this chapter were probably inevitable. In the past, recognizing problems and potential solutions was based mostly on randomness. No one could really describe how it happened, therefore the techniques utilized relied heavily on the influence of random inspiration. In this chapter we are going to look at some of those tactics for creating ideas and why they produce lackluster results. It's not that they are necessarily bad tactics for idea generation, just bad tactics for *business* idea generation. They may be applicable to the writer, the artist or the inventor looking for new sources of stimuli, however, they are not well suited to the needs of the entrepreneur. Some of the methods described do create unique results. However, the chances of the techniques we are going to talk about generating useful business ideas is low, in my opinion. These methods need to be tweaked and molded for the tasks of an entrepreneur.

Many "techniques" for being creative and generating new ideas stem from the notion that ideas are a flash of genius or a bolt of lightning at an unexpected moment. Humans have associated idea generation with this notion. I think, however, that this association is incorrect. My entrepreneurship professor, Michael Camp, pointed out that a lightning bolt or flash-in-the-pan more accurately describes the speed at which a thought fires through the brain. The essence of what an idea is, however, is much more than this. The elements and occurrences that come together to produce this instantaneous thought have taken much longer than that to come together. Whether the process is consciously thought through or simmering in the subconscious, the idea has been bouncing around for some time before that instant of genius. Humans rarely question how ideas came together or reason them back through our thought process. If we did, we would most likely find that the components of an idea are not all that amazing. If we reason backward, the combination of stimuli seems obvious. If we reason backward, we can tweak the "idea generating" strategies and fit them to be more useful to the entrepreneur. Unfortunately, many of the tactics out there prescribed for business idea creation rely on the idea that a random stimulus will set the necessary spark in your brain. Quite often it will set a spark down a completely irrelevant path.

A recent speaker event that I attended on the topic of creativity and idea generation illustrates the above point quite well. In order to spark your creative genius, he proceeded to tell us, you have to get out of your daily routine. He suggested taking a new route to work or giving up television. He also suggested spending time with people you don't normally associate with. His basic tactic was to apply broad brush suggestions for creativity to the business world. Now these are all creative and I do believe that they will change your outlook on various aspects of life. But I was irritated by the fact that I had attended to hear such advice in a *business* creation setting. Now that I am writing this book, however, I am glad I attended if only to understand why I thought his ideas were useless. It occurs to me now that the speaker had hit on a key point, it just needed some tweaking to be useful. His key point was that bringing in new stimuli will facilitate your creativity and idea creation sessions. However, I think the walk in the park or the random coffee house conversations are better left to other applications of creativity. You never know what you might encounter in these situations, but for business building applications this has to be too random to be useful. I believe that if you are trying to conceive of ideas in the realm of business then your new stimuli could be much better focused.

What do I mean by being more focused? Try bringing new stimuli into your life in the form of business stimuli. Try subscribing to new publications about business in general or your industry specifically. For an entrepreneur, there is nothing better than magazines such as Fast Company, MIT Technology Review and Inc. magazine. Try reading books on business and especially entrepreneurship. For instance, I would recommend Clayton Christensen's series on innovation as a starting point. Have random conversations with other entrepreneurs instead of mixed background strangers. Read websites like TechCrunch, VentureBeat and Springwise. All of these activities will provide you with tons of new stimuli. More importantly, they are chock full of new relevant stimuli which differentiates itself from a walk in the park, or idle chat with a stranger. The information inside one edition of these magazines, one book or one conversation will be more relevant than 50 random, non-business activities you could choose to do. On top of reading, you could also visit a start-up or business incubator and talk to people doing the same things you are doing. The point is to focus your new stimuli. "New" random stimuli are going to produce "new" random results. Focused new stimuli are going to produce focused new results and, in the case of the entrepreneur, will be much more relevant to their needs. To understand the difference, compare and contrast these suggestions against some of the more common tactics out there today that I am going to list for you now.

The second technique I want to talk about deals with random association. In the association technique, you take your product and transpose aspects of another product or random object onto the product. I had read about this method but I was also in attendance at another event where the keynote speaker offered his version of random association. His first step was to decide what we were going to be producing. After a moment, he selected that we would be the manufacturers of the chairs in the ball room. He then had an audience member randomly pick an object to associate with. The object they chose was cabbage. So we started to talk about the aspects of cabbage and how it could be transposed onto the chair. The first thing that was mentioned about cabbage was its structure. He said that each layer of cabbage fit inside the other in an interlocking type fashion. Since stackable, interlocking chairs already exist, he moved on. His second observation was that cabbage was edible. The speaker then shouted out, AN EDIBLE CHAIR!! THERE IS A MILLION DOLLAR IDEA, I GUARANTEE IT! No. No. No. This is not a million dollar idea. It is quite the opposite of a million dollar idea. It is a useless idea, not to mention that it is disgusting and impractical. But it does show what kind of results random association techniques are going to provide you with. They are creative and funny but they are not business ideas. If you are going to use this association technique, focus the association. Again, try and introduce relevant business inspiration as opposed to random items such as cabbage. Take different business models from other industries and see if they could fit on your product. Take the Southwest Airlines way of low cost, no-frills and see if it applies. Take Wal-Mart's distribution strategy and see if you could dominate your competition in the same way. Take a technology like RFID tagging and see if it fits some aspect of your area of interest. You can associate anything in business; design, processes, services, pricing models, et cetera. It may not be as creative or produce as amusing results, but it will be more applicable and it will be more useful. Once again, to tweak random association techniques, we need to focus on incorporating random *business* inspiration.

A third technique that is commonly used is an attribute listing. This technique takes all of the attributes of your product and dissects each one. Essentially, you break your product down into each individual piece that comprises it. Once you have broken it down, you start looking at substitutes for the current inputs you are utilizing. This technique starts off more practically than the previous two. Looking at all the attributes of your product gives you a chance to look at each element in a new light and in isolation. You should start to consider what other possibilities could be used in place of each element that currently makes up your product. Looking at alternatives for each element can provide insights into how to alter a product offering. The caution here is to not take this to the level that some creativity people would suggest. You do not have to think so far outside the box when you brainstorm alternative inputs that it makes the process useless. Take the tip of a pen as an example. Instead of a "tip," a "stock tip" was one of the alternatives that I have seen people use to demonstrate this method. While it is original and creative and thought provoking, it does no good for solving any real business problems. At the same time these "leaps" of creativity have now taken you away from your core competencies in most situations. Yes, the leap was creative and thought provoking, but what is the probability that this process will provide something relevant without consuming half of your life? In my opinion the chances are low. This technique is useful but, like the others, don't use it so randomly that it makes your results utterly pointless.

The fourth method, one that I actually think is very valuable, is the old staple of idea creation. I put it down a little bit in an earlier chapter, but it wasn't to take away from the actual method, it is to take away from the community that hasn't changed in decades. That method is the "brainstorming" method. We have all been exposed to brainstorming. You define the problem, and then you begin to jot down ways that you might solve it. The brainstorming method is good and I think one of the most applicable because it brings all the relevant stimuli to the table and leaves out the random stimulus aspects. In brainstorming you are drawing on your experience and your knowledge. You draw on the elements of the problem and the elements of your conscious. If you could brainstorm long enough you most likely have all of the components of the final idea right in front of you in writing. The only downfall to brainstorming is that it might be constrained by prevailing norms and ideas of how things must work. Brainstorming can be useful if you allow your mind to break down those norms and rules of industry. Brainstorming is also much more focused. It is a good way to let the problem simmer in your mind. Hopefully, you will let that problem meld with knowledge across the sources for innovation that we talk about in future chapters.

The last method is a checklist method. I think it is important to save until last because, in many ways, it is how I hope you can think through business problems or ideas after you have read this book. The checklist method involves taking all aspects of a product or business idea and subjecting it to outside stimuli.8 It can be very effective if you are subjecting it to relevant stimuli. For example, a checklist might ask; Can I make it smaller? Bigger? More Transportable? Faster? Incorporate the Wal-Mart Business Model? Eliminate Waste? Can I complement it with another service? Can I make the process more efficient? The list goes on and on. It allows you to subject known successful ideas in business onto your own personal situation. I also feel like this method is the most similar to the way in which humans dissect and question what we know about the world. We run down checklists of other similar stimuli that occupy our mind. The more business models a person knows, the more a brain can project those onto a business venture. The more a person knows about new technology, the more he or she can project that knowledge and ask where else it can be used. I think the checklist model is good but I do not think it has to be written. You just have to be conscious of how to mentally walk through it in your brain. Take your idea or your problem and subject it to all the different solutions and stimuli you have in your business mind. Take the concepts and sources in this book as a mental checklist and run down the list to generate novel business ideas in whatever realm or industry you are attempting to innovate.

The whole point of this chapter was to show you what currently dominates the idea creation landscape. It was to point out first and foremost how our current techniques seem to be catered to the "flash-in-the-pan" moment of genius and how randomness

---

8 Hisrich, D Robert, Michael P. Peters and Dean A. Shepherd. <u>Entrepreneurship</u>. New York, NY; McGraw-Hill/Irwin, 2005, sixth edition.

is used to jump start that moment. I think a lot of people give these tactics credit because they do seem to provide us with instantaneous new thoughts. For a moment, they do feel like they reproduce that glorious moment when an idea flashes onto the scene in your mind. However, I'd be surprised to meet many people who have used these tactics to create anything beyond a line of novelty toy products. Just like the random stimulus that was utilized to get a spark, it sparks randomness. The ideas that we end up with are definitely new and novel. Unfortunately, they are generally not relevant nor do they solve any real world business problems.

Lots of suggestions, tactics and processes for being creative exist, yet people still seem to have an extremely hard time coming up with ideas they can use. I feel that in order to change that, we have to change the way we look at idea creation. The speed at which an idea comes to us may be fast, however the bases and knowledge for creating them comes over much longer periods of time. Random objects beget random ideas. Relevant, focused stimuli produce relevant, focused ideas. Work on feeding your mind with relevant business stimuli rather than random non-business stimuli. Our processes need to evolve and be studied as opposed to waiting around for an AHA! experience. You should be honing your idea skills and actively pursuing ideas as opposed to passively waiting. Great business ideas are rarely random. Do not let your success or failure as an entrepreneur be either.

Choose Your Own Ending

From here on out, you have a choice. The next four chapters take a look at the origin of ideas, their relevance in becoming an entrepreneur and how to focus your thinking for the task at hand. However, I realize that they are not the core of what you are searching for. With that in mind, this is your invitation to skip around. If you are anxious to get to the answers and the "how-to innovate" type of information, proceed to "solutions" and chapter 9. If you are not in a hurry and trust that my chapter ordering will pay off in the end, proceed to the next chapter. It's kind of like the choose-your-own-ending adventure novel. You know you'll read them all anyways, if the book is any good.

Chapter 5:
The Origin of Ideas and Creativity

"We have got to abandon that sense of amazement in the face of creativity, as if it were a miracle if anybody created anything."
-Abraham Maslow

To be able to suggest a framework and develop analytical techniques for idea creation, it is necessary to understand exactly what an idea is and what exactly creativity is. What is this brain spark that humans have such a hard time conceptualizing and putting into words? Put simply, what is an idea? What are its base elements? In order to conceptualize them, it is necessary to understand these factors. Once the inputs are understood, the output of a creative business idea is less spectacular. The following is an attempt to lay some groundwork to describe what we know to be the AHA! moment.

An idea at a basic level comes from a human's aggregate knowledge of the world. It is what is all around us. At its most basic level, knowledge is formed by the aggregation of stimuli. Before any products, services or businesses existed, humans had only their senses and the earth around them to take in stimuli. These stimuli that included touch, taste, smell, hearing and sight formed the basis of existence. Based on these stimuli, humans began to make sense of the world around them. By experiencing the five senses and interacting with the world, humans began to accumulate knowledge. They "knew" or could predict certain things based on past stimuli. This is still how the world is today. Humans interact with the environment, receive stimuli and process it into knowledge of how the world works. The process is ongoing and will continue forever. Stimulus is what forms the bases of knowledge. Ideas, then, stem from the connection of one or more stimuli.

If stimuli are the base of ideas, then it is important to understand how these stimuli are triggered into an idea. What sets off the spark? I believe that the idea spark is triggered when humans are forced to digest new stimuli or re-digest old stimuli in our daily lives. Stimuli that form our knowledge and beliefs tend to stay in the background of our conscious thought. As long as we have no reason to question it, or re-evaluate it, it is not at the forefront of our thoughts. Humans do not generate ideas until we encounter something new or rethink the established. New stimuli are what I believe pull the trigger on ideas. They are the catalyst. New stimuli have a natural tendency to do this because you have to fit the new information somewhere in your belief system about the world. New stimuli force you to recall old, related stimuli. They force you to find a place for the new information and reconcile it in your head with everything you already think you "know." By finding a place for new stimuli in your head, you are then forced to re-evaluate the things you don't often question. You shed new light on old thoughts and give them new meaning and potential. I believe that when you are forced to evaluate the place for new stimuli in your mind, and are forced to rearrange old stimuli, you create the spark that is the idea. Sometimes that spark and reorganization will produce nothing new for you, or maybe only something marginally interesting. Other times, it is just what you needed to create the AHA! moment that is referred to so reverently. That is what I believe the essence of the idea is. Entrepreneurs combine existing resources in new and novel ways to create ventures. In much the same way, combining existing stimuli in new and novel ways creates ideas.

So if this is how ideas are sparked, how do we translate that knowledge into creating meaningful business ideas? How are successful business ideas created? Too often, when we consult outside sources for how to generate business ideas, we get a lot of meaningless fluff. Everyone is telling you one way or another to spark ideas. Most often the suggestions stem from employing creativity. The problem is that the ways they suggest to employ creativity are so broad, they are almost useless. Creativity gets blanketed across disciplines. The same suggestions for generating it are given to the business man, the scientist and the artist alike. Why is it that the creativity suggestions for generating artistic ideas are the same creativity suggestions for the business mind? Do the creative bases for creating the next painting era and creating the next multi-national have anything in common? I personally think they are quite different mindsets. Yet business people are getting the same advice for stimulating creativity as artists. Take a walk in the park. Project attributes from random objects. Take a new route to work. Read a book you wouldn't normally read. A majority of the suggestions stem from random association and random events that should spark new ideas. While the suggestions might be helpful, what is more interesting is what is at the core of all these suggestions. They all suggest that you introduce new stimuli as a way to spark ideas. They all suggest that these experiences will force you to reorganize some of your knowledge about the world around you. So being creative gets equated with being random in more or less words. This stems from randomness being different from the established. But the question we must tackle is whether the methods out there to induce creativity are relevant to the business mind. Fun? Yes. Interesting? Yes. Enlightening? Yes. Relevant? Doubtful.

When the artist has taken a walk through the park, they have encountered nature, colors, movement, forms, etc. Relevant? Yes. When the business person takes a walk in the park, what are they supposed to encounter? What are the chances that this experience will truly lead to some breakthrough idea? In the case of the artist, they have sought creativity by surrounding themselves with what I would call relevant randomness. It is relevant because nature and all its elements are often the subject of the artist's work. The stimuli are always changing in the park and what you will encounter will be random. However, ideas will spark from new forms, new colors and new movement because they were relevant random observations. It is a random act but driven by relevance to their profession. Why then would we blanket this creativity exercise across all disciplines? Does business have all that much relevance to park visits? I think not. How many times have the observations of geese or blowing leaves lead to new ideas for a great product? Not many. Beyond the park example, does any old random association tactic really create that many great, relevant business ideas? Again, I think not. Creativity is not a blanketing concept. Scientists are creative in science in different ways than businessmen in business or artists in the art world. What makes you creative in one field can have utterly no relevance in another. The world may prize artistic creativity over business and science creativity, but that is not the point. The point of this book is to create great business ideas. The point is to deliver the relevant stimuli your "creativity" needs in order to come through. It most likely won't happen in a park or randomly in your shower unless you are focused on providing your mind with relevant random stimulation.

I chose the quote at the beginning of the chapter from Maslow very purposefully to precede the breakdown of ideas and creativity. Great ideas and creativity are not a feat of the mind beyond explanation. They are not concepts that deserve as much mystique and awe as people like to accredit them. They are both attainable with the right mindset and the right processes to let them come forth. The purpose of the rest of the book is to better understand the framework to get your creativity to come forth. The rest of this book is about feeding your mind with relevant stimuli, not randomness. The art world already seems to know how to be creative within their field. Now it is time to provide the business world with the right tools for creativity. Understanding why your approach to creativity needs to be different from the approaches of other disciplines is a key first step. We will now look to providing you with the equivalent in the business world of the artist's walk in the park. The sources of ideas, starting in chapter 9, will be those equivalents. They are the common areas that business people dive into looking for new, entrepreneurial ideas. By understanding the commonalities of business ideas, we can uncover some of the paths for creative *business* inspiration. By doing this we will reduce the randomness involved in the task and drive relevance into your proactive search for ideas.

Creating great business ideas is about understanding what exactly makes up an idea. It is about understanding the role of creativity and what creativity actually is in its most basic form. The above paragraphs should give you those understandings. They should at least take ideas and creativity to a practical level versus the sense of amazement most people attribute to these intangibles. Creating viable business ideas is about taking in relevant stimuli. Even when it is random, it still should be relevant. Ideas and creativity are not a fuzzy art. They can be somewhat of a process that, contrary to popular belief, can have a loose framework for achieving results. When you can abandon the sense of amazement that Maslow referred to, idea creation can be an active pursuit rather than an AHA! moment when you least expect it.

Chapter 6:
The Importance of the Idea

"We live in an age in which superfluous ideas abound and essential ideas are lacking."

- Joseph Joubert

The process of starting and growing a business is manageable. The process of capturing a unique business idea is nonexistent. Think about it. Once an idea has been conceived, the processes involved in bringing it to fruition in the business world are more concrete. For instance, the respective state you live in has a process for setting up a corporation. Negotiating a lease on your office space is a process. Books upon books can be read for ways to market and sell your product or service. After the original creative nugget of an idea, the rest of the equation of starting a business is more of a manageable process. In this chapter we are going to look at the importance of ideas in the business world. Should we accept that ideas are a dime a dozen like many people would assert? Or is it the case that those dime a dozen ideas are superfluous in the face of truly great business ideas?

There are differing opinions on just how important the original idea for a business venture is. Many people have made the claim that ideas are "a dime a dozen" and dismiss the importance of the original idea. Certainly the ideas that fly around your head but never get communicated, written down or put into action definitely are. What about the ones that do get put into action? It is widely accepted that a majority of new ventures will fail within their first five years. The percentages vary from 50% to 80% depending on the source and what they are measuring, but that is not the real point here. These are cases where action was taken on what people thought were worthy enough ideas for the markets. It might be more accurate to say that ideas are worth a dime for seven dozen. In any event, it is certain that once the idea is set into action, the original direction of the business is going to change and alter many times over. This is necessary and important for the firm to learn where they fit in the market landscape. It is the way that businesses grow and adapt that set them up for their future triumphs or failures. In that respect the original idea loses some relevance. The idea that you thought was going to be the cornerstone of the business may have been set up on faulty assumptions. The direction of your new venture may change. Some would say that this

renders the original idea minimally relevant because you will learn
how to adapt to be successful over time. But there are also other ways
to look at the importance and relevance of the idea.

On the other hand, the power of the original idea might be
more substantial than the critics think. The original idea is how
you got started in the first place. It had to exist. It was the tipping
point that brought you out of the realm of the employee and into
the realm of the entrepreneur. Had it not been for this dime a dozen
idea, you wouldn't be championing a start-up venture. It had to be
powerful enough to consider putting yourself in such a position. The
original creating, formulating and shaping was necessary to take your
entrepreneurial tendencies from hopes and turn them into a reality.
The original idea may not be fully intact over time, but the core of the
idea is going to guide the business venture. The assumptions and
ideas you start with are going to guide you through the most crucial
financial stages of the young company. You would not begin selling
brooms on day one and find yourself selling software components on
day 300 without running out of money. In this respect the original
idea is crucial. It will determine the degree of innovation that the
company is undertaking. It will determine allocation of funds. It
will determine the markets and the consumers you are attacking.
The business model around the original idea is going to determine
the initial exposure to risk. It will also determine the initial potential
for profitability. No matter how far down the road you get, that
original idea formed the basis of your undertakings. It will have at
least partially determined whether you are a small time firm forever,
poised for growth or bankrupt. In these regards, the original idea is
crucially important.

Either way that you look at it, consider the opening quote
to this chapter. Granted, it was penned hundreds of years ago, but
can the same still be said today? How important are our original
ideas? You can obviously make cases for both sides of the story. I
would make the case, however, that the average entrepreneur does
not have the luxury of using average, dime a dozen ideas that we so
often have running through our heads. It might be the case that ideas
are a dime a dozen for the established players in markets. They have
the funds and they have a much larger margin of error. With novice
entrepreneurs we are talking about ideas that need to be truly original
and powerful in the marketplace. Your first ideas for the direction of
a venture are going to make or break your shot at self employment.
The big players can afford to bet money on knock offs, add-ons,

sequels and run of the mill material. They will probably be profitable and their ideas probably are a dime a dozen. But you do not have the luxury of employing superfluous ideas. If you are an aspiring entrepreneur of average income, you are only going to have a couple of shots in life at being successful with new ventures. In that regard, your ideas and how you attack them are going to be crucial.

Whichever side of the argument you believe, this chapter was not meant to be contradictory to chapter one. The original idea doesn't have to be a grand scale innovation. It shouldn't be just any old industry you choose, either. The idea is not going to be a roadmap for your undertaking. At the same time, it is not just a randomly chosen direction. The original idea is a guide. It is going to serve as a basis for starting and a guiding light for the rest of the venture creation process. The relevance of the original idea can be debated, but it must exist and it was important enough to be your tipping point. Just remember that superfluous, dime a dozen ideas do exist all over. You do not have the luxury of employing them. The ideas that you employ must be "essential."

Chapter 7:
Focusing the Idea

"Nobody can be successful unless he loves his work."
- David Sarnoff

The past few chapters were about catching you up to speed with the problems of our current methods for generating business ideas. At this point we are going to depart from belaboring what is wrong with the process and start to lay the ground work for improving your idea generation process. In this chapter we are going to look at how to focus your idea creation process. By focusing I mean laying a framework for uncovering ideas that you are excited to pursue. To date, this topic has been one of my personal weaknesses. I formulate business ideas and entertain them for about two weeks before the excitement wears off for me. The problem is that I haven't found a business idea that I am passionate enough about pursuing each and every day for the coming years of my life. If you haven't found an idea to pursue yet, then you are probably in the same boat. I am positive that I do not want to work for someone else for the next 40 years of my life, but at the same time I cannot stay focused on just one idea. That is why I am writing this book. It is the only idea that I have found that I enjoy contemplating each and every day. So that is the goal of this chapter; to start you down the path to creating ideas that you will stay passionate about in the face of the uncertainty inherent with entrepreneurship.

Part of the problem with finding ideas is that most people's process for uncovering opportunities is random. This randomness provides us opportunities, but opportunities that often do not interest us. Random processes beget random results. Part of reducing dependence on such randomness is about understanding what types of ventures you are willing to pursue. Generating or recognizing great ideas for business may not be difficult, however, generating ideas that you are excited to pursue may be a different story. Part of the frustration of wanting to be an entrepreneur is seeing ideas that present great opportunities, but that you could care less about starting. Sure, biotechnology and RFID tagging might provide a wave of opportunities in the future, but that doesn't make them "your" opportunity. Part of your new mindset for innovation has to be about uncovering the right places to search. This chapter is about finding the core of the right places and uncovering "your" opportunities.

Starting off my career with no money, minimal experience, few contacts and a sea of industries to choose from, I feel confident that I represent a novice entrepreneur. The point of that is that I had no idea what business I wanted to start when I first became interested in entrepreneurship. I just knew I wanted to start one. This book is written for people like me or at least in similar circumstances. When this is your prevailing mindset, you are willing to entertain almost any possibility for a new venture. However, after you have entertained many ideas and haven't found one you are interested in, this mindset becomes problematic. The problem is that you have millions of avenues to consider and 99% of them aren't of interest to you. Think about the options you are leaving open. You could choose any industry from Artist to Zebra Rescue. Then choose whether you are going to have a product or a service. Then choose the point where you will be on the supply chain from supplier to retailer. Then choose how you will frame your business model. The list goes on and on. You have literally millions of options at your disposal. However, consciously or not, you are only willing to consider a small percentage of these options. Thus, we need to focus in. We need to isolate those areas that you are willing to pursue for the coming years of your life and eliminate the possibilities that you are not willing to consider.

Now prepare yourself to be annoyed with the answer to how you focus in, because I was. The answer is short and annoyingly cliché, but it is true nonetheless. You focus your ideas by finding the things you are passionate about in life. Nothing else will drive you to follow through with a business. I didn't want to hear that answer when I started researching this topic. This idea is something I still have trouble grasping. I would like to think that I could start a business in any industry just because the idea is original, innovative and profitable. However, after cycling through hundreds of ideas since my early teenage years, I realize why none of them ever stuck. I could have started those businesses but I wouldn't be any happier than I would have been working for someone else. Sure, they were original and interesting to think about, but after a couple of weeks the novelty wore off. Looking back on all the business ideas that I threw out the window, I realize that they didn't keep my interest. I wouldn't follow through with any of them because the only enjoyable part was dreaming them up and thinking, what if? Unless you really enjoy the work you are about to undertake, you won't care to see the details through to fruition. You won't care to dive deep into the underlying bases of the industry for the next few years of your life.

You simply won't care beyond the fact that it is an interesting, novel business idea that no one else is doing. If you aren't jumping at the prospects of finding out all that you can about an idea for the next few years of your life, then you haven't found something that you truly enjoy.

So now you have to ask yourself, do you know what your passions are? On the surface it would seem that everyone would know what their passions are. It seems obvious enough. However, many people do not know or can't articulate it. Many people who will read this book are stuck in dead end jobs or careers that they find unfulfilling. Many of us, even if we know our passions, aren't following through on them. In fact, as we speak, beyond my passion for problem solving and idea creation, I have little clue as to what I am passionate about doing in life. Just like most other Americans who have precious little free time to spare, I have my hand in a hundred different activities but none of them to a great extent. I have interests but nothing that jumps out to me as being a "passion." With that being the case, I went on a search to figure out what I am passionate about in life. The two suggestions I am about to make are two things that helped me get a better picture of where I want to head in the future. These sources also helped me identify what types of business ventures I will be pursuing in the coming years. Undertaking the same or similar steps that I have is one way that I feel you can "focus in" for your idea generating mindset.

The first source is included for free at the end of the chapter and the second is something I would recommend you purchase or read at the library. At the end of the chapter I inserted something that resembles a cheesy self help book. Use it or skip it, it is up to you. You might even think that no one should need this. However, it is a collection of general questions about your life and your interests that everyone should have the answers to. Understanding what drives you and what you truly enjoy is something that we must be able to articulate. By considering the questions and being able to articulate an answer, you get closer to understanding where you should be headed in the future. This knowledge is imperative if you ever plan on doing something you enjoy in your career. These answers will also be the vague beginning of where you are headed entrepreneurially. Utilizing the answers from this chapter and what we are going to discuss in chapter 8, you will be prepared to undertake the process of business idea formulation much more productively. Feel free to check out the section at the end of the chapter now or read through it after you have finished this chapter.

The second source of finding my passions came when I read
Strengths Finder 2.0 by Tom Rath.9 The book is a follow-up to the
bestseller Now, Discover Your Strengths by Markus Buckingham
and Donald Clifton.10 The actual reading element of the book is
extremely short, but the value is in the online assessment. What the
assessment seeks to do is identify your top five talents in life out of
the 34 categories that the poll considers. Subsequently, the book
offers insights into your talents and how to build them into strengths.
It also gives you ideas for action and ways to implement and leverage
your strengths in your career. My suggestion would be to read one of
the two titles mentioned above. They are free at your public library
if you do not want to make the investment. Just for an example, my
top 5 strengths are; ideation, futuristic, strategic, intellection and self
assurance. After reading the descriptions and action steps in the
book, I have a much better idea of my strengths. The descriptions of
these five strengths are something that I knew in myself but would
never have been able to articulate prior to reading the book. Having
that knowledge, and a source to refer back to, gives me the chance to
take proactive steps to building on those ideas. Instead of wandering
aimlessly in search of something I will enjoy, I now feel I am better
prepared to proactively target where I am headed for the future. This
is a huge help when you begin thinking about the businesses you
should attempt to tackle. Understanding your strengths and passions
is about knowing your core competencies. Starting a business in areas
that you do not excel in makes no sense at all. The key to innovating
and starting successful businesses is about leveraging your inherent
strengths that other people lack.

So go out and find out what it is that you enjoy doing. Find
out what your passions are. You are going to be spending the next
40 odd years of your life pursuing something, why not take a little
time now to avoid years of misery later? I know what each and
every one of you will do, at least the first time you look at the list
below. You will read each line, barely consider it, be annoyed that
I included it because YOU of all people do not need self help. I also
realize that by including this I run the risk that you will either stop
reading or continue on as if this "passion" stuff didn't occur. Suit

9 Rath, Tom. Strengthsfinder 2.0. New York, NY: Gallup Press, 2007.

10 Buckingham, Markus and Donald O. Clifton. Now, Discover Your Strengths. New York,
NY: The Free Press, 2001.

yourself. In any event, yes it is cheesy, but if you do not figure it out now, you may spend the next forty years being someone who hasn't yet figured out what they want to do with their life. It might take you until retirement before you get to start doing the things you enjoy for extended periods of time again. The upside is that you might find things you didn't realize you were interested in. You might find areas that you couldn't articulate or were brewing in your subconscious. Use the sources I mentioned to find something that is relevant to what you love doing or might love to do. Dave Sarnoff put it pretty simply, "Nobody can be successful unless he loves his work."

Note: This isn't a self help workbook, although it does resemble one. Run through the list mentally or write down your answers, whichever is more helpful. Also, I concede that some are cheesy and cliché-ridden, but hey, you have to start somewhere.

1. What activities can you spend hours participating in without realizing how much time has passed?
   Do you do it because you enjoy it or because it is a necessity?
   If you enjoy it, what specifically?
   If someone would pay you to do it would you quit your job?
   Could you create a business around this activity?
   Did you put aside time especially to do this activity? Why?

2. What magazines do you subscribe to?
   Which magazines have you subscribed to for more than 1 year?
   Even if you don't subscribe, what magazine would you look at if stranded in an airport?
   What category of magazines do you go to first?
   Do your various magazine preferences relate to each other?
   (ie. Dog Fancy and Travel)
   Could they be mixed for a business idea?

3. If you could live vicariously through your child (or future children), what would you have them doing and attempting to accomplish?
   What would you have them do differently than you did? Why?
   What profession would you choose for them? Why?

If money was not an issue what profession would you have them pursue? Why?

4. What are your goals in life?
Where should you be in ten, twenty or fifty years?
Where would you like to be ideally?
What is it going to take to get there?
What would be the ideal job to be in while accomplishing these goals?

5. What gifts do you ask for?
When you do not have to spend the money, you tend to treat yourself.
Why are these gifts a treat?
Think about various gifts that weren't necessities. Why did you ask for them?

6. What do people come to you for help with?
You're more advanced than most people at a few things in life.
What are they?
Why do people come to get help from you?
Is there any way to fashion your help to more people?

7. What are you better at doing than other people?
Does it annoy you to see other people attempting tasks and succeeding when you know you could do a better job?
What jobs do you tend to take leadership in?
What situations do you feel the need to take control of because it is the only way it will get done right?

8. What do other people claim you are good at?
When you get compliments in any area, why?
What do other people urge you to pursue full time that you don't?
What tasks do you do that inside you are hoping for great compliments on?

9. If you could trade places with anyone professionally who would it be? Why?
If you are not already in professional sports or on your way, don't choose professional sports.
What is it about the profession that draws you to their successes?

What professions do you dream about that are attainable? ie, not based on genes and years of practice that you didn't put in.

10. What are your casual hobbies?
Is there a common base interest across these hobbies?
Why aren't they passions?
Are there any that you would like to pursue on a grander scale?

11. What do you ideally picture yourself being in life?
How do you want to be remembered professionally?
What profession would you like to have dominated the majority of your career?
What professions do you dream about but are inhibited because of the money involved in pursuing them?

If you made it all the way through to this point I must say that I am impressed. Although it may have made you a bit nauseous, you'll be more focused and more prepared to tackle the next steps than those who skipped it. Keep your answers in mind as you continue on in the book as you will probably need to revisit them.

Chapter 8:
Getting to the Core

"The perplexity of life arises from there being too many interesting things in it for us to be interested properly in any of them."
- Gilbert K. Chesterton

Hopefully you have thought through the previous chapter and came up with at least some idea of where your passions lie. You might still be saying, "so what?" That didn't give me much more information than I had before I read the chapter. But did you really get to the heart of what you enjoy? It is easy enough to say that you are interested in travel or entertainment or sales. It's a good starting point for sure, but that is not going to be enough digging to get you focused. Chances are you have defined some broad categories of interest while reading the last chapter. Chances are you are still leaving too many options on the table for your brain to drift between. There are thousands of options, thousands of inputs and thousands of processes for the mind to consider within each broad marketplace of the world. With each industry comes many layers. With each layer of industry comes opportunity for innovation. We need to look at where we can innovate within the industry on a deeper level. Getting to the core of it all will give us a better picture and bring us closer to the core of your passions.

Consider the following example. If someone says they are passionate about "cars" what did they actually mean? Are they interested in being a car producer? An aftermarket parts provider? A custom car refinisher? Maybe the person isn't even consciously aware themselves what they meant. In this chapter we want to start to understand the "why" elements of our passions and the actual underlying factors to our enjoyment. They might have simply liked cars without considering what specifically brings them enjoyment. They might never have needed to describe or understand "why", but it is imperative to the entrepreneur to understand what drives them. What you have to do is dig deeper into what you are claiming your passions to be. You have to get to the core of your passions. You have to be able to answer the "what" about cars that brings you your passion. Let's take this example a little further.

Let's go back to the original thought. The person has decided they enjoy "cars." They really haven't told us anything. They could produce cars, service cars, sell cars, provide after market products for cars, et cetera. If you break down each component of the car and the myriad of products and services surrounding the car industry, you begin to peel back the layers of how wide an industry can be. Now your interest in "cars" can lead you into a hundred different areas of expertise. You could focus on car bodies, paint, tires, rims, et cetera. Even then, those categories can be broken down further. If you choose car tires as your area of interest, what type of tire? Will you innovate in the area of tire traction? Will you produce the tire valve? Will you recycle the tires? Areas that are more specific will hone your actual passion and be more meaningful to this exercise. You could also spawn a hundred more companies by looking at the after market parts for cars. Let's say that you are interested in wheels but you don't want to be an original equipment manufacturer to the Fords, GMs or Chryslers of the world. You may produce your own line of after market parts, start the next Pirelli racing tire or produce custom wheels and rims. Inventing a tire valve that automatically reports tire pressure might be your enjoyment. In any event, you get the point. Picking apart an industry that you know and getting to the core of your passions will allow you to see where all the areas for opportunity lie. It might help you figure out that your interest in "cars" actually means that you really enjoy the thrill of a much more specific aspect of the car industry. Once your area of interest has been dissected and focused, you can understand that your interest in "cars" could have lead you down a thousand different paths to new venture possibilities. At the same time, none of the thousands would have been given any great thought considering the vagueness that you were pondering.

Another important thing to remember is that each industry that is associated with the Car Industry has their own bases of competition, their own business models, their own pricing schemes and their own "industry norms," each of which can be an area in which to innovate. Even a very specific passion is going to have a plethora of factors to take into consideration. When you get to the core you begin to see how ideas can truly be focused. Innovating in the realm of tire pressure is a lot easier to construe than making as broad a statement as "I want to be an innovator in the car industry." Getting to the core, considering what you actually mean and focusing the idea hones your thought process. By doing so, you will make the rest of this book much more interesting and applicable to your search for business ideas.

This is a short chapter because I think you are smart enough to understand the concept without beating a dead horse. The whole point of this chapter is to build on the previous one. I felt it was necessary considering my own personal search for finding the core of my passions. I knew that I had an interest in business when I chose to go to college. Along the way I figured out that marketing was the best fit as a more specific major for me. The Business Builders Club allowed me to expand my knowledge of entrepreneurship. Through that club and my classes I learned that my main passion was not the start-up process or the development of a business plan. I realized that I liked hearing about new and innovative ideas, reading about them and creating them. My passion is for ideas. My passion is to understand, describe and actively pursue the creation of business ideas. I have gone from an inkling of a passion for business to writing this book about ideas. That is what you need to do in order to get moving in the right direction. Peel back the layers of your interests and figure out what you are truly passionate about. Once you have figured this out, you are in a position to utilize the rest of the "solutions" in a much more productive manner.

The Sources

The following chapters are probably the reason you picked up this book in the first place. They are the "answers" you were looking for, so to speak. To make it easier for you, I have grouped the chapters so that similar sources of innovation appear close to each other. Peter Drucker and Joseph Schumpeter made my job easy. They weren't especially concerned in telling you "how-to" innovate but they were excellent at describing the sources and end products of innovation. For that reason I will be using a combination of their categorizations to organize the sources. Under each broad categorization, then, you will find the specific "how-to" type frameworks. The categorizations are as follows; New Market Strategies, New Product Strategies, New Process Strategies, Consumer Based Strategies, Business Model Strategies and a chapter on New Inputs. Just to clarify, I did leave out two categories of Drucker's in my ordering. Drucker's chapter on Incongruities was already covered by "the most basic answer" and his chapter titled "The unexpected" refers to randomness, which we covered in chapter 4.

In chapter 1 I briefly mentioned that not all problems are equal. With that in mind, the categories of sources range from broad levels to the more specific. I felt putting them in order would make it somewhat of a boring read but felt the need to clarify that here.

Also, keep in mind that "sources" operate in a few different ways. One way is that they point you to a problem or unmet need. They are not necessarily ends in themselves but rather indicators of where to look. After reading such chapters, it will be up to the reader to identify the markets they will target and search out these indicators. The second way is that the "sources" are the ends in themselves, meaning that employing the steps in the chapter will inherently create novel solutions. I will try to mention which chapters are which as we go along, but keep this in mind as you read so you understand how to utilize the information.

Finally, innovation is still a tricky subject despite our best efforts to harness it. There are no absolutes. Therefore, the categorizations are not all encompassing or black-and-white. Some of the categories and sources will overlap. You may feel that I put one of the "how-to" chapters under the wrong general category or that a source may span three of the categories. Getting caught up on details like this is not the point. Innovation will never be 100% clear cut. There will never be a 1-2-3 process. Just realize that exposure to this information, no matter how it is organized, is going to greatly improve the way you look at innovation.

New Market Strategies

Chapter 9:
Exploiting Technology

"We live in a society exquisitely dependent on science and technology, in which hardly anyone knows anything about science and technology."

- Carl Sagan

    The diffusion of technology in our society is an interesting way to see how products and services evolve over the lifespan of industries. Marketing, pricing and application strategies can all change as the cost of technology decreases and the diffusion of a product increases. Some very powerful observations in the world of technology, such as Moore's law, have helped us to understand the progression of technological capabilities and the effect on the price of those technologies over the same period. While Moore's semiconductor observations are not necessarily relevant to this chapter, generalizing his law can beget some powerful observation tools. Generally speaking, technological capabilities will increase over a period while the price of those technologies stays the same or decreases over the same period.[11] Every day, more and more powerful technologies are becoming cheaper. When this happens, it opens up new markets in which the application of such technology can become financially viable for use. Technologies that were price prohibitive to some industries in the past are now ripe for integration. Entrepreneurs can capitalize on such a phenomenon. The interesting thing about technology is that many industries know that great potential exists in some technologies but have no idea how to integrate it for competitive advantage. This is your opportunity. It is up to you to determine the future states of industries and how technology can be used to create them.

    The idea that technology can revolutionize industries is pretty obvious. But few people watch technology day to day. Few people realize just how far things have progressed. Few people realize the efforts that must go into making breakthroughs happen. Even if they do, even fewer understand it. It is unfortunate because most people trying to innovate are not focused on researching and following ground breaking technologies. Most people trying to innovate are walking around brainstorming ways to produce flash-in-the-pan

---

11 http://www.webopedia.com/TERM/M/Moores_Law.html (Moore's Law Generalization)

gadgetry or novelty items. Instead of reading industry magazines and researching industry uses for the latest breakthroughs, we walk around thinking about how to create self-cooling cup holders or dream about opening a niche pet salon. But if you are dreaming of making it big time in this life, that mindset is pretty counterintuitive. One of the first things you can do to have the innovation lens of technology at your fingertips is to start learning. You do not have to know how to create the next semiconductor chip, but at least start understanding what technologies exist and read where people think they are headed in the future. You'll be surprised with just how little you do know about most of the ideas and equipment that are appearing in the marketplace. Take the internet as a generic example. Most people these days have access to it, know how to generally navigate it and might be able to pull off a few cool tricks with it. But how many people understand it? What separates you from the founders of Youtube or Facebook? Probably not a whole lot. Take the time now to realize how technology creates and destroys industries. Take stock of what exists and where it is going. Take the time to get a general knowledge of what is coming in the world of technology and brainstorm as to how you could use it to start your own venture.

Let's look at an example to show just how powerful technology can be. I am going to refer to the movie industry multiple times in this book, but specifically for this chapter think about the technological advances of the industry. Consider the history of Hollywood and take a look at how fast technology can revolutionize industries. If you had thought about producing a major motion picture 40 years ago, people would have called you crazy. They still may call you crazy. Access to making major motion pictures was an uphill climb considering the initial resources required to undertake such a venture. The technology was in its nascent stages and took a lot of skill to be able to shoot, edit and produce a full-length film. Back when television and film were in their beginning stages, professional grade cameras were almost the size of refrigerators.12 They produced low end pictures and were limited in their applications. The film that motion pictures were shot on was clumsy and even had a tendency to melt. Editing was done with razor blades and scotch tape, not USB cords and digital studios. This was the technology of the 1960s. Over time, the video camera evolved. It moved to briefcase size and then shoebox size. Video

---

12 http://www.internetvideomag.com/articles2002/historyofcamcorders.htm

Cameras made the move from the Hollywood set to the American living room. The evolution of technology allowed a whole new set of consumers the chance to shoot their own videos outside of any studio walls. Now-a-days the video quality on most cell phones far exceeds the capabilities of video cameras of past generations. At the same time that hordes of consumers bought video cameras to capture home movies, high end cameras were getting cheaper and more refined. In today's world the average consumer can purchase a camera of the same quality as that of a major studio for about $4000. Videos of today operate on digital film and are streamed into TVs and computers in High Definition. Recent hits such as Saw, 28 Days Later and Napoleon Dynamite were bootstrapped on very low funds, no name actors and a few nice cameras. The picture and production quality of the major studios was out of reach until now. The technology was cost prohibitive until recently, and the effort to create a high quality product in the past took lots of effort. Thanks to the phenomenon like the type described by Moore, high end technology is becoming available to entrepreneurs at very economical prices. The technological capabilities have been increasing exponentially over the years while the price has been falling. This phenomenon changes the rules of the game and allows for a new industry structure. It allows for innovation by a whole range of people as opposed to the select few. These advances have spawned a generation of do it yourself videographers and published amateur material. It is opportunities like this that technology presents to the entrepreneur. As technology becomes more readily available, what is going to be its impact in the future? What industries and what consumers will embrace it to change the way things are done?

Movies are just one example. Think about what a desktop computer could do ten years ago that can now be done on a cell phone in most places in the world. What used to take minutes to download on the laptop at the office can now be retrieved wirelessly from your iPhone in the subway. We have gone from main frame computers to desktops to laptops to palm pilots and cell phone computing in the course of two decades. This example has tremendous implications for the entrepreneurial thinker. Technology is being diffused throughout markets daily. Every day, technologies that could revolutionize markets creep closer to economic viability. The question is, will you be ahead of the curve to see it coming? Every time you think about a technology you should be thinking about where else it could be used and a timeline for when it will become economically viable to do so. Think about the possibilities outside of where everyone is watching. Everyone is eyeing up the next computer gadget, but in places like the good old boys group in Hollywood, the revolution is just beginning. Within the next few years access to powerful, cheap technology could reshape an entire industry. No one knows how or what will work. Your guess is as good as theirs. Now see where else this phenomenon could have an impact. Revolutionize an industry that people didn't think would be touched. Use your cognitive abilities to spot opportunities and technological gaps. Extrapolate on where technology is going for the future based loosely on ideas such as Moore's law. Look to places that you know are going to leave unexploited gaps in the future states of things and see how you could put the pieces in motion to fill those gaps.

Technology that is increasing in capability while becoming more inexpensive is only one opportunity that this lens of innovation can provide. Let's go beyond cheap new technology. If faster, better technology is being sold everyday for less, what is happening to technology of our recent past or even outdated technology? Think about how cheap technology that is past its "prime" can be. What is outdated garbage for the forward-looking computer industry may well be a giant leap forward for some other industry out there. Integrating old technology into completely new areas can have just as much of an innovative effect as lowering the cost of brand new stuff. Older technology is limited compared to the newest gadgetry, but if it never existed in an industry in the first place, then the integration of it may as well be a revolution.

A great example of this type of innovation can be seen in the company Microchip Technology and the man in charge, Steve Sanghi.[13] Sanghi's company thrives by using technology straight out of the 1970s. He and his company use microcontrollers as their primary product for innovation. Microcontrollers are generally a slow, rudimentary chip that the likes of Intel and AMD have more or less abandoned for years. They are on par with some of the slowest laptop chips available on the consumer market. However, Microchip continues to find ways to make profitable businesses with them. Sanghi has taken this type of chip that most people would view as junk and has implemented it in places outside of the realm of computers to create waves. While the other chipmakers focus on producing super chips where one component runs all

13 Parks, Bob. "Tiny Chip, Giant Ambition." Business 2.0; Oct. 2006, pp. 98-103.

the functions, Microchip focuses on multitudes of less advanced
chips, each controlling a small function within the overall scheme
of the operations. Sanghi has used microchips in such products as
the Segway scooter, the Adidas-1 running shoe, the Tesla roadster
and the underwater LED display at the Wynn casino in Las Vegas.
Each product is as different as the next, yet they all have similar,
modest processing needs. These products didn't need the fastest,
most advanced processor in the world. Adidas-1 running shoes, for
instance, needed a processor to soften of stiffen the shoe based on
the impact with the ground. While any modern chip would suffice,
the price would not. A simple microcontroller based on technology
from 30 years ago does the trick. This tactic brings technology never
seen before to the shoe industry, while keeping the price tag in
line with what consumers might shell out for such a device. While
Sanghi's competitors look for the next implication of Moore's law,
he looks to industries that were never influenced by such a law. He
creates innovation with outdated technology in industries that have
rarely seen its influence. Sanghi is a great example of how a unique
perspective on innovation with technology can have a profound effect
in industries people never saw coming. Using old technology in
new places can be as equally entrepreneurial as trying to predict the
technological landscape of the future.

If the idea of theorizing the future of new radical technologies
had you a little worried, then the idea of employing outdated
technology in new industries should be a bit more comforting. It is
an area that you can start brainstorming about right now. This lens
of innovation with technology is actionable today. Most of us are
aware of technologies that are no longer practical for the industries
they initially were intended for. We encounter them every day. We
all own technology that is outdated and technology that is on its way
to being forgotten by the major markets. It is these types of situations
where innovative people can thrive. And in the case of outdated Tech,
thrive relatively cheaply. It is about brainstorming other industries in
which the outdated technology could be a major improvement. It's
about projection. It is about extrapolation. The capabilities of recent
and outdated technology are well known. Where else could these
capabilities be useful? What other industries need processing speed?
Even beyond that, what other industries would it just be cool and
novel to infuse technology and processing speed? (I.e. the Adidas-1
and the shoe industry) Projecting the task that is accomplished
by outdated technology and then comparing and locating similar

markets to implement it in can be a great source of ideas for the entrepreneurial thinker.

   A third area for innovating with technology lies with the idea that technologies of today that are not quite good enough for some markets might be beyond "good enough" for innovation in other markets. This might include technologies that can't be classified as ultra new and at the same time they are not classified as outdated. They are technologies of the present that are simply not up to par for the industries people have envisioned for them. These technologies might still be in their development stages and can still be pricey due to the low levels of diffusion. This idea of "not quite good enough" was expounded on by Clayton Christensen in his series of books on innovation starting with The Innovator's Dilemma.14 In essence, the major industries that are expected to be revolutionized by a technology are waiting. The technologies have to be "good enough" efficiency-wise and available at a specific price point in order for it to make sense for implementation. They are waiting for the technology to live up to the expectations for it before they utilize it in their markets. While these major industries are waiting, what is happening to the technology? It sits and waits. This is where the entrepreneur can be savvy in the marketplace and use this to her advantage. There are opportunities to take technologies that are "not quite good enough" in some industries and apply them to other industries where such a capability would be a leap forward. Take, for example, the electric engine. The technology was and still probably is a ways off from being viewed as a viable alternative to the combustion engine. We have yet to see mass adoption of the technology. It is not outdated and the technology is not cheap. So while everyone is waiting for the R&D labs to come back with a practical version for cars, what else could we be doing with these inferior electric engines? What other industries could benefit from an inferior electric car engine? It's a simple mind exercise. Where else could it be used? For starters, what else uses an engine? Sure, they can't run a car practically yet, but could they run a lawnmower? Could they run a snowmobile? Could they run a dirtbike or 4-wheeler? You'll find many industries that could replace the output of combustion engines with an electric engine but do not necessarily need the energy required by an automobile. Why not insert the inferior electric engine there? Technology that is "not good enough" for some industries is

---

14 Christensen, Clayton. The Innovator's Dilemma. Cambridge, MA: Harvard Business School Press, 1997.

a prime source of innovation in others. Understanding all three of these applications can shed light on ways in which entrepreneurs can redefine industries. It is about taking in stimuli and actively pursuing opportunities using technology that can empower the entrepreneur.

Technologies of yesterday, today and the future all represent opportunities for the entrepreneur. It is when you begin to realize the implications of all three types that the entrepreneur begins to see how powerful a source of innovation that technology can be. It is not a hard source to begin thinking about. You can begin with what exists. You can see it, touch it and use it. Many times, technology is something tangible for us to experiment with. From there it is about learning. It is about looking around you. It is about asking questions. It is about projecting products, concepts and ideas. There are literally thousands of industries at varying technological levels. There are thousands of industries that could be revolutionized by creatively utilizing past, present and future technologies. Take stock of what is out there and now you have the tools to theorize what is to come.

Chapter 10:
Non-Innovators

"Be daring, be different, be impractical, be anything that will assert integrity of purpose and imaginative vision against the play-it-safers, the creatures of the commonplace, the slaves of the ordinary."
- Cecil Beaton

The only thing that is constant is change. At least that's what we're commonly told. But what should be occurring in theory doesn't always translate into real life. In fact, it is interesting to note that while industries are purportedly in a state of constant change, statistics show a completely different picture. By some estimates, 80% of industries are actually in stagnated maturity. Demand has leveled off, products are indifferentiable and industry players compete mainly on price. What has happened in many cases is that the firms in an industry have stopped innovating. They have stopped trying to push the envelope with their respective products and services. Hence the title "Non-Innovators." While this is contrary to the ideal progress of society, this is good news for people like you. Utilization of innovative ideas and ingenuity on the behalf of the entrepreneur can completely upend or reinvigorate these stagnant markets of the past. The rest of this chapter is going to focus on the characteristics of these industries and what we can do to shake things up. Innovating in this type of situation is a classic example of entrepreneurs becoming a catalyst for growth in the marketplace.

To get started, we are going to revisit Economics 101 for a moment. The idea is to illustrate how industry lifecycles can provide a good picture of the degree of innovation in an industry. As many of you already know and some of you may not, the lifecycle that industries generally go through is as follows; it starts when they originate, proceeds through a growth period, levels off at maturity and eventually declines. (see the black curve on the graph on the next page) This can be measured in a variety of ways, but the trend is the important thing worth noting. The life cycle of an industry may be extremely fast, and measured in months, or it may be drawn out over many years or decades. At any point along that lifecycle path, another product could displace the need for the original and start the cycle all over again, thereby creating a new market. Reread the last sentence. That is where you come in. That new path is the new growth curve, or S curve as it is commonly referred to, due to its shape. (see the dotted curve on the graph below) It represents the new path of the altered market. This observation can be especially useful when you begin to look at industries that have reached their maturity or decline stage. You will see these companies that, in general, are no longer innovating or have reached a ceiling on product capabilities. In such cases, the bases of competition are set, the industry structure is set and the competitive advantages of the firms have been whittled down to where the players compete mainly on price. Basically, the market is drifting along in a constant state. Industries like these are ripe for innovation. This is where entrepreneurs can enter and shake things up. It becomes the job of the entrepreneurially minded to create the new growth curve.

Graph 1.1:15 The original product life cycle from introduction to maturity is shown by the black "original S curve." The dotted line indicates the introduction of innovation into an industry that allows for a new product life cycle to start somewhere on the curve. Often we see this occur to industries in the maturity stage, but it can happen at any point along the graph.

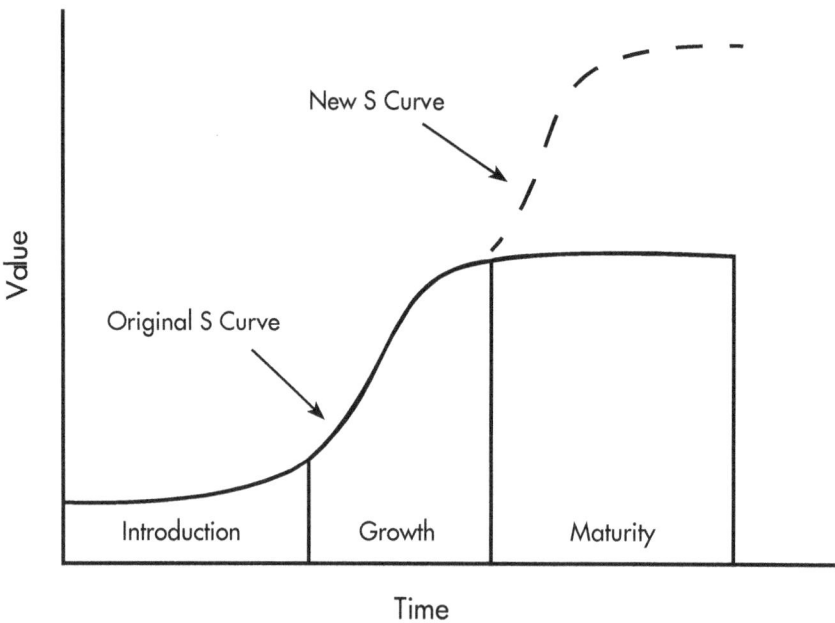

---

15 Graph 1.1 is loosely based on Clayton Christensen's graph from The Innovator's Dilemma - Christensen, Clayton M. The Innovator's Dilemma. Boston, MA: Harvard Business School Press, 1997, pp. 39 – 40.

The best way to see a new growth curve brought on by entrepreneurs is with a few examples. I was recently reading an issue of Fast Company magazine and saw a prime example of non-innovators. The companies I am about to highlight are a few of the new entrants into the "death" industry, if you will. These companies are staging an attack on the traditional funeral and burial industry. As you follow along with the story, keep in mind the ideas we mentioned above.

Burial and funeral services have been around for thousands of years. It's a recurring need as long as humans continue to be subject to the laws of nature. The point of the story was that the death industry, as we have known it in recent history, has been cruising along in maturity. The process has been the same. Someone passes away, coffins and flowers are picked out, services are held, they are laid to rest and a chiseled piece of stone adorns their resting spot. The firms in place around the country operate much in the same way as one another. Choosing between them is usually a matter of price or family connections. You might be thinking that this is a pretty odd place to innovate. At the same time I hope this story gives you a good perspective on industries that may be in line for an overhaul. (the ones we never question) Anyway, the process has been the same. The rules of the game and the industry norms were taken for granted. Individuals delivering funeral services could count on a steady flow of "customers." They counted on things to stay the same. Why wouldn't they? Business has been conducted the same way for many decades. Funerals and burials are as much as an established ritual in our society as anything else. However, a few new entrepreneurial firms hope to shake things up a bit.

One of the companies featured in the article, Vidstone, is creating their own new growth curve by adding technology to the mix. Instead of simply having a traditional gravestone, the monuments of the recently deceased can now be outfitted with solar powered video players.[16] Once attached, the device plays a loop of videos from the life of the deceased. The qualities of a person that once might have been chiseled in stone can now spring to life on the monitor. The advantage of this is pretty obvious. Any memories we can hold on to of the ones we miss are nearly invaluable. The advances in solar power allow for this innovation to be self-sustaining and a renewable source of memories year after year. The idea will not

---

16 "The future of...Death." <u>Fastcompany</u>. Dec. 2005: pp. 46.

completely replace gravestones, but it is one more way to celebrate the life of those who are dearly missed.

Another company in the article focused on a similar, yet slightly different, form of the final resting state; cremation. Traditionally, after the body has been cremated, the family of the recently deceased places the ashes in an urn or scatters them at a spot of significance. What Lifestone has done is create a third option or complement to this tradition. They take the ashes of the recently deceased and form them into decorative, colored diamonds. These stones can then be incorporated into any piece of jewelry. Now, instead of the morbid jar of ashes, families have the option to keep their relatives close, conspicuously and tactfully. The company offers rings and necklace stones that appear as normal jewelry to the average person. Again, this innovation in the death industry is not necessarily going to replace urns or the practice of scattering ashes. However, what it does do is reinvigorate growth and create new markets within an industry that had long been stagnant. These are examples of "new S curves" that allow an otherwise mature industry to add value to their product offering. The new products create a new level of value and a new chance at growth and differentiation among funeral and funeral service providers. They are great examples of how industries that are cruising along in maturity are a prime target for entrepreneurs.

What is more disturbing than the industry of choice for these entrepreneurs is the question as to why people within the funeral business did not see this opportunity? Being that the benefits are so obvious, why did it take entrepreneurial intervention from outside the industry to capture new growth? Let's face it, people saw solar power coming for years before it became economically viable. Using video clips to celebrate people's lives is nothing new either. But funeral operators and cemetery owners still missed the boat. The answer is pretty simple. Industries that have cruised along in the maturity or the decline stages of their lifecycle generally become complacent. Things have not changed for years, why would they now? They also become myopic, a term that marketing guru Theodore Levitt brought to popularity.[17] Myopic meaning that they define their business too narrowly. Basically, the death industry didn't "do" technology. They weren't "in the business of" creating jewelry. They buried dead people and they had a system. Unfortunately for them, they missed an opportunity. Some of them are probably still resisting.

---

17 Levitt, T., "Marketing Myopia", Harvard Business Review, July- August, 1960.

As unfortunate as that is, the better it is for entrepreneurs. For the myriad of reasons that companies miss their chances at opportunity, we are the beneficiaries. Don't worry too much about why they miss their chances, just be happy that they do.

Think of all the industries that we take for granted. They may have operated on the same premises for as long as you can remember, and few people question why it should be done this way. A good example is the relatively recent onslaught of the United States Postal Service package delivery. Innovators who thought up UPS, Fed-Ex and DHL saw an industry ripe for the picking. The industry had been run the same way for years. The fact was that the USPS was a monopoly thanks to the federal government. Their service was slow and did less than OK at getting packages where they needed to be and intact. All it takes is a few entrepreneurs and second mover competitors to take a monopolistic, non-innovating industry and turn it into one that is currently fierce with competition and options. Just think of all of the services offered and the rates that can be given just among the three aforementioned companies. Thirty years ago that was not the case. When the firms in a non-innovating industry get lazy and have concretely defined their product offerings, there is an excellent chance for innovators to come in and reap the benefits of years of complacency.

In order to put a framework around this, it is crucial to understand the things that characterize industries that are ending or have ended their growth phases. There are some telltale signs that will help you recognize industries that are in the mature stage or about to be. The following are the characteristics of mature markets according to the Merrifield Consulting Group.[18]

1. Demand that is saturated and slow growing if not declining

This is an obvious one when you consider the industry life cycle graph I referenced earlier. When products are first introduced there are only a few industry players. Demand is high for the new product and sales begin to grow. For a period of time, demand will continue and the growth of the business will proceed along the S curve. Then, in most cases, entrepreneurs and other firms will recognize the profits that are being made and enter the market to satisfy demand and reap a profit. Eventually, demand for a product will be met and sales will level off. This is the first sign of a mature market. When a product has been diffused well enough and enough

18 http://www.merrifield.com/articles/1_1.asp

suppliers exist to satisfy demand, a market is coming into the mature stage. Mature markets may grow slightly or they might decline. In any event, it is a sign that the market is mature, saturated with product and generally there is a lack of differentiation between offerings from the various suppliers. It is time to reinvigorate the industry or continue along the curve.

2. Excess supply of competition too willing to discount

As we mentioned above, mature markets generally lack differentiation among the products offered. If the consumer cannot rationalize a difference between two products, they will most likely seek the lowest price. This brings us to our second sign of a mature market. Since the demand in a mature market is being met, the producers of that product have to find some way to move product. Since the consumers are mainly buying based on lowest price, competitors in a market are motivated to discount the cost of their product to move more of it or to get rid of inventory. When they do that the other competitors have little choice but to match or lower their price as well. If the consumers cannot tell the difference between products, they have no reason to buy at a higher price. It is pretty obvious that this is not a market that you want to be in, yet 80% of businesses are. You either have to differentiate, cruise along or get out of a market space.

3. Eroding profits, margins and returns

Since the mature markets are mainly competing on price, initiatives to discount or lower prices have an obvious effect on the rest of the financials. In mature markets the players are going to have to endure lower returns on their sales. Likewise, their margins decrease in order to stay afloat and their overall profit margins decline from the days of the growth phase when demand still outweighed supply.

4. Emphasis on cost cutting to stay ahead of market erosion

It is brought up many times in business that saving $1 in the production of a product is as good as selling $5 more of the product. Cost cutting in production or any aspect of product creation goes straight to the bottom line of a company's financials. A sure sign of a mature market is when an emphasis is put on cost cutting. If you cannot create more demand or sell more of a product, the only way to preserve your profitability and margins is to reduce the costs involved in creating a product. When an industry is focused on these things, entrepreneurs should be figuring out why.

5. Consolidation of competition

If you can't sell more of your own product in the market place, it stands to reason that an alternate way to grow sales is to acquire the sales of other industry players. Consolidation of market players is common in mature markets. For one, it lets you grow your sales volume when you have no other way to do so. At the same time, since there are many competitors willing to discount their prices to get sales, consolidation lessens the number of players able to affect an industry. Consolidation is somewhat of a safeguard against competitors discounting you out of an industry. The fewer players there are and the more volume you have will determine your level of price control in an industry.

These are just some of the warning signs of mature markets. They are all around us, but most of us just do not take the time to think about them. So the key is to start looking for them. They aren't on your radar for a reason. You have never had a reason to question their existence or their way of doing business. Now you do. Actively comparing industries against these signs of maturity will give you a pretty good idea of where innovation is not occurring. Again, it is said that 80% of industries are in this phase. Traditional strategy will tell you to focus on serving niches within a market space to be able to find a specific source of revenue for your product line. Another route is the consolidation method and buying your way to increased business. But too often these strategies still aren't effective and eventually companies end up divesting in certain product and service categories. Unfortunately, one of the main reasons that these strategies often do not work is that they are focused on doing more within the confines of known bases of competition. Rarely do the strategies of companies take them outside of what they have been doing for years. Rarely do companies survive long enough to thrive again in mature market spaces. They simply keep cruising along and riding out the profits as long as it makes sense to do so.

It wouldn't be very innovative to suggest that you, the entrepreneur, should employ the strategy of the incumbents. While they are busy segmenting with a fine tooth comb and buying up all the competitors, you should be focused on upending their bases of competition. The problem that mature markets run into is that the major players generally refuse to venture far from their knowledge base and the competencies that they have had in place for many years. They are usually so heavily invested in a market space and a business model that they often can't venture far from their base. This is where you can come in. The consumer is buying strictly on price because they cannot see a reason to spend more money on two products or services that have an indifferentiable utility. Value propositions and competitive advantages are based on having a product that is differentiated from your competitors. Products in a mature market lack these characteristics. You have to be the catalyst and find a way to create differentiation. You have to be the one to analyze how an industry operates and then decide how to alter it to improve the value proposition for the consumer. Once the consumer can see an increased value proposition again within a market, they will be willing to compensate you for that. The incumbent players will be busy trying to protect what they have been doing for many years and you can slowly gain the business of their consumer base.

Recognizing mature markets is not an innovative end in itself. Many of the sources that we discuss in this book are about ways to create differentiation. Simply recognizing a market as mature does not create this, it is just the beginning. At the same time, it is a source of innovation because it points you to the source of a problem. If consumers are buying products strictly on price then there is a problem, in my opinion, with the solutions being offered. Being aware of and searching out mature markets is going to be a big step to defining your thought process and setting the stage for innovation to take place. When you search out mature markets you are focusing in. You are being pointed in a relevant direction towards a problem. With the other sources, you may be trying to innovate within industries that are not ready for or in need of innovation at the current time. Maybe your ideas are a couple years away or not economically feasible at this time. With mature markets you are being directed to a space that already has a problem. The industry is well laid out and the time is at hand for a new growth curve. So go out, search out these markets. Compare them to some of the signs in this chapter. Read some more about them beyond these basics. Then use other sources in this book or your own thought process to create the new S curve.

The moral here is to simply start looking around you. You are probably taking many sources of opportunity for granted because you never questioned why things are done the way they are. Just like the

USPS and the funeral industry, there are examples of non-innovators all around you. 80% of industries in the United States are in the maturity stage. Think of the recent history of things. What happened to railroads? The full service airline companies? What about the big 3 automakers? The point is that if industries are not constantly innovating, they have a big bullseye on their chest. Fat, lazy and complacent should have an entrepreneur foaming at the mouth. So go out and find these people. Chances are, 80% of the markets you interact with on a daily basis are ripe for you to pick.

Chapter 11:
Combining Alternatives

"It is the power of creative men to perceive the relations between thoughts, or things, or forms of expression that may seem utterly different, and to be able to combine them into some new forms–the power to connect the seemingly unconnected."

- William Plomer

Plomer states that the creative mind connects the seemingly unconnected. To start off this chapter let's consider two things that are seemingly unrelated and test that assertion. Take, for instance, business ideas and dragons. What is the relationship? It is not obvious, and quite frankly, I developed this connection as I wrote the book. However, this chapter could theoretically be taught using a dragon as the primary illustration of the concept. When you break down what comprises this mythical creature, you find that the inputs that combine to create it are not mythical at all. A dragon, when broken down, is simply a combination of a bird and a lizard; two commonplace inputs. However, after a simple combination and a few tweaks - add fire for effect - the resulting whole is something "mythical." The point of this observation is that it is exactly what entrepreneurs do in the world of business. They combine ordinary inputs in new ways, and then they tweak the result to create something innovative. The concept is simple but, much like a mythical creature, innovative businesses have the power to inspire awe in the minds of others. Thus the rest of the chapter is going to look at how we use this idea in the business world. I am going to show you how combining alternatives is a powerful source of innovation and how one exploits ordinary concepts to create extraordinary ones.

The first thing we need to establish to use this source is a working definition of "alternatives." Any number of marketing books will give you an answer to this, but I want to use one that is maybe a little more accessible if you don't own a marketing textbook. I think the book <u>Blue Ocean Strategy</u> sums up the idea of "alternatives" well for our purposes. To summarize Kim and Mauborgne, alternatives are; those things that are not direct substitutes for each other, but they accomplish the same general purpose.19 Alternatives are products or markets that satisfy the same needs but in a different way. For instance, the authors make the point that when you have some free time, you have many options to fill that free time. You could go out to eat, you could go to the mall or you could go to a concert. While these things do not directly compete head to head, such as restaurant versus restaurant, they still compete on a general level for your free time and money. This is the idea of alternatives. Alternatives are products, services, ideas and even entire industries that are not directly connected but might vie for the same time and money investments of consumers. They are different solutions to the same problem that indirectly compete in the marketplace.

Now that we have a definition, what is the point of combining alternatives? What does it accomplish? The idea is to bring together two alternative solutions that compete for time and money out there in the economy, and fuse them into one product offering. By doing this, the consumer does not have to make a decision between one or the other. Often times, combining alternatives allows them to experience the benefits of two or more solutions in one product form. In the Blue Ocean Strategy, Kim and Mauborgne explain that by using alternatives, the goal is to combine the best aspects of two or more products and get rid of the least desirable aspects. Now the consumer has a third option at their disposal. Let's look at an example for illustration purposes.

The recent onslaught of "minute clinics" provides a great example of what I am talking about with regards to the benefits of this source. Minute Clinics are popping up around the nation at Target stores and CVS pharmacies as a third option between consumers having to go to a doctor and self-medicating themselves. The base idea is that the minute clinic combines the convenience and accessibility of a drugstore pharmacy while providing the basic treatments that a private doctor can offer, all at one location. The minute clinic offers sixty or more straightforward procedures such as immunizations, physicals, disease testing, cold treatments, et cetera, without the hassle of scheduling and driving to a private doctor.20 It then also incorporates the convenience of a pharmacy on-site so

---

19 Kim, W. Chan and Renee Mauborgne. Blue Ocean Strategy. "How to create uncontested market space and make the competition irrelevant." Boston, MA: Harvard Business School Press, 2005.

20 www.minuteclinic.com

the consumer does not have to go to a separate location to follow up the visit. Again, this allows the consumer a third option between self treatment or waiting multiple days for an appointment at a traditional office. It combines the positive side of both alternatives while reducing the pain of having to choose between the two when they exist separately. This is a real life example of what we are trying to explain. The combination that you create can produce something entirely new but using elements that already exist. Much like the idea of the MinuteClinic, your combination can create a superior solution by finding a better use of everyday inputs.

Before we dive into the framework for using this source, I want to preface the main argument with a short observation. Specifically, I want to look at why "combining alternatives" jumped out at me as one of the more important sources of this book. I want you to see why it may be better suited for the way our minds operate than most of the other sources of innovation. If you don't mind, I am going to return to the mythical creature thing again for just a moment.

Think about all of the mythical creatures that mankind has invented over the years. Then think about all of the rituals, fables and stories that accompany these creations. It would seem that the things that inspire so much awe in our minds would be absolutely amazing conceptually. However, when you break them down, "mythical" animals and creatures are just a hodge-podge of characteristics from other creatures in nature. Combine half of a horse and half of a human, you get a centaur. Theorize reptiles that fly like birds, you get a dragon. Put the horn of any number of animals on a horse, you have a unicorn. Rarely does the human mind think beyond the things that it has encountered in its lifetime. These "awesome" incarnations are simply a cut and paste of what we see every day. It is only natural that our imaginations are based on the familiar constructs of our lives. With a few tweaks, once ordinary inputs can become extraordinary ideas. So, in my opinion, a baby step to innovation for humans is naturally the combination of two or more business concepts we are already familiar with. Much like a centaur or a dragon, a cut and paste of what we are already comfortable with is a way to create something completely new without stepping beyond the boundaries of daily thought. Fusing the alternatives is novel because it creates something entirely new, but with elements of familiarity. At the same time, new combinations have the power to awe the mind and jump start the imagination. As entrepreneurs, we need to embrace this idea and figure out how to exploit it. Powerful business ideas can be constructed when you think about ideas in this light.

By now I think you understand the concept, but putting this idea into application is an entirely different beast. For instance, the first thing you might ask is, what alternatives should I fuse? When you consider "alternatives" you realize how broad and vague a term it can be. The things you fuse could be anything. Alternatives could be products, services, ideas, theories, processes, et cetera. Fusing alternatives could be as easy as matching up two products or as difficult as matching up a dream with a theory. The products, industries and categories are numerous and the combinations are exponential. Being that we are seeking a systematic look at innovation, we need to focus in.

Remember a good place to ground yourself is in the smaller subset of ideas that are your life passions. The goal when using this source is to eliminate as much dependence on randomness as possible. I believe your search into fusing alternatives should begin through the lens of your passions. It's your work, your hobbies, what you do in your free time, what you dream about and what you aspire to. These are the things that you know and are a good starting point of reference. Starting with a smaller subset of all of the possible categories you could fuse will help you to become more productive and generate more meaningful results. Whatever way you choose to narrow your search for a starting point, don't rely on randomness. The needs and problems of the customer are not random. They can be identified. Chapters 5-8 will help you with this if you skipped over them or are having a hard time. Find your passion, then find your focus.

Once you have found an area to focus on, you want to start looking at the current options available to consumers that could be viewed as alternatives to your product category or service. What exists to satisfy their needs? What else do they employ for their needs when they aren't using your industry? What is the consumer trying to do by utilizing products and services within your industry and in industries closely related to yours? By understanding the total solution that consumers are trying to accomplish, you start to see how they trade between solutions and why. You need to analyze what issues and factors cause them to choose and what drives them toward a decision. In the process, you want to note what they have given up by employing a specific solution. Decisions between alternatives are never black and white. There are always internal debates. Consumers give up a lot by employing one alternative over another. Understanding the upsides and downsides of each decision a consumer has to make within your industry should give you a way to key in on what frustrates them. You can focus in on the problems they face when they have to choose. Say for decision X, the consumer gets Y benefits but gives up Z benefits of another product. Fusing alternatives is about improving the overall solution. How can you create a fusion in which the consumer can get the best of both worlds? How can we eliminate some of the downsides of choosing between two or more solutions? Start to think about new markets and new combinations that are superior to two or more products existing separately. Analyzing the customer, their total solution and the tradeoffs they make is a great way to unearth potential opportunities for utilizing this source.

By focusing on your passions, you should at least have a starting point and possibly one part of the "alternatives" equation you are seeking. The second part of your fusion is going to be based on your analysis of what the consumer is trying to accomplish as a total solution. When you figure out the "task to be done," you start to see how they trade across industries. Now it is time to figure out how to innovatively combine those multiple solutions to the same needs. Again we are faced with many possibilities to match up. Again we have the chance to let our mind wander. How do you choose?

While I was editing this chapter I was also in the process of reading Small is the New Big by Seth Godin. It you haven't read it, this is another book I highly recommend. I could have tried to put this in my own words, but I think his concept of "zooming" is a great way to start thinking about what to fuse with your base industry. His observations are in regards to change and how people deal with it. Seth said that "zooming" is about "doing the same things we normally do, only different." "Zooming is about stretching your limits without threatening your foundation."[21] For our purposes that means by combining alternatives you are taking your base industry and stretching it. You do this by introducing new elements to your base from the other solutions that consumers employ as alternatives to your industry. Industries that are related, such as fishing and boating, are a close zoom. On the other hand, industries such as steel manufacturing and finger nail polish are a huge zoom. How far away from your passions you go to pull in alternatives to fuse is going to be

21 Godin, Seth. Small is the New Big. "And 183 other riffs, rants, and remarkable business ideas." New York, NY; Portfolio, 2006.

your "zoomwidth." This will determine how far away you stray from your core. If the two or more elements you use in the fusion are close to your base passion, you will have a small zoomwidth. The further apart the elements are from your base of knowledge, the larger your zoomwidth is going to be. So when you set out to use the idea of "alternatives" as a source for innovation, start considering your zoomwidth. How far across related industries do I have to zoom to pull in elements that are relevant? Much of this determination will be based on what the customer is trying to accomplish. Your decision as to what to fuse with your base is based on the needs of the customer. Focus in, figure out related solutions and then zoom across industries until you find the right fusion of products for your target consumer.

Let's look at an example because this can all get a little confusing. This is a theoretical situation, but I think it will illustrate the point well. For this example we are going to make the following assumptions:

Your Industry: Creating and producing video games for home game consoles (ie. Playstation, X-Box, Nintendo Wii)
Solution Consumers are Seeking: Playing games that mimic reality as closely as possible

So now that we have made these assumptions, let's look at how we could fashion an entrepreneurial venture out of this situation. You, the entrepreneur, have to start finding industries to fuse with your base industry, video games. The first thing to do is identify the solutions consumers employ as alternatives to playing video games on a home console. Remember that those alternatives could be any industry where a game mimics reality. Your list of alternative solutions might include arcade gaming, computer gaming and virtual reality gaming, to name a few. These are all pretty similar alternatives that might occupy one's time and a close zoom to your industry of focus. Once you have uncovered all of the industries, you can start zooming across them and toying with ideas for combinations. An actual set of real world examples comes to mind with these possibilities. Recently video games such as Guitar Hero have brought elements of arcade gaming into the living rooms of the average video game user. Players buy a special guitar controller to mimic the real life actions of playing a guitar while following along on the video game screen. In this scenario the gamer is given props like an arcade game but for use in their own home. Also, the recent release of the Nintendo Wii has integrated the physical motion aspect of virtual reality into its most recent console release. Gamers swing around a motion sensing controller in real life and the characters of the game mimic those actions in the game. Now consumers can recreate elements of virtual reality in their own living room. Both of these examples illustrate a "zoom" across the alternative solutions to playing a standard video game. These industries –arcades and virtual reality- that were once distinct from your average video game are now starting to merge to better suit the needs that video gamers have. Instead of the two or three industries existing in entirely separate realms, they are being fused to create a better overall solution for gamers seeking to mimic reality when they play. But these examples were pretty basic. You didn't have to go far from your base industry to find alternatives. Let's now look at how we could have found an entrepreneurial venture with a large zoomwidth, using the same assumptions as above.

For our large zoomwidth example we are going to consider alternative solutions that are a far cry from your industry of focus. In this example we are going to assume that you would like to bring a radical level of interactivity to video gaming. Let's say you want players to physically act out their video games in a real environment. Now you might look at industries such as laser tag, paintball and theme parks where the person is immersed in a real environment but still ultimately playing a game. From there you start to zoom and see how to fuse these industries with your base. You might theorize a theme park based on game environments in which players can gain admission to and act out their fantasies in real life. This is much more ambitious and further from your core focus but a very interesting fusion to toy with. You see, with the arcade and virtual reality examples, you are still a video game producer at your core. With a theme park based on video games, you are now at extreme opposites and it is questionable if you are a theme park operator or a video game producer. This second example was a much larger, more ambitious zoom. Your "zoomwidth" is going to be determined if you stay within the same or similar industries or whether you pull from multiple, non-related industries. Similar industries are generally small, less radical zoomwidths, whereas pulling from two highly different industries can create a huge zoomwidth. Be conscious of this as you choose your industries and elements to fuse. The solutions that consumers desire could be anywhere along the zoomwidth spectrum. Consider my example and try to figure out the scope of what you want to accomplish. These are the steps to gaining insights on what to fuse.

As you start to get comfortable with combining alternatives and understanding the nuances of it, you can start to build on the base idea. For instance, keep in mind that a fusion doesn't have to be 50% of one product and 50% of another. Part of the nuance of fusing alternatives comes in when you tweak how much influence you will draw from each of the alternatives. It might be the case that you fuse 75% of one product with 25% of another. You might even fuse 40%, 30% and 30% over three alternatives. Figuring out how much and why is the key. What percentage combination is going to produce the best overall solution for the customer? Take water planes as an example. In the case of water planes the fusion is 90% airplane, 10% boat. This is a small zooomwidth. You are dealing with 90% of what you know and only 10% or so with what you do not. On the other hand, the theme park based on video games is only about 25% video game and 75% theme park. You as a video game person are stepping well out of your element. But that is the beauty of entrepreneurship. If you give two industries to two different people and ask them to combine them, it is highly unlikely that their respective hybrids will be very similar at all. An infinite amount of combinations and small tweaks exists between even a small subset of products, ideas or industries. Understand the nuances and use them for your gain.

Ideas like the water plane we just talked about, or even the goal of a flying car that inventors dream of, are about as simple of a fusion as you can get. Combining the most generic elements of two alternatives and slapping them together 50-50 takes no time at all. The amazing thing is that people are actually working on these projects. Concepts that took less than ten seconds to spew onto paper are having considerable time, effort and money thrusted at them. That's good news. That means that thinking through this exercise for any serious amount of time should produce even more intriguing ideas. Those ten seconds of application provide more access to innovative ideas than most people's understanding of innovation currently provides. The more you think through ideas, the more options you give yourself for areas to pursue for innovation. People are actually working on flying cars. Water planes already work. If you put your mind to it, you can come up with better ideas than this. You are smarter than the guy trying to be the next George Jetson. Start "zooming" and actually put your mind into creating fusions.

In order to get away from slap together, basic innovations, this source and the rest of the sources in this book deserve a good amount of time and effort on your part to be meaningful. You are going to create businesses that will consume years of your life. It would be a big step forward if people would take a couple of hours, days, even weeks to fully analyze the possibilities and directions that idea formation can take you in. If you take this source further, beyond the 50-50 slap together combinations that you get off of the top of your head, you are going to start producing some very interesting ideas. This exercise should take your brain down many relevant paths. Kim and Mauborgne talk about ideas such as Netjets, a fusion of private jet ownership and commercial travel, and Cirque du Soleil, a fusion of the circus and Broadway plotlines, as great examples of success stories who created markets via alternatives. These markets are out there for you to create if you really put your mind to it. Use this source to its full potential by fully fleshing out all of the possibilities that are out there for you to create.

Finally, let's look at one last real world example, since most of the others were theoretical. Let's take a look at the "gum" industry; an industry that hadn't seen much innovation since its inception. It used to be that consumers were presented with a couple of new flavors of gum each year and possibly a new texture or two to boot. However, more recently gum has become more multipurpose. You can now buy gum that is infused with caffeine to wake you up. You can buy gum that touts certain health benefits, such as vitamin and nutrient infused gum. You can also combat smoking with nicotine infused gum. Nowadays gum makers are looking to alternatives such as food, beverages and addictive substances that may replace gum chewing and combining them with their base industry for unique product lines. The resulting value propositions are great for consumers. You can now quit smoking by gnawing on an everlasting piece of goop. You can also get your daily vitamins or a morning pick me up without even glancing at the breakfast table. The benefits of the food and other sustenance have been coupled with the value and convenience of chewing gum in order to produce a whole new breed of products. These products not only compete with other gum manufacturers, but also begin to "eat" away at the profits of other industries, especially big tobacco. Integration of the benefits of multiple alternatives can be a powerful source of innovation, as these real world examples illustrate. Combining the benefits of two or more products can substantially boost the value proposition and create new market spaces for entrepreneurs to exploit.

I realize that this chapter holds a great deal to be digested, and that is why I tried to present as many examples as possible. The key framework is; focus on what you know, zoom across alternative solutions, integrate the benefits and drop the least desirable aspects. There are many products that consumers have not yet thought of bundling. There are many market opportunities that consumers would never think to ask for. But, if somebody offered a compelling solution to a need that people didn't realize they had, they would be more than happy to purchase that solution. Think outside of the status quo and think hard about the possibilities. People will integrate the obvious alternatives. The smart entrepreneur has the opportunity to soar beyond the obvious and create extreme value propositions. Chances are that not only will people enjoy the fusion that you create, they will also be willing to pay you handsomely for it.

Chapter 12:
International Markets

"Globalization is a bottom-up phenomenon with all actions initiated by millions of individuals, the sum total of which is 'globalization.' No one is in charge, and no one can anticipate what the sum of all the individual initiatives will be before the result manifest."
                                                          - John Naisbitt

The United States in recent history has been known as being an epicenter of technology and innovation. For years the US has been a frontrunner in developing and bringing to market new ideas, innovations and technologies. We design it here and work out the kinks while we can still afford to produce in America. Ultimately, the technology peaks and we outsource large portions of the operations to places around the world with cheaper inputs. Such a timeline can be seen over and over again. Consequently, international markets have become a huge topic in the world of business. We have evolved from a domestic economy into a global one, with each playing off of and contributing to one another. Technology, cultural phenomena and popular products of one culture are constantly being integrated into other areas around the globe. Not only does this occur when we take our products and services overseas, but also when we integrate the products and services of other cultures into our own. Competitors, both foreign and domestic, are free to adopt, imitate and improve upon the ingenuity of other countries. In this chapter I want to discuss the idea of international markets as a source of innovation and the array of possibilities it presents for entrepreneurs.

For thousands of years civilizations have been trading, copying and sharing ideas. When a new technology, skill, business model, et cetera is proven in one place, chances are that it will soon be emulated in other areas of the globe. The firms in our present economy not only have to consider domestic competition, but also the competition that will inevitably follow in similar economies around the world. In the past the diffusion of innovation across geographic boundaries was slower than we are experiencing today. The diffusion of ideas had more lead time in a global economy. However, today the information flow is lightning fast. The dissemination of ideas occurs at an exponential speed and the torch is passed to would be competition around the globe in a matter of moments.

As entrepreneurs, this can be both a problem and an opportunity. It means that the opportunities our ideas represent in the global economy are quickly fleeting. It also means that the ideas of other firms around the globe are being served up at the click of a mouse for our convenience. Let's consider an example from recent history to show just how innovation travels.

Consider for a moment Southwest Airlines and their approach to providing no-frills, regional jet service. The company was started in 1971 in the United States by Herb Kelleher and Rollin King.[22] The objective was to provide low cost, efficient and timely airline service by eliminating the frills and superfluous costs of traditional airlines. A pretty simple notion by most accounts. In 1971 they were the first airline in the world to take this approach. However, if we flash forward to today, we can see how, once proven, their business model spread like wildfire. Just look across the Atlantic and you see companies in Europe such as RyanAir, which was started in 1985, and EasyJet, which started in 1995, that borrowed and transplanted Southwest's concept into their home countries. Along with the concept, they are also emulating Southwest's success. RyanAir is to this day Europe's largest low fare carrier. The two companies are doing exactly what Southwest did to United Airways, USAir and others by undercutting the offerings of their European equals, Air France and British Airways. Entrepreneurs around the globe quickly figured out that the unique business model that Southwest enjoys in the United States was transferable almost anywhere. Our neighbors in South America are familiar with Gol Airlines that provides low fare air travel in Brazil. Similarly you can look at Mexico and you see Vuela Airlines or India and you see Jet Airways. The examples abound. All of these airlines in other countries saw the value in taking a proven concept and transplanting into their situation. They not only replicated the new business model, but they are also replicating similar success and profits.

The lessons for the entrepreneur are pretty obvious. Replicating successful ideas in foreign countries is one avenue to championing a successful business. If you've missed the first mover position in America, you can still capitalize on existing innovation in markets that first movers in America have yet to branch into. By the time they get there, you will be the incumbent. This source is powerful because you don't have to be a genius to recognize successful businesses. Take success and replicate it in similar

22 http://www.southwest.com/about_swa/airborne.html

environments around the globe. Figure out where similar voids exist in the global market and fill them. Instead of fighting tooth and nail in the United States, go to other places and be the trail blazer. Transplanting innovations into other areas is a great way to start down the road to entrepreneurship.

The lesson just articulated works equally as well in reverse. Chances are that if RyanAir was the first low fare, no-frills airline in the world, Southwest may have been the one to transplant the idea into America. International companies that offer technologies and products that are not found in your geographic area of the world are ripe for copying onto your own turf. This international transfer is interesting because it puts a spin on being a competitor and entering markets. If you choose to copy a business model domestically and three firms already exist in that market space in America, you are probably in for a bloody fight for market share. Conversely, if you transplant the ideas of a group of international firms onto your home markets, you might as well have been the original innovator. You could have the exact same idea, but entirely different results depending on how you position yourself in the global economy. Finding commonalities across cultures can be an indication of what types of foreign products and services could be integrated into your home location. Go and actively search for things that might transfer. Recognize similar economies and group values. Business models, technology, et cetera can all be things that humans can appreciate across cultural boundaries. All you need is to locate a void that a proven concept from abroad can fill. Entrepreneurs have the chance to capitalize by locating these things and bringing them home.

The concept of mimicking companies in the international marketplace is a basic starting point for taking advantage of this source. However, the concept of international markets goes beyond simple copying. Consider for a moment countries such as India or China. If you look at the recent history, these countries are undergoing radical growth and transformation. Whether it's governmental changes, changes in social values or simply an efforts to modernize their economies, these catalysts have sparked remarkable progress. The infrastructure, markets and technologies that took years or decades to adopt in other modern nations are being integrated in a fraction of the time in these countries. It's similar to watching history repeat itself at warp speed. These countries desire to set up the same or similar economies and infrastructures that other modern nations currently enjoy. Maybe they lack infrastructure that we had ten years ago. Maybe they lack the power grids and phone grids in a majority of the country. It might also be that they lack technology and other hallmarks of the modern world. Consequently, those of us who live or work in the cultures these countries are trying to emulate know what these nations need to do to ramp up to a modern world economy. We know the end situation they desire and we know the inputs that are necessary to get them there. Thus we must recognize the opportunities abroad to contribute our knowledge. If a country is ten years behind most of the modern world, we won't necessarily transplant the technology from ten years ago and expect them to always be behind. It is our opportunity to create businesses that exploit the knowledge curve we have experienced and implement the ideas we have internationally to bring other countries up to speed. If you recognize a need for, say, modern warehouses and transportation systems in India and have the knowledge to implement it there, then you have a huge opportunity to provide your services abroad. The things that a culture lacks but desires could be anything. It could be a complete reinvention of their farmer's markets into modern day retailing. It is up to you to recognize the need gaps in nations outside of your own. Again, in a sense you are watching history repeat itself. Nations around the world are at varying points of progress. Once a country aspires to grow, most of the things they need and the problems they will encounter have already transpired elsewhere in the world. It is a matter of recognizing the gap, knowing how to close it based on experience and closing it for developing nations that desire it so badly.

The last topic I want to cover in this chapter is how ideas, products and services have different implications for different countries. When we export or import them, often times the use and meaning to the new culture encountering them is different than what the products meant to the home country. The business models get tweaked, the execution is varied, et cetera. The notion of how ideas, products and services are useful to them will be unique. For instance, consider the use of technology abroad. A recent throng of ventures have sprung up across the globe to bring technology to third world countries. Instead of the typical uses that we find here in the United States, these impoverished nations are finding unique ways to be able to afford technology. For instance, foreign phone companies are selling one cell phone per village that can be used on a per minute basis by the rest of the residents. Others are providing internet kiosks where people can't afford access in their homes. We are also seeing solar power put into villages that never had a power grid and e-mail being delivered to grass huts. Even though the markets have an entirely new context, entrepreneurs like you are finding ways to cater ideas, products and services to the contextual needs of other societies. You can use known technologies and applications and see how they fit around the globe. Sharp entrepreneurs will find ways to transplant products and services abroad in new and meaningful ways to each respective society. It may be using the exact same models as domestically, or it may entail inventing entirely new business models. The point is that the world is full of opportunities to adapt existing knowledge for profit abroad.

Each and every country around the world has unique contributions that they can make to the global society. Likewise, each and every country has unique needs that the global society can help them out with. The citizens of every country are privy to innovations that can change lives and make money in many locations across the globe. Whether you import ideas, export ideas or tweak existing ideas for incorporation, the opportunities that a global market present are far reaching. Open your eyes, recognize the opportunities, fill in the gaps of the global market and figure out a way to profit from your efforts.

New Process Strategies

Chapter 13:
Reducing Transaction Costs

"Technological advances in everything from product design software to digital video cameras are breaking down the cost barriers that once separated amateurs from professionals. Hobbyists, part-timers, and dabblers suddenly have a market for their efforts..."
                                              - Jeff Howe, Wired Magazine

      One of the first topics that you cover in economics is the topic of costs. We talk about fixed costs, variable costs and opportunity costs. We talk about the cost to produce a product and also the costs associated with consuming a product. The concepts of economic costs are at the heart of all business transactions. With this in mind, it is easy to see how altering the cost makeup of a given industry can have dramatic effects on how it operates. My entrepreneurship professor, Michael Camp, used to say that creating value can be as simple as squeezing $1.01 out of the same inputs that used to be used to create $1.00 worth of value. One of the ways this is accomplished is by reducing transaction costs. A transaction cost is any cost incurred in making an economic exchange.[23] Reducing transaction costs has a double meaning in that it can mean reducing the costs for businesses to compete in a market, or in the case of the consumer, the cost to utilize a product or service. If the heart of entrepreneurship is creating more value from existing inputs, then it stands to reason that a great source of entrepreneurial ideas can come from reducing transaction costs. It inherently creates value to the consumer.

      "Reducing transaction costs" sounds like a boring topic you might find as a lecture title in a college syllabus. Let's break this down into more interesting layman's terms. More simply put, "reducing transaction costs" means that you reduce or remove a cost associated with producing or consuming a product or service. That may even mean subtraction by addition. An advance in technology that reduces the cost of a product or service is a great example of subtracting costs by adding new inputs. Either way, all else being equal, reducing or removing a cost gives the same value as before, but at a reduced investment. This either; A) increases the value to consumers by providing the same product only cheaper, or

---

23 http://www.riskglossary.com/link/transaction_costs.htm

B) allows a new group of consumers to utilize your product who couldn't afford to do so before. Part A is nice and may give you a temporary advantage over your competition, but it is part B that can be so powerful to the entrepreneur. When transaction costs have been reduced enough to allow a new group of consumers to utilize a product, amazing things can happen. Great entrepreneurial ideas can ensue.

One of the industries that stands out right now as a great example of item "B" above is the current state of Hollywood. I referred to this example in an earlier chapter, but for this chapter we are specifically looking at the cost structure. For years the major motion picture studios have been pounding out multi-million dollar productions. Some shows today top hundreds of millions in production costs, with big name actors and special effects extravaganzas. That is before the $30 million advertising blitz. It is also before the millions associated with bringing the show to home video and licensing associated products. Even the physical film on which the movie is shot is equivalent to burning $100 bills by the minute. The sum of the transaction costs is astronomical. The transaction costs are so large that they are prohibitive for a vast majority of the public and many firms. What has happened, however, is that over the last decade or so the transaction costs have been coming down exponentially. With the onset of things such as digital photography, at 1/200th the cost of 35mm film, the industry is being transformed.[24] Films can be shot on digital film at a fraction of the price of the traditional film medium. Even the initial costs of the cameras have been dropped to the point where casual film buffs can produce top end images for $5000 or less. The internet has also played a key role. The capabilities of the internet and computers to download large complex files and stream them to the user is a huge step in the distribution of media. Sites such as Youtube allow users to disseminate high quality media quickly and easily. Even massive advertising budgets have given way to the marketing ploys of the day, such as "word of mouth" marketing and blogging. The costs of promoting a film have been slashed as social networks such as Myspace and Facebook allow this word of mouth phenomenon to occur at a rapid speed. The reductions in transaction costs in each of these areas have combined to allow a whole new set of producers to create an end product that used to be cost prohibitive. The power of this is that it didn't just create new value to existing users. It allowed

---

24 Penenberg, Adam L. "Revenge of the Nerds." Fast Company. Aug. 2006: pp.62-69.

a whole new set of users to partake. The digital era is just beginning. Reduction of these transaction costs in the movie industry has changed the rules of the game or will in the near future. It is going to be up to the new consumers, the entrepreneurs, to innovate and change the movie experience. It is when transaction costs are reduced to levels like this that entrepreneurs can change the faces of industry. So as the big studios roll out Garfield 7 in theaters, look for the next great movies to come streaming into your living room from people just like you.

Along the same lines as the revamping of the movie industry, there has been an amazing drop in transaction costs associated with writing a book. The publishing game used to consist of many hours of labor on the author's part in the slim hopes of being published. Even of that slim percentage that actually do put the ink on the paper, even fewer get the reward of a publishing contract. It used to be that the process of writing a book would be so time and cost prohibitive that few people actually did it. Most authors go through 20 or more rejected book proposals before getting one "yes." On top of that, most of the proceeds would go to the publisher even after the author had covered the "advance" on their book contract. It plain and simply meant that transaction costs were just too high for most aspiring writers, and coincidentally, for a majority of the population. But that is all behind us now as entrepreneurs have changed the face of publishing. The computer and the wide dissemination of internet content have allowed for everyday writers to put their work into physical form. Companies such as Lulu.com have come along to greatly reduce the cost of publishing.[25] At Lulu, the writer can upload their word processor documents into PDF format. After some formatting and tweaking, the author can then go on to select a binding, hard or soft cover and upload images for the outside of the book. Once the author is ready to OK the final product, Lulu can print just one copy or hundreds for a similar cost to the author as the traditional methods. The author can then go on to list her book in the largest bookstore in the world, Amazon, and have her work available on a global scale at the click of a button. The transaction costs of publishing have been slashed. The would-be writer is now published, and the entrepreneur who developed the system is getting paid a nice fee for their efforts. It is reducing transaction costs, such as this example, that allow entrepreneurs to exploit new opportunities and make a lot of money by opening markets to new and original ideas.

---

25 Heilemann, John. "Freedom of the Press." Business 2.0. Jun. 2006: pp. 38-40.

These two intriguing examples beg the question of how entrepreneurially minded people can recognize and exploit such opportunities. How can we see which industries are heading in the right direction and will be fertile for growth in the near future? Once again we will try to create a framework for the entrepreneurially minded to think through. It is about finding a lens to look through so that we may recognize where opportunities may lie. The following is how I believe you can actively pursue opportunities to change an industry by focusing on reducing transaction costs.

It would seem to go without saying at this point that you need to have selected your industry of focus. Once you have done that, the first step is quite intuitive. In order to reduce any costs within an industry, you have to know where they are. As we stated above, it could be fixed costs, variable costs or opportunity costs. It could be overhead costs, labor costs or raw material costs. A cost is an expenditure, whether it be tangible or intangible, to consumers to consume or producers to produce. Find them, know them. You want to physically put the costs to paper. It helps you to understand, it helps you to remember. Break down all costs associated with production and consumption in your industry of focus. You have to begin to understand how each cost affects every aspect of business transactions. It is very easy to brush off the importance of doing this because it seems so obvious. Below I am going to list some of the most basic costs that you will find in any entry level economics textbook. Know these and understand them. At the same time, there are hundreds of economics books available for free at your local library. These books can expand your understanding of costs exponentially. The burden lies on you to supplement your knowledge and pursuit of ideas with all necessary tools to succeed. Therefore, if you know nothing of costs, start doing your homework. It's free.

Costs:

Fixed Costs - A cost that remains constant, regardless of any change in a company's activity.[26]

Fixed costs are thus the costs that you must incur whether you produce 0 items of product or 1 million items. Fixed costs are things

---

26 http://www.investopedia.com/terms/f/fixedcost.asp

such as rent, overhead and salaries. Many times, the cost of buildings and machines are also considered fixed costs. Fixed costs are the costs you have to incur in order to do business regardless of your sales. Some times fixed costs are minimal, as with opening a website for instance. Other times fixed costs are extraordinary. Think of businesses such as telephone providers or railroad companies. These types of companies have to make enormous capital outlays before they turn one cent of profit. For the entrepreneur, reducing the fixed costs of doing business can open the door for many new producers. As we mentioned in the Hollywood example above, the capital required for equipment has been slashed. In the past, millions would have had to be spent before one second of a movie could be produced.

Variable Costs - A cost that changes in proportion to a change in a company's activity or business.[27]

Variable costs include such things as material costs, labor costs and transportation costs. These are costs that are going to change depending on how many units of a product or service you produce. Variable costs will increase as you produce more and more units. Variable costs have the power to enable or disable production and consumption as well. If the price of raw materials for your product increases greatly, you may not be able to profitably produce your product or service any more. Finding ways to eliminate variable costs or reduce them in any way can be very powerful to companies who depend on them to provide their products and services.

Transaction Costs - The direct costs associated with transacting trades.[28]

Transaction costs are the costs that are required in order for exchange to take place. The cost of doing research on suppliers is a transaction cost. The cost of finding the best prices in the marketplace is a transaction cost. The time and energy associated with producing or purchasing a product are transaction costs. These are all costs that go into exchanges in the marketplace. When transaction costs are prohibitively high it excludes some would-be producers or consumers. It is important for the entrepreneur to understand what

---

27 http://www.investopedia.com/terms/v/variablecost.asp

28 http://www.riskglossary.com/link/transaction_costs.htm

the barriers are to production or consumption. If people want to
purchase or produce but are incapable due to transaction costs, there
is a problem. It is up to the entrepreneur to reduce these costs and
enable a new subset of the population to partake.

Opportunity Costs - The cost of an alternative that must be forgone in
order to pursue a certain action.29

Opportunity costs are what you give up in order to pursue the option
you are considering. If you decide to invest your time pursuing a
certain business venture, you give up the opportunity to pursue the
other ventures you were considering. Consumers that choose to
go to see a movie for two hours give up the opportunity to see one
of the other movies that is playing. They might also be giving up a
walk in the park or a chance to read a book. Opportunity costs are
important because people are seeking to maximize their time. With
the little free time we have, we would like to think that we are not
wasting it. If you are standing in line for 45 minutes to eat at your
favorite restaurant, what opportunity costs are you incurring? How
can you as an entrepreneur reduce the opportunity costs of a product
or service so more people could produce or consume something?
Reducing opportunity costs creates value because it saves people
time, money and effort.

      Recognizing the costs of production and consumption gives
you an insight into who can produce/consume and who cannot. High
barriers to entry are what allow only a few companies to control
markets. High barriers to entry are also what can restrict only a few
people to consuming a product level. On the other hand, low barriers
to entry allow the masses to participate. Keeping in mind that not
every cost is in monetary terms, which costs that you've identified
are turning out to be these barriers? Which transaction costs are
the crucial elements that either enable or inhibit production and
consumption? It is quite possible that what you thought might be the
barrier to production or consumption is not the case. Some costs are
going to be miniscule in the overall scheme of including or excluding
producers or consumers, and others will be giant walls. Sometimes it
is an issue of money and sometimes it's not. Below are some common
costs that can turn out to be huge barriers. You should build on the
list that I am about to detail. Add and subtract to your framework

29 http://www.investopedia.com/terms/o/opportunitycost.asp

until it makes sense for your purposes. The key is to understand them. If you understand what enables or disables each party involved in an industry, then you come closer to understanding where the market could go in the future. You get closer to prediction. Also, the more you understand them the more you will be able to manipulate them, which we will get to in a minute. So here they are:

Common Barriers to Production and Consumption:

Price / Capital – Sometimes it comes down to the almighty dollar. Price / Capital is one of the most obvious barriers to production and consumption. High prices and heavy monetary investment can deter a lot of people from starting a business and a lot of people from consuming certain products and services. This goes back to the opening of the chapter. If you can figure out how far the monetary investment needs to be lowered in order to allow new people to produce or consume, you can assess whether it is possible from an entrepreneurial standpoint to pull it off. It might be squeezing $1.01 out of the same inputs that used to create $1.00 worth of value. On the other hand it might be squeezing $2.00 out of the same inputs that used to create $1.00 worth of value. Knowing the barriers and when markets become economically feasible is crucial to the success or failure of your venture. Figure out when the opportunity is going to be accessible. Predict where prices are headed for the future, extrapolate on when the opportunity is going to be economically feasible and take action accordingly.

Time – Time is something that we all value. In the hectic American workplace, free time seems to get reduced year after year. Time obligations to family, friends, sleep and work seem to all but exhaust the days away. In a world where every second counts and time is equated with money, it goes without saying that large time investments can be a huge deterrent to producing or consuming products and services. As an entrepreneur, if you can find ways to save time, maximize time or create more time for producers or consumers, you will have many ears listening to your pitch. Find ways to free up time for people and they will pay you for the opportunity.

Knowledge / Skill – Sometime we have the heart and desire to do something but we just don't have the knowledge or skills it takes to get it done. Going back to the issue of time that we talked about a second ago, many people have a great deal of knowledge about a very specific industry or job they are in. Many of us do not have time to become properly knowledgeable about another industry or skill in order to capitalize on its opportunities. Finding ways to make it easy to acquire knowledge and skills can be a very powerful proposition. This can be as basic as providing drag and drop websites instead of the necessity of learning code. Companies such as Spotrunner are creating template type commercials that users can purchase and customize as opposed to attempting to create their own marketing efforts.[30] If you as an entrepreneur can enable people by doing the detail work for them, you can be very successful. Of all the dreams and aspirations that Americans have, it just takes one person like you to conveniently package knowledge and skills in order for them to reach a tipping point to producing or consuming.

To exploit the opportunity that transaction costs afford, you have to change them. Entering a market and not changing the cost structure or the inputs creates no value. Maintaining transaction costs is basically maintaining the industry norms. It maintains the barriers to entry on both ends and it enters a firm into a fierce competitive battle. Without change, you have little differentiation and are another me-too firm. You have to change the cost structure in order to create new opportunities for both producers and consumers.

When you begin to toy with ideas for changing the cost structure of an industry you have to analyze what sort of reactions you are most likely going to draw. Many producers and consumers alike accept all of the above as established norms and "the way things have always been done." How will they and consumers react given a new value proposition? By this point you have identified the key barriers to either production or consumption and are toying with ideas to change them. As you start to think through ideas, you have to constantly be evaluating what consumers and other firms will do. Will they be motivated to smash your idea or will they ignore it? Is your idea enough of a change in value to get consumers to switch, or is the value proposition only marginally better than what they have? One of the most interesting things is that companies will usually

---

30 http://www.wired.com/wired/archive/14.06/crowds.html

not change immediately because they are still profitable under the old system. Some ideas for change can trap the competition. Let's say they are so heavily invested in a mode of doing one thing that switching to compete with you would bankrupt them. They do not see the problem with their business as long as they continue to be profitable. Fortunately for you, the entrepreneur, you should be aligned to recognize and exploit the changes they don't see. It is not about keeping things the same because they are working. It is about changing and aligning for what is going to work in the years to come. What are the market conditions right now? Where will they be in a year? Five years?

One of the things I find to be very valuable to a framework regarding costs is a comparison between costs and derived value. When you evaluate an industry you figure out the task at hand that the consumer is attempting to solve. You should know the core utility that they are trying to gain by using a product, service or combination. As an entrepreneur you have the opportunity to look at industries and markets from the outside in. Look at what costs are sticking around. What hasn't changed in years? Are those costs providing the same amount of value as they once did? Look at it in a generic sense for your framework. Spending X amount of dollars on this on day 1 provided us with Y amount of value to the consumer. Does spending X amount of dollars still provide us with Y or more value on day 400? Have things changed? The reason I mention this is that things change, as we said above. Consumer attitudes could have shifted. New technology may have become available. Whatever it is that could have influenced markets, you have to ask the question: If spending X dollars on day 400 provides less value than it did on day 1, have the incumbents' business models changed to reflect that? If they haven't, then there is a potential opportunity for the entrepreneur. If the value proposition has changed or is less than it once was in an industry and the incumbents aren't changing, then you should change them!

The last thing I want to add to the framework is the "what if?" question. When you are trying to figure out how to innovate within an industry, posing this question will allow you to break out of the norms of the industry and pose some aggressive (maybe ridiculous) questions. The point is that it gets your mind going. It gets you thinking along the right path. WHAT IF the costs of producing a movie were reduced 10 fold? WHAT IF the time to produce something was reduced by a month? WHAT IF consumers only had to have one tenth of the technical skill to operate a product that current consumers are required to have? WHAT IF? There are millions of theoretical questions that you could pose about the products and services that exist in the world. Posing them takes your mind to a new level. By posing sometimes audacious questions, it removes the roadblocks that your mind puts up about how industries are supposed to operate. It is about questioning everything. It expands your thought process and makes you think about the ramifications to producers and consumers alike. It allows you to see into an ideal world or possibly where the future is going. Constantly posing "what if?" is one of the easiest ways to start thinking about innovation. It gets your mind going every time. Start posing these questions because your "what if" today might be the future of an industry of tomorrow.

So whether you are the company who figures out how to slash transaction costs in an industry or you build a new company once the transaction costs have already been slashed, reducing transaction costs is a great way to be entrepreneurial. One of the themes that is reiterated time and time again in this book is that no one knows what the future holds, your answer for what the future should be is as good as anyone else's. If transaction costs are slashed to let a whole new group of entrants into a market, who knows the potential of where the industry could go? Hollywood is already talking about day and date releases (movies released in home at the same time as the theater) and other concepts that were unfathomable before.[31] How could you capitalize when transaction costs of your industry are slashed? Find industries that are prohibitive to some consumers and find ways to reduce costs and open them up to a new subset of the population. A reduction in transaction costs is a ripe opportunity for the entrepreneurially minded.

---

31 Heilemann, John. "Commercial Interest." Business 2.0. Mar. 2007: pp. 72-74.

Chapter 14:
Support Systems

"Look at today's leaders and you'll see no contenders for 'the next iPod.' You will, however, find two companies selling iPod accessories."

- Pat Regnier, Money Magazine

    Innovation begets new and exciting products, services and even entire industries. It has the power to open up a world of possibilities where there seemed as though none existed prior. What happens when entrepreneurs succeed is that they not only open doors for themselves, they also open doors of opportunity for the rest of us. For instance, some of us will enter the market as competitors. Others will carry the idea to other industries. You may decide to incorporate the knowledge to enhance your competitive advantage. The possibilities go on and on. The reason for this chapter is that while observing new and creative ideas over the years, I found that a common source of opportunities exists in playing off the innovation of others. Every industry and market in the world has this. You're like the supporting cast. A source of innovative business ideas exists by being the person or organization to provide supporting products, services and back-end systems.

    What happens with innovation in the nascent stages of a market is that the idea is being molded and shaped by the original entrepreneur. They are trying to find out where the firm fits in the competitive landscape. They are concentrated on catering the product to the fickle consumer. They are focused and driven on making it succeed. For a time, the original innovator is going to have very focused, specific pursuits. Their time, money and eventual success or failure is dependent on such a focus. The opportunity that is posed to the rest of us, then, is how we can use this to form our own profitable venture. The original innovator cannot be a one stop shop for all of the new avenues of possibilities that their creation has opened. This is especially true when markets are trying to gain traction and firms are just getting up on their feet. That is where you come in. If you are not the trailblazer, you at least have the opportunity to start laying down the road to the door of the original entrepreneur.

    If we refer back to the quote at the opening of the chapter, it shows us the essence of what we mean by producing supporting products, services and back-end systems. The iPod was an innovation that transformed a fragmented market. It changed the face of the game in personal music and then in personal entertainment in general. This is somewhat of a generic example to use, but think of all the products that flooded the market after the successful launch of the product line. Hundreds of aftermarket products came into existence. Anywhere and everywhere you could possibly listen to music became a space for a supporting product. Think of ideas such as the "iShower" or the waterproof cases that let you listen while you swim. Also, every type of wearable accessory, stationary accessory, computer and car accessory began to roll out. You can also look to the ways in which the actual iPods and the iTunes are sold and distributed. I have seen them online, in stores, in kiosks and in vending machines. Many people and many firms are contributors to the success of Apple's vision. Many people have found ways to play off of the ideas presented by Apple and form profitable ventures. The lesson is that entrepreneurs can ride the success of other innovations and create their own venture with supporting products and back-end systems.

Google is another company that shows us the power of support systems and creating ventures around the ideas of others. Take for example Google Earth and the map feature. Revolutionary companies like Zillow.com and Trulia.com have used the map resource to find the basis for their own ventures.32 With the map feature, you can illustrate statistics by transposing them onto the geographic pictures provided by Google. You project the data to create a visual picture of what is going on with that statistic in a geographic area. Zillow and Trulia both decided to frame their business with real estate. With the two sites, consumers can compare and contrast the prices of homes in a given market. It allows transparency to potential buyers or sellers. Consumers can see the prices and estimates of homes in a given area. They then framed the information and resulting mapping of the info as a business. Consumers can utilize the information and purchase the mapped statistics. The information is invaluable when you consider the size of the purchase. Knowing whether homes are overpriced or under-priced in a market can give consumers a leg up when it comes time to purchase or negotiate the price of property. The point is again that profitable business ideas are created daily by playing off of the ingenuity of others. Seeing the benefits of Google Maps and success

32 McNichol, Tom. "Map Mashups Made Easy." <u>Business 2.0</u>. Jul. 2007: pp. 23.

stories like Zillow, other entrepreneurs are now moving on to all types of other statistical data. Consumers can see everything from real estate prices in their neighborhood to traffic congestion and strength of the school systems. Google was a necessary component for these businesses to even exist. Their original vision and venture paved the way. Once the technology and resources came into being, entrepreneurs took the opportunity and spawned numerous new ventures that support and add on to the capabilities of the initial product.

Putting a framework around supporting systems is about asking questions. What else could this product be used for? What other consumer needs does this idea have implications for? Could we produce an add-on? Could we provide an alternative distribution strategy? When a new firm chooses a point along the supply chain to establish their business, they are opening a world of possibilities for other people. If the firm is a manufacturer, then the door is opened to be a retailer or a distributor of their goods. Ideas such as 3-D printers and air-taxis are some of the industries that come to mind. Once the original innovators chose to be the manufacturers of the planes and printers, it was up to the rest of the entrepreneurial community to decide what to do with those innovations. In the world of air-taxis you have the case where people started businesses to buy up the jets and actually sell flight plans to consumers. We also saw companies enter to be the online booking agencies for the air-taxis. In the 3-D printing market, firms are buying up the printers and then contracting out printing services to firms that need rapid prototyping.[33] The list of possibilities goes on and on. The original innovator can only do a certain set of focused tasks when they bring an innovation into the world. It is up to you to figure out what other implications their innovations have. Start looking for ways to support and play off of other entrepreneurs en route to starting a venture of your own.

So that is the lesson for you. When you encounter industries, when you encounter new ideas, when you are thinking about business ventures in your daily life, start to think about the doors of possibility that have been opened by a given innovation. Whether you choose to start a supporting business that is crucial to the operations of the original innovator or whether you simply develop an add-on perk, you need to ask yourself, what is going to be necessary to be in place in order for an industry to succeed? The original firm is not going to be able to successfully cater to the entire

33 Morrison, Chris. "3-D Printing For The Rest of US." Business 2.0. Sept. 2007: pp. 46-47.

target market that has opened up from their ingenuity. Entrepreneurs can enter the market and pick up the slack. You can capitalize on the successful ideas of others. Innovation begets innovation. Search for it and exploit it.

Chapter 15:
Constraint Innovation

"Man built most nobly when limitations were at their greatest."
- Frank Lloyd Wright

There aren't a lot of exciting things that pop into your head when someone mentions the words "process innovation." I couldn't even bring myself to title the chapter as such out of fear that I may never finish it. While process innovation may not get your wheels spinning as fast as some of the other sources of innovation, it is still undeniably important. Instead of focusing on what the phrase elicits in our mind, try to think of the more appealing end products. Vast fortune, pioneer status, industry disruptor or whatever you can muster up to get motivated. Because when we look at entrepreneurs such as Henry Ford, Sam Walton and Ray Croc, who have changed the faces of industry, we can see how powerful process innovation can be. At the heart of their innovations and success stories lies the not so sexy world of pioneering process innovations. In order to put a new spin on the concept, I am calling this chapter "constraint innovation." If for no other reason, it is just to reset you to an unbiased mindset about the topic. I also called it this because the core of innovating within processes has a lot to do with constraints. We'll get to that in a minute. For the time being, try to reset. Look at some of the innovators I just mentioned and think about the ways in which their ideas about processes changed the world and influenced society. Process innovation may not have you jumping out of your chair, but the opportunities it presents for innovation are substantial.

So just what is a process and why does the term elicit painful boredom in our minds? The most applicable definition, in my mind, is found in the Merriam-Webster Dictionary, which defines it as such: "a series of actions or operations conducing to an end."[34] The key part is "conducing to an end." We put processes in place when we know that doing a specific set of actions will bring about the end product we want or need. A process is a way to achieve consistency. Part of the reason processes are so boring is that they inherently have to be. If there were high levels of variability in our end product, we do not have a good process at all. To achieve consistent results, processes demand that the actions be straightforward and

---

34 Merriam-Webster Collegiate Dictionary, tenth edition

methodical. The ability to repeat the actions over and over again is important. Thus, boredom ensues when the elements of creativity and original thought are sucked out of the task at hand. But to be a process innovator is actually quite the opposite of boring. The aforementioned innovators became industry giants and household names by employing innovative ideas with regards to processes in their focus industries. Process innovation is the epitome of entrepreneurship if you think about it. As entrepreneurs, it is our job to recombine all of the available inputs to create something entirely new. When you change a process this is exactly what happens. Once you change or recombine one or more inputs in a process, the whole system can be disrupted. What once created X, now creates Y. Changing elements of a process eliminates the consistency you had in the previous arrangement of actions. The new set of actions creates an entirely new end product. In doing so you have the capacity to greatly increase the value proposition of an entire system. Whether it be cost savings, time savings or what have you, any incremental change in the value proposition can have major implications on an industry level and possibly across industries. Let's now move on to see how we can identify opportunities for process innovations and how it works.

When you start to think about innovating at a process level, where do you look? First it is important to note that a process can be as broad as an entire firm's operations and as specific as one part of a machine within a manufacturing plant. It is important to define exactly what sort of ideal state you are trying to achieve. Are you trying to reduce a constraint to allow a business to go global or are you simply trying to increase the efficiency of the stamping press? The scope of your process is going to determine how large of an innovative lens you are taking. The smaller the lens, the more likely the differentiation level will be low. The larger the lens, the more complex but also the more innovative an outcome might be.

Let's get back to the whole point of renaming this chapter. As I said at the beginning of the chapter, much of process innovation stems from constraints. If you have the opportunity to read up on the subject or take a class on process control, this concept comes up often. This is especially true in the world of manufacturing and production. These are areas where consistent end products are a necessity. For that reason, manufacturers are obsessed with the processes they employ. Methods such as Six Sigma and Just-In-Time inventory management abound. What you would also learn about is the way in which companies continuously try to improve their processes. Much of the focus is on constraints.

When we talk about constraints, we are talking about the things that hold a process back. These constraints are something that keep the process from achieving an ideal state as defined by the user. Sound familiar? What this is basically saying is that there is a problem. An ideal solution eludes us. We would like to have 100% output but we are only getting 67%. We would like to cater to millions of customers but our current business model only reaches thousands. We would like to have finished goods in stores in two months but it currently takes four, et cetera. What it all goes back to is that anything less than an ideal output has to do with a constraint on the process we are employing. Something is holding it back. That something is the problem. That is where we focus in. When we can identify the elements of a process that constrain it, we isolate the area where a problem needs to be solved. That is where the job of the entrepreneur comes in. A way to recognize problems exists in finding constraints within an overall process and theorizing and developing ways to reduce or eliminate that constraint. In doing so, you will have created an entirely different process and, hopefully, something differentiated enough from the previous solution that consumers are willing to pay you for your innovation.

The process of finding constraints is mostly observation. The only prerequisite is that you have to have defined the ideal solution you are seeking. If you have not done that, then you do not know where to look to see what part of the current process is holding back your vision. So try and define what you are trying to do. If you are trying to tweak a business model to go global, what are the current roadblocks? Once you have defined it, you need to dissect the process. Take it apart piece by piece. A technique I learned in college was very helpful for defining where to look for constraints and how to break down processes. The technique was dubbed "Value Stream Mapping." In essence, once you have defined what creates value in a process with your ideal state, you map out each element in the process to see where the most value added steps occur and where the most counterproductive steps, or constraints, occur. Then you begin reducing and solving for ways to decrease the effects of the constraint and provide more value to the overall picture. Eventually the original source of the constraint will cease to be the problem. Firms and entrepreneurs who practice continual improvement constantly shift focus to where the next constraint lies. Over time, gradual improvements will occur. Other times, dramatic shifts in the way things are done will occur. Either way, the key to constraint innovation is realizing that they always exist. There is no perpetual motion machine, there is no process that is 100% energy efficient. Constraints always exist, and the entrepreneur can systematically analyze processes to find these constraints and innovate in such a way as to solve them.

To round out the topic of constraint innovation we're going to take a look at an example. The company I am about to talk about took the idea of reinventing a process to a whole new level. That company, Apollo Diamonds, has one of the most intriguing new processes I have seen in a long time. The problem? Well, it takes mother earth thousands of years to form the gems and stones that mankind values.35 On top of that, in the case of a diamond, it might take millions, or even billions, of years to bring those stones close to the surface of our earth via volcanic eruptions. The result is a short supply of precious stones at a high price of acquisition. Leaving this process up to nature results in a finite supply of diamonds and limited applications based on their scarcity. However, Apollo Diamonds has found a process for reinventing the way we think about diamonds. They can create them. Through a process called "chemical vapor deposition," Apollo can shorten the time of creating diamonds from millions of years to one or two weeks.36 "The [founders] spray heated carbon gas over diamond chips; under extreme pressure, the carbon atoms settle on the chips and conform to the structure, building on it." The result is a near flawless diamond. Although this is an extreme example, the implications of this technology are enormous. Everything from semi-conductors to engagement rings take on a whole new meaning. If we can take a finite resource and effectively make it nearly infinite in supply, the implications are staggering. Applications expand dramatically and the cost of obtaining these sought after stones should effectively be reduced. While I don't expect that most of us will develop such an intricate process, this example should illustrate the possibilities that new processes can open up. Much like the concepts of franchising and assembly lines, this example has the potential to completely topple the way things are currently being done in our society. What processes are out there that you see need to be changed? Even if you can't completely topple industry norms, how could you greatly increase the value

---

35 http://www.answers.com/topic/diamond?cat=biz-fin

36 LC. "Man-Made Diamonds." Fast Company. Mar. 2006, pp. 116-117.

proposition? What processes are slow, inefficient or downright useless? Search them out and start taking steps to improve on what is there.

Innovation is not always the sexy magazine cover, wild idea. Sometimes it is tedious and has the potential to be downright boring. However, if you look at a business as a process or a process within a business, you can freely choose to define where those processes go and what they will create for the future. The interesting side of process innovation is determining what consumers will value in the future and theorizing what the future state of things will look like. Even though analyzing processes might be a boring prerequisite for innovation, defining the future states of industries is not. Define an ideal state far from the current norms and all of a sudden process innovation can become a very exciting endeavor. It is up to entrepreneurs to determine the capabilities we will have in the future. You could be the one to create those capabilities, and process innovation is just one more way to make that a reality.

Chapter 16:
Waste

"Oh! waste thou not the smallest thing…For grains of sand do mountains make."
- Edward F. Knight

A prime area for a new venture can be found in the most unexpected of places. The inescapable production of waste in any society provides fertile ground for innovation. Whether the waste is physical, such as grass clippings, intangible, such as a waste of time, or unusable, such as scrap metal, it matters not. Any area of waste is an area of opportunity, especially for aspiring entrepreneurs. Waste is an unwanted by-product of any realm of industry or human activity, yet waste has given birth to many highly profitable organizations. Waste Management, founded by Wayne Hyzuinga, was started by one man and with one garbage truck. His company, which literally takes care of waste, has since grown into a multi-billion dollar empire. Likewise, mini-mills were spawned from the idea that scrap steel could be put to profitable use and have presented a highly profitable business model for many years. More recently, the internet has spawned thousands of online retailers that save you time by not having to travel to purchase the goods you desire. Any way in which waste can be reduced or eliminated is a place where there is a business potential and a profit opportunity. Entrepreneurs who can frame waste as a potential profit can flourish in the marketplace.

So, how do we start identifying areas of waste that might present an opportunity for entrepreneurs? Given my background in marketing and logistics, I don't think I will be the next complex plastics recycler. I start with what I know. I start with what I encounter in every day activities. Where is the waste? Write it down. I personally have a pet peeve with waiting for a table at restaurants. The other evening I was Christmas shopping in a busy urban area. Upon entering an Olive Garden I was told that the wait for two people would be about 45 minutes. I do not know how to solve the problem, nor would it particularly interest me to do so, but I see waste. When people can pay some money to save time or gain some time to make money, there is a profit potential there. In this instance I was unable to find a shorter wait anywhere in town. I still had shopping to do, but the store I was going to would have taken more time than this. So there I sat for 45 minutes. I was a member of a captive audience with

20 other individuals in the same boat. We were wasting time, and the loud, crowded waiting area was not especially good for conversation. Like most restaurants, this one would not take reservations during this busy time. In any event I had little choice, and wasted 45 minutes of my day and hard to find free time. However, we as consumers are accustomed to restaurant wait times. Few people question why they exist, they just do. I would be happy to pay for a solution to gain back these valuable moments of my life if someone would provide me a solution. The point here is to analyze where you encounter waste in your daily activities. It can be a catalyst for new ideas.

Along the same lines, my entrepreneurship class in college discussed a company that collects and recycles grass clippings for consumers for a fee, turns them into a base for mulch, and then resells the mulch back to consumers. The founders of this company didn't have to be geniuses to figure out that grass clippings could be turned into a profit. People have been keeping compost piles for years. Everyone who does yard work knows that compost turns into a valuable fertilizer in the spring when it is time to plant a garden. These same consumers run into resistance by the city waste removal programs who do not want to haul away their leaves or grass clippings and eat up room in the landfill. Enter the entrepreneur. The featured company realized an opportunity to make money on both ends. They bought some land and some collection equipment and charged to haul away the waste from consumers for an initial fee. Then, they stored it over the winter until it was a nice fertilizer. They then sold it back to consumers in the form of nutrient rich mulch in the spring. Everyone is happy and someone is making a nice profit. The companies doing this aren't all that old and anyone watching for waste on a daily basis could have put these variables together many years ago. You've been staring at a stink heap of opportunity for years in your back yard. What else is going unnoticed?

Waste is not a hard source to comprehend. It happens every day in every facet of life. You just have to recognize it and formulate ways to take advantage. Nonetheless, I am going to attempt to at least throw some categories of waste out there for a framework. That way your mind has some more concrete things to wrap itself around as opposed to randomly searching for an abstract term. So here they are in no particular order. Please add, subtract or reword for your own benefit. Start identifying sources of them today.

1. Byproducts

Every day, in every industry, humans and machines are creating byproducts. These are generally unwanted results of manufacturing, services and product consumption. Byproducts can be physical or intangible. Since every industry has them, it would be futile to try to develop a list of all the things that could be considered "byproducts." But you are smart enough to realize what I mean. Pose the questions to yourself; What are the unwanted byproducts of this industry? Why? What is being done about them? What *could* be done about them? You're looking for any tangible or intangible results. You are looking to recognize the byproducts, write them down and then let your mind contemplate how you could create a business out of the things noone else wants. You can also take the route of the wholesale elimination of byproduct. Think along the line of substitutes and alternatives that can accomplish similar ends without the byproducts.

2. Unused Resources

The use for certain resources in an industry comes and goes with the product life cycle. Machinery becomes obsolete. New technology replaces older technology. Businesses go paperless. Whatever the event that sparks the move from the current way we accomplish tasks, in the process we tend to leave resources behind. We perceive that they no longer have much value. I have to add the obligatory cliché that "one man's trash is another man's treasure." (sorry) But, it is a true statement. Resources and inputs often fall from grace, but that only makes them irrelevant to one company, one industry or one person. There are plenty of other places where those resources are valued. Referring to international markets, think of how valuable many unused technologies could be to third world and developing countries. Read the technology chapter and you see how old technology can be given new life in another industry. In any event, look around at what you no longer value for your business or in your life. Figure out who would value these things. Figure out what industries have resources that can be bought at a very low price and reinvented to create value elsewhere.

3. Non-sustainable Resources

Every day the environment is affected by the industries, products and processes we as humans use to live. In the past it seemed as though the resources we were consuming were virtually unlimited and only slightly affected by the actions we took. However, with the growing case for global warming, ozone depletion and rampant pollution, it is pretty obvious that things are going to have to change. All of the resources from trees, clean air, water, et cetera are affected by what we are doing in industry. The past has been focused on using up resources such as trees for lumber without much regard for the consequences. When all we do is take from the world around us, eventually our supply of resources is going to falter. Many opportunities lie in the ability of people to develop processes, products and services that allow for resources to be sustainable once again. You don't have to look far for evidence of this type of waste. Consumers will one day not have a choice but to embrace it. When will you?

4. Inefficiencies

There are no perfect businesses, no perfect industries and no perfect people. Inefficiencies exist throughout our world today. Some industries are pretty good with efficient use of inputs, while other industries are absolutely terrible. Whenever you encounter an inefficient product, an inefficient process or an inefficient service, you should see the chance for opportunity. It could be a waste of time or a waste of materials. They are tangible and intangible but they exist everywhere. Instead of blindly accepting that the inefficiencies have always just been there, why not question them? Why not change them? Obviously, other people are too lazy or tied up to change it themselves, but I am sure they would be glad to pay you to do it.

5. Man Made Compounds and Non-recyclables

This is similar but still different from byproducts. Sometimes the problem isn't a byproduct of something humans value, it is the product! Of all of the science and engineering marvels we have created over the years, we have also created huge problems. Many of the man-made compounds, materials and products that we have produced are not good for our own health, the health of the environment and for the health of other animals. We have produced thousands of non-biodegradable materials. We have formed thousands of toxic compounds. We have been careless with what we do with those items. A source of waste in this sense is two fold. It is wasteful because products cannot be broken down and reused after their relevance is obsolete. At the same time it is actually wasting away our environment through pollution and disease. Entrepreneurs who can find ways to recycle the non-recyclables are the winners. Entrepreneurs who at least find new uses for such materials save them from the environment. Entrepreneurs who find natural or at least less toxic substitutes are the winners.

6. Using less than 100% of any input

If you are trying to innovate in the area of waste, understand everything that goes into an industry, product or service. A big focus today is being put on energy used to accomplish various tasks. Companies are determined to rid the earth of polluting fossil fuels. They are determined to find alternative sources for anything in the home, car and office that uses energy. Another focus is the time factor involved in the creation or consumption of a product. Time is money, and therefore wasting time is wasting money. Look to find where your time is being wasted on a daily basis or how it could be used more effectively. Raw materials that go unused or partially used are another source of waste. Land and natural resources that are not being fully utilized are a source of waste. (think back to the grass clipping example)

In today's high paced, fast action world of productivity there is no excuse or time for waste. Companies are realizing that instead of focusing on increasing sales volume, they can profit just as much if they cut out the waste within the organization. One dollar in cost savings is essentially the same as finding five dollars in new sales. Eliminating waste goes straight to the bottom line and generally with less effort. If the market is saturated or the industry has stopped growing, one of the easiest ways to generate money is to cut waste out to improve bottom line profitability. You could be the person to show them how.

New Product Strategies

Chapter 17:
Substitutes

"Creative thinking may simply mean the realization that there is no particular virtue in doing things the way they have always been done."

- Rudolph Flesch

You must realize that all consumers are currently satisfying their needs with some product or service on the market or they are choosing not to consume. It is probable that they will continue to do so as long as they have no reason to change. But, as Flesch points out, there is no particular virtue in doing this. The current solutions to consumer problems are not necessarily the pinnacle of possible solutions. However, consumers are generally not beating down the door asking for new solutions to their problems. It is up to the creative minds out there. It is up to entrepreneurs to question the established ideas and find new answers. One way to do this, and the topic of this chapter, is to locate and implement substitutes for the current solutions. Employing substitution as a source of innovation is about showing consumers how it can be done better, or cheaper, or more efficiently, et cetera. In a general sense, all entrepreneurial firms are naturally employing some degree of substitution as a means of creating opportunities. The money that flows into successful new firms has to be drawn away from somewhere. For that reason, it is important for your mindset to include a proactive search for substitutes. Questioning the established market solutions and developing new ways of solving the same problem is a way to progress and find profitable new venture ideas in our society.

It is often hard to differentiate between some sources of innovation and where concepts should fall. Usually they overlap, resulting in gray areas that are left up to interpretation. When you read through this, you might struggle somewhat to differentiate some ideas as "substitutes" versus "alternatives." There are gray areas. To add to the confusion, there are also two different types of substitutes that need mentioning. The first thing I want to do, then, is lay out the definition of "substitute" that I will use in this chapter. The first part of doing that is understanding the difference between two types of substitutes; "perfect substitutes" and "close substitutes." Economic theory tells us about perfect substitutes.

A perfect substitute would be two products or services that are indifferentiable to consumers. A good example of this would be most agricultural crops. Crops from across the nation are produced by different people but are mostly indifferentiable to the consumer. The characteristic differences between say, two ears of corn are generally not obvious or noticeable. This is the idea of a perfect substitute. Unless demand exceeds supply, having an undifferentiated product from competitors is a bad idea for an entrepreneur to have. On the other hand, you have close substitutes. I like to think of imperfect rhymes in poetry as a good analogy for this idea. Two words that are imperfect rhymes are similar in sound, but not the exact same sound. For instance, wing and caring are imperfect rhymes.[37] In the same sense, close substitutes in business would be two products that solve the same problem but not in the exact same way. Picturing two different brands of the same product is a good way to illustrate this concept. Different brand names from the same industry are often close substitutes for each other, but they are not exactly the same, differentiation exists. Close substitutes are what I am referring to when I talk about substitutes for this chapter. A substitute, then, is a product that serves the same core utility as another product, but not in the exact same way. You can see how the gray areas will come into play when we try to make the distinction between similar and same. Just in case there is any confusion, I will provide an example.

For our example, think about buying a car. There are many car manufacturers in our country. None of them produce the exact same product, yet all of their products serve the same core purpose or utility to the consumer. They all seek to transport you over land from point A to point B in a hunk of metal on multiple tires. Most cars are substitutes for one another. Yet each car manufacturer has differentiated product lines that allow them to be successful. No other car is a perfect substitute for their competitor's line of cars. The cars may be close substitutes, but not perfect. This is the idea of a close substitute and how I will be using the word throughout this chapter.

At the same time that we have to make a distinction between types of substitutes, we also need to take into consideration the idea of "alternatives," that we touched on in an earlier chapter. With the car example you were looking for a specific core utility; a multi-wheeled hunk of metal that transports you over land and roads to get from point A to point B. It is a pretty specific core utility. With

37 http://www.public.asu.edu/~aarios/formsofverse/furtherreading/page2.html

alternatives, the need being fulfilled is less specific. An alternative to a car might be any vehicle that can transport you over land, sea or air to get from point A to point B. It could be a plane, boat, et cetera. You are still accomplishing a similar task to be done, getting from point A to point B, but in a very different way. Think of substitutes as being different brands within a market space, whereas alternatives compete in entirely different markets. Even with such examples, the gray areas will always exist. It is not that important. Just remember that there is going to be a spectrum from perfect substitutes to polar opposite alternatives. Distinctly categorizing these concepts is not nearly as important as understanding how to utilize each of them.

Now let's get back to the important part of the chapter and try to form a base framework for using "substitutes" as a source of innovation. Anytime you think, "how could this be done differently?" you are asking yourself what kind of substitute could solve the same need or problem. If you look around, you can pose the question about any number of things. Why are humans bound to a screen in a set location to be connected to the world? Why do we still use electric lights placed in strategic locations to light our homes? Why do we do anything that we take for granted? What other solutions could we use? The point is that when you start to look around your world you should be questioning why things are done the way they are. How could we solve it better? What products, services or inputs could we utilize to solve a problem in a new way? This is the essence of substitution. It is about questioning the established solutions. We are all solving our problems, but until someone shows us how to solve the same problem more efficiently and get the same core utility, we rarely question the methods we employ. Successful entrepreneurs have the ability to see where conventional wisdom is flawed. Successful entrepreneurs have the ability to pose new solutions to old problems. Entrepreneurs can capitalize where poor and outdated solutions abound by exploiting the idea of substitution.

The entrepreneur who actively questions the world around him or her should have a constant flow of ideas for business opportunities. They just have to be looking. The first thing you need to do is choose an industry to focus on. Once you have done that, start looking at how consumers are currently solving their needs in your industry. You have to analyze what products and services are currently being employed as solutions to their problems. What is the core utility that this product, service or idea is providing? Why are they buying? I suggest you steal a page out of the book of random idea generators in order to do this. When employing substitution, you need to break down the products that are currently being used to solve problems or satisfy needs. You want to break them down into all of the inputs that combine to produce the total solution. Inputs could be anything; raw materials, physical characteristics, emotional characteristics, aesthetic characteristics, design characteristics, et cetera. Any input that comes together to form the product, tangible or intangible, is something that should be considered. Break them down and understand the role that each plays. What does each input accomplish? What does it cost to incorporate that input? How much value does each element of the product add to the whole solution? Analyzing each individual input will give you the perspective you need to see why consumers buy. Understanding why consumers buy a product and the core utility they are seeking is crucial if you plan on selling anything to replace it.

After you have broken down the attributes of a solution, the next step is figuring out how to replace it. Randomly replacing inputs won't get you far. Random substitutions will produce random results. Your substitutions have to be purposeful and anchored by the needs of consumers. The next step is about analyzing all of those reasons you came up with for why people buy. What do consumers value in each input? What adds to the product? What detracts from it? Ultimately, how can we improve on what exists? Just like we did with the chapter on alternatives, you start looking for ways to improve on what is out there. Start theorizing ways to change the elements of a product or service that detract from the overall solution. Start thinking of ways to enhance those elements that consumers already value. When you've broken down the reasons people buy into distinct elements, you start to understand where substitutions can have a meaningful impact on the product. What do you see that others are missing? What can you change to improve the overall solution? What needs improvement or could be done differently?

When you think about substitutes, what you are really doing is taking all of the stimuli that you have at your disposal and inserting relevant stimuli in place of what currently exists to improve the overall solution. What experiences and knowledge do you have that could contribute to an industry and create new solutions? What theories do you have about the ways you think an industry *should* work? What is your unique perspective? Most of us do this to some degree already in our daily lives. However, there is a reason you and I haven't launched an array of successful inventions. In order to utilize this source of innovation you have to be willing to dive deeper than most people. If the ideas that come off the top of your head were obvious successes, we would have a nation full of millionaire inventors. But remember, most inventors have the word "toiling" in front of their title. In order to use this source, be prepared to fail with many, many ideas before you find a winner. The more ideas you are willing to entertain, the better your chances for success.

All of us have entertained thought streams of how we could better solve one of our daily problems. We have all dreamed up novelty gadgets and widgets to help us in our daily lives. However, our brainstorming on the topic generally stops after that first vague thought stream. Unless the problem is in a field that we are steeped in, we often come up with tentative solutions and imaginary products that we are incapable of pulling off. Instead of digging in to do more research, most people decide to give up. If you can relate to such a situation then you should realize that the ideas that you pull off of the top of your head are only going to get you so far. Brainstorming for thirty minutes or a couple of hours probably isn't going to provide you with the answers you are seeking. Seeking out sources of innovation is much more than that. It is about research and answering unknowns. It is about posing and testing theories multiple times over. You are going to go through many failures before you encounter success. When most people come up with a theoretical input, they will discard it quickly unless it is something they believe they could easily produce. If you think good ideas come this easily then you will shrug them off too. Good ideas take time, effort and research. If you are interested in solving a problem in a new way, take the time to explore it. See what is out there. Learn something. Take the time and invest it to research substitution possibilities in the world. By doing this you are at an advantage, because most people will stop before you do. Substitution, like many sources, is simple on the surface, but the results will not come to you without effort.

Finally, remember that a consumer is unlikely to substitute your solution unless they can see an obvious increase in the value proposition and a reason to abandon the current way they are solving a problem. Raising the value proposition is going to mean different things to different industries. It may mean lowering the cost. It may mean integrating better technology. It may mean lowering the time commitment involved in consuming a product. It is about staying focused on the core utility that consumers are trying to accomplish. Improving ways to accomplish that core utility is going to be the way to increase your value proposition. Keep this in mind or you may be creating ideas that are novel but not necessarily viable in the marketplace you are going to be targeting. Once you have learned everything about what you want to replace, then you can truly begin to understand where making a substitution can have an impact. Remember to keep your substitutions relevant.

Although the concept of substitutes is a simple one, I think it is always interesting to see how entrepreneurs are utilizing sources of innovation for success in the present day. I want to close out this chapter with a few real world entrepreneurs employing the idea of substitution. The following are a few examples that I thought might get your mind going and cement the idea of substitutes in your brain.

Astroturf For Horses

In October of 2006, Fastcompany magazine reported on entrepreneur Michael Dickinson and his development of a synthetic racing surface for horse tracks. Dickinson's "Polytrack" is a mixture of "sand, rubber and wax coated fibers" that replaces the need for dirt as the base of a track.38 However, he didn't replace the need for dirt out of randomness. The idea behind Polytrack is that it provides a more forgiving surface on which the horses can run.39 The track prevents impact injuries to animals that commonly plague the industry. At the same time, the synthetic track also reduces the amount of maintenance necessary to keep a track in top condition. Polytrack is a great example of purposefully substituting inputs to raise the value proposition. These expensive competition animals are now safer while they compete, thereby easing the minds of their owners. At the same time, the tracks utilizing Polytrack are realizing monetary gains from reduced maintenance.

Foie Gras Reinvented

As you most likely know, "foie gras" is the French terminology for a fattened goose liver. Restaurants around the globe serve the dish as a delicacy to their patrons. However, in the United States, the process for creating this dish has come under fire. The reason for this is that geese are often force fed to fatten them up. Many local and state governments have already banned, or are considering banning, this practice that is considered unnecessarily

38 Swindler, Josie. "Astroturf for Horses." FastCompany. Oct. 2006, pp. 42-43.

39 http://www.polytrack.com/

cruel to the animal. The point of all this is that one entrepreneur has taken this problem and flipped it into an opportunity. Even if restaurants cannot get traditional foie gras, the demand does not go away. So, being a longtime goose farmer, Jim Schiltz thought he might have a viable substitute for the controversial product. Schiltz has observed that the livers of older geese tend to be fattier than younger geese. Instead of force feeding the animals, he has opted to let part of his flock age and let them get naturally fatter over time. By setting aside 10,000 geese specifically for this purpose, he is hoping that his product will become a viable substitute for foie gras.[40] Schiltz's idea is an excellent example of how substitutes can provide new solutions to old problems. In this scenario, both consumers and local governments should be able to compromise by preserving this famous dish while improving the standards for how it is created.

Bamboo For You

Bamboo is an agricultural crop that most people associate with the diet of pandas. However, all that is changing as Chinese manufacturing firms have found a method for turning the stuff into a fiber for clothing and related textiles. Traditionally, cotton and other fibers have dominated the textile industry, but that may now be changing. Business 2.0 reports that bamboo "yields 50 times as much fiber per acre as cotton." [41] With that being the case, bamboo is quickly turning into an economically viable substitute for its predecessor. The price should steadily decline as people realize the higher crop yields and the process for creating bamboo fiber becomes more widely known. Bamboo fiber is also supposedly "far softer, easier to dye, and better at fighting odor than cotton." With all of these factors becoming apparent, it should be easy to see how bamboo is quickly becoming a substitute fiber in many products. When we can increase the yield of scarce land, improve product quality and have a method for doing so that is economically viable, cotton products that have remained unchanged for years are going to get a run for their money. The trend towards utilizing more bamboo is expected to continue and entrepreneurs who find a way to exploit its popularity should see their business grow along with the trend.

With these examples I think it makes the topic of substitutes a

---

40 Newman, Kara. "Can This Guy's Goose Lay a Golden Egg." Business 2.0. Nov. 2006, pp. 42.

41 Durst, Sidra. "The Panda Food in Your Pants." Business 2.0. Oct. 2006, pp. 34.

bit more intriguing. Entrepreneurs out there just like you are finding opportunities in the markets by exploiting the idea of substitution. What implications does this source have for you? How can you employ this idea to change the future in your industry? Start questioning established norms in your industry and question them often. Do your due diligence and really dig into the problems out in the marketplace. The current solutions to consumer problems are not the pinnacle accomplishments of an industry. It is up to you to show consumers what else is possible.

Chapter 18:
Complementary Products

"There are two ways of spreading light: to be the candle or the mirror that reflects it."

- Edith Wharton

In our modern world people are constantly looking for extra time to squeeze out of each day. Multitasking has become a necessity of everyday life. Squeezing more value out of our resource of time is one of the keys to innovating in today's world. Whether it's e-mailing on the Blackberry while at the grocery store or paying bills online over dinner, each saved minute is value for the consumer. Only a few short years ago, consumers had to juggle telephones, cameras, planners and notepads. Now we have digital camera phones with typing capabilities and the internet. Women might have had to choose whether to work or to stay at home with children. Now they have corporate offices with daycare services.[42] Among the myriad of product offerings, sometimes consumers have to go to extra lengths to be able to do all the things he or she would like to do at one time. Enter the entrepreneur. A great source of ideas comes from creating products and services that complement the solutions that consumers are using to solve their daily problems. Successful complements can save time, increase efficiency and allow multiple tasks to be completed at once. All of these things combined make the idea of complementary products a great source of opportunities for the entrepreneur.

Start to think about all the things in your life that have been conveniently bundled for you, the consumer. Most of the products you encounter on a daily basis need other products and services in place in order to consume them. Often we cannot fathom operating without these ancillary products once we have been introduced to them. Sometimes these products are critically necessary and other times life is simply more convenient with their existence. Enabling one activity with a complementary product or service can be one way for entrepreneurs to capitalize in the market.

A good example of this concept comes from the relatively

---

42 Influenced by: Kim, W. Chan and Renee Mauborgne. Blue Ocean Strategy. "How to create uncontested market space and make the competition irrelevant." Boston, MA: Harvard Business School Press, 2005.

recent introduction of eBay drop sites. EBay is a service that millions of people use. It has revolutionized the world of auctions and garage sale type transactions. EBay by itself was good. However, entrepreneurs came along and made it more convenient for potential sellers. EBay drop sites allow people to drop off the items they wish to sell and, for a cut of the sale price, have the items listed, sold and shipped on their behalf. The drop site owner gets his or her cut and then pays the person who owned the property. This has allowed many people beyond the typical eBay seller to utilize the power of eBay's service in a fraction of the time. By upping the amount of items that people can sell, and by bringing in consumers who otherwise would not have the knowledge, skills or time to sell on eBay, these sites have raised the value proposition. For many people, the time saved utilizing this complementary selling product is well worth the percentage cut that the drop site takes as commission. It allows consumers to sell items while they watch their kid's soccer game or go see a movie. It gives busy consumers another source of multitasking and, in this case, an opportunity to make money while they do it. The sum of these benefits to the eBay users illustrates how complementary products operate. Being the person or venture to offer these solutions to consumers is the opportunity for you, the entrepreneur.

We have all had ideas for complementary products in our lives. Any time during the day when you think; "If I only had a ____ right now," or " This would be much easier if I could _____," you are having inspirations for complementary products and services. Anything that facilitates the main activity at hand is something that complements it. Chances are, if you are experiencing the problem, then other people are as well. It's probable that consumers in a similar situation would also like a viable solution for their pain. On top of that, like eBay drop sites, most consumers would pay you for saving them the time, effort or energy wasted on ancillary events that divert them from the main activity.

As an entrepreneur, one of the main concerns with developing complementary products is that your ideas for products or services are not too closely related to the main product. You have to step back and figure out if the addition of a complement is really valuable enough for the consumer to pay for it. If the price they pay is more than the value they perceive they will get out of your product or service, they may not buy. Many times complementary products come off as more of a gadget or a perk, and not a separate product in itself. You also have to avoid simply making incremental improvements to products and services. Additions and upgrades to products that only incrementally increase the value should be left to the people who are producing the original product. The original producers will be likely to adopt your upgrade and defend their market space, which is not your desired goal. The key to successfully innovating in the area of complementary products is to bring something valuable enough to the main event but yet differentiated enough to create a new market space. The next cell phone gadget is not going to cut it. If the producer of the main product can easily integrate your complementary product, they will, and you will lose the battle in the long run.

So how can you create something so closely related to one product while remaining sufficiently differentiated to create value and fend off the competition? The formula is about bringing together two very different core competencies that are interrelated. Take for example the babysitting services at corporate offices that we mentioned above. The service enables once stay-at-home moms to work while still having their children close by and adequately cared for. The babysitting company knows little about running a corporation, nor would they want to. At the same time, the corporate office knows little about running a babysitting facility, nor would they want to either. But the two core competencies combined creates value for working mothers and the firms that employ them. This complementary arrangement guarantees the sitting service a steady flow of customers and the corporation a steady flow of competent employees. Thus the two products complementing each other drives up the value proposition for both parties. You can look all around and find complementary services that coexist without one stepping on the other's toes. Valet parking is another example. Most restaurants and malls have the service available but are subcontracting it out to the people who do these types of things on a day-to-day basis. It all goes back to core competencies. Complementary products work when you can facilitate the total solution and the core competencies of the two companies are differentiated enough to where they are not competing in the same market space.

Typing out the idea of complementary products makes it seem like more of a difficult phenomenon than it really is. We've mentioned core competencies, differentiation, value propositions and the like, but this is one of the sources that is actually easier to comprehend than it is to write out. In a minute you will see what I mean with the last example. Sometimes complementary products and services can be as simple as expanding to new methods of distribution or offering the exact same product and service in a new light. Let's look at my local oil changing facility as an example.

Recently, at my jobsite, I was offered an onsite oil change and car detailing service while I worked. I had never heard of the service but it made complete sense. The local lube company was charging a slight premium on the service to come out and perform the task while I was inside working. I jumped at the chance to pay the $8 extra to have my oil changed at work considering the time and effort it saved me. I didn't have to drive anywhere special. I didn't have to wait in line. I didn't have to wait while the service was being performed. They complemented their product offering by performing a service I needed while I spent my time doing other things. At the end of the day I exchanged $8 to save 45 minutes of my life, a very fair trade. Complementary services, like this one, demonstrate perfectly the concept of adding value to all parties involved. The oil and lube company complemented their main business by offering an on-site service that saved me valuable time. At the same time, they expanded their business to perform their service at times when the brick and mortar locations were slow. My transportation brokerage employer would not have been interested in setting up a full-time mechanic to change employees' oil at work. Likewise, the oil house wouldn't be interested in starting a transportation brokerage on the side either. By offering this complementary service, three parties benefited from the transaction. This is the essence of a complementary situation and innovative thinking on the part of the oil house.

I struggled to put a framework around searching out complementary products as a source of innovation. At first glance it is as simple and as difficult as remembering all those times you said "If I only had a ____ right now," or " This would be much easier if I could ____." We've all done it hundreds of times, yet the mind quickly forgets its woes after the task has been finished. Finding ideas for complementary products is essentially recognizing problems in our lives as they occur. The problem is we often we fail to think about all of the problems and inconveniences that we encounter in our daily routine. Even more often we fail to even recognize something as a problem or an inconvenience. As humans we generally get conditioned to keep employing the same solutions to solve our daily problems. We find ways around the glitches and the setbacks. We integrate those solutions into the entire process, rarely considering ways to cut out the problems. Our solutions proliferate the mindset that "this is the way it has always been done." It creeps into our thought process and into our decision process. It is another reason why identifying problems is so difficult. We don't even recognize many daily inconveniences as problems! Until someone like you comes along and shows us a better way, we do not realize there were any major issues to be solved in the first place. Forgetting problems after a task and not recognizing the solutions we use as problematic combine to make thinking of complementary products quite difficult at times.

Before we get too technical with developing a framework for this source, the first thing you want to do is exploit the "most basic answer" as much as you can. If you've forgotten, the most basic answer is simply recognizing there is a problem. Like I mentioned above, when you encounter one, you will most likely forget or stop caring once the task has been completed. So, first make an effort to recognize in your mind when you are frustrated with a solution. It may be a serious problem or it may be a minor drawback to the current solution. You are going to forget either way, so make an effort to recognize your chain of expletives as a sign. Use it as a sign to write something down. It sounds cliché and it sounds dumb, but how many times have you uttered the words "I thought of that ____ years ago," or "I've said that a thousand times, why didn't I think of that." So you can either start to realize your system for recognizing potential products is flawed, or you can continue to miss opportunities for new venture ideas. Either way, it is as simple as writing down the problems you encounter in daily life as you go. I personally make it a point to keep a mini notebook and a pen in my coat at all times. My computer desk is littered with random Post-it notes for all the ideas I thought of through the course of writing this book. Some people advise keeping something near your bed. However you feel like doing it, it doesn't matter. You will forget, so make the best of the opportunities you uncover in your daily life and make sure to write them down.

Now let's get to the task of developing a more systematic framework. As usual, have an industry or product in mind before proceeding. Once you have that, the following ideas are an attempt to eliminate the randomness inherent in just recognizing a problem when you cross it. Without further ado, here is what I found out.

I found some key elements for a framework in a book titled the Blue Ocean Strategy by W. Chan Kim and Renee Mauborgne. Two sentences in particular on the topic of complementary products struck me as important. Let's look at what they said, one sentence at a time. In the first sentence they said, "The key is to define the total solution buyers seek when they choose a product or service."[43] So the first step is really about focusing in on exactly what the consumer is trying to accomplish and the total solution they are seeking. It is important to lay it out and completely understand it. Their needs are going to be a guide for the actions your venture should take. Many companies miss the boat because they are basing their product offerings on misguided ideas of what the consumer needs. Thus, it is important to nail down the core of what the consumer is seeking. When you see consumers juggling multiple tasks or multiple products, what are they trying to accomplish? What elements have to come together to represent the complete solution? We need to see how closely their reality matches their ideal total solution. Complementary products are one way to bring them closer to an ideal solution to a problem. The more we understand the total solution, the better we can locate problems to solve and issues that we can address with new products or services. Figure out this part as your first step.

In the second sentence Kim and Mauborgne said, "A simple way to [define the total solution] is to think about what happens before, during and after your product is used." This sentence seems obvious, however, when we are in the shoes of the consumer, we rarely think about the elements that Kim and Mauborgne mention. When the process is random, you are just stumbling across problems in your daily life. You are living the sentence rather than thinking about what you are actually doing. Consumers do not consciously recognize most times that in order to satisfy a need they have to jump through hoops one, two and three before they can get to the heart of what it is that they are trying to accomplish. We as consumers do not break down all the steps involved and consciously consider the importance or annoyance of having to do any of them. Being able to think through the second sentence is how I think a loose framework can be created to generate innovative ideas through the lens of complementary products. By doing so, we can rely on something that we can consciously pursue instead of stumbling on an epiphany in the middle of doing a specified task.

Like the Blue Ocean Strategy suggests, you should start

---

43 Kim, W. Chan and Renee Mauborgne. Blue Ocean Strategy. "How to create uncontested market space and make the competition irrelevant." Boston, MA: Harvard Business School Press, 2005.

analyzing what happens before, during and after consumption of
a product or service. The point of this exercise is to start locating
where problems might lie. It starts with everything you have to do
before consuming. You need to list out what inputs are necessary
to prepare. It may be physical items or intangible items. You need
to consider the raw materials, the time involved, the costs incurred,
the processes to be done and the overall value of each step. You
need to figure out what facilitates the solution and also what detracts
from it, or prevents some consumers from employing it. The same
process needs to be applied to your analysis of what happens during
the consumption of a product or service and after consumption. It
is about laying out every single input from the outset to the finish,
similar to the process of attribute listing that we mentioned in an
earlier chapter. It is about analyzing how each element affects the
total utility of a product. Any element that is not adding value or is
detracting from the value is something that needs to be looked at for
improvement. You'll find in some instances that a consumer desires
to consume a product or service, but one of the inputs involved
prevents them from doing so. How do you change this? How could
it be done better? What is the problem and why does it exist in
the first place? Breaking down the steps of consumption will help
you uncover these details. It is about analyzing, brainstorming and
theorizing about how a market or product could be different.

The end goal of employing complementary products is to raise
the value proposition. As you go through this process you want to
find ways to bring the consumer closer to the ideal situation with a
facilitating product or service. What product or service is needed?
What could be implemented to make this better? You will come up
with plenty of ideas for improving products and services by following
the above framework. Some will be incremental improvements and
not worth pursuing. Other ideas will have the power to change the
way things are done. Know when to throw out ideas that take the
competition head on. Know when to keep the ideas that they will
never see coming. Stay focused, keep thinking, and good things will
come.

Your task as an entrepreneur is to uncover problems and
create opportunities. Often times this means that you have to go
well beyond what the consumers are telling you are the main issues
with a product or service. Utilizing this source has a lot to do with
detecting issues consumers would never think to articulate for
you. Use this chapter to dig in and observe the underlying issues

that consumers are experiencing. Recognize where people have to
jump through hoops or completely abandon a product because the
solutions available do not fit their needs. Lay out the total solutions
people seek and start to pick them apart from beginning to end. How
can you help consumers multitask and create value by reinventing the
way things are done? What can we do to complement and improve
what is already being done? Start searching for these opportunities
on a daily basis and you will be well on your way to creating new
ideas and new possibilities for entrepreneurial ventures.

Chapter 19:
Product Design

"For me, the concept of design is more than object-oriented; it encompasses the design of processes, systems and institutions as well."

- John Seely Brown

    One aspect of product creation that has been getting a lot of attention these days is the element of "design." Firms across a wide array of industries are beginning to realize the effect that a quality design can have on the sales of a product. This rise to popularity is for good reason too. A good design has the potential to transform your product offering and rescue it from relative obscurity. It is a source of differentiation and uniqueness. Just look at Apple's dominance in the mp3 market. Design can speak to the consumer about what they get when they buy the product. A good design can sell the *benefits* of a product to the consumer just by looking at it. In today's world of mass advertising and message overkill, reaching consumers is an uphill battle for many firms. A great design has the power to break through the clutter. When a concept can have this kind of effect in the market, entrepreneurs need to take notice. Harnessing that power and being able to innovate using design can prove to be a lucrative process for savvy entrepreneurs.

    In the past, tweaking product designs was generally left up to the incumbent firms in an industry, not entrepreneurs. Design was more of an afterthought for many firms. It was a way to tweak products and provide incremental improvements so that firms could keep offering new versions each year. However, that mindset seems to have changed in recent years. The element of design is now closer to the forefront of concern when firms seek to launch new product initiatives. It seems to me that people finally started to realize how powerful design can be. As John Seely Brown points out, design is now considered more than just a way to manipulate objects. The topic of design now encompasses "processes, systems and institutions." Essentially people have realized its impact is much further reaching than most people had given it credit for. Design isn't just a way to spiff up a product offering, it is a way to completely redesign the way things are done. For entrepreneurs, that is a key concept to grasp. Using design to slightly improve a product and create incremental value is not your opportunity. Throwing a slightly improved product in the ring with the gigantic industry players is a good way to be crushed. However, when entrepreneurs can embrace the idea that design is much more than a new color or feature, they can start using the idea to transform the way things have been done in the past. Design in an entrepreneurial context is really about redesigning product and service offerings. It is about changing the way things were done in the past.

Take one look at James Dyson and you see an entrepreneur who has redefined markets again and again using the power of design. From wheelbarrows and washing machines to vacuum cleaners and boats, he and his firm continuously re-evaluate and redesign products that are out there in the consumer market. Most of you will probably recognize his name from his inventions in the world of vacuum cleaners. The Dyson Cyclones, as they have come to be known, are the product that James Dyson has built over a billion dollar fortune around. The cyclones use the power of centrifugal force to separate dust particles in a vacuum cleaner and eliminate clogging.44 It was the first vacuum that was able to prove no loss of suction. At the same time it incorporated a bag-less design to eliminate the need for further purchases on the part of the consumer. Essentially Dyson finally found a way to manifest the ideal solution for consumers with innovative design. The funny thing is that the first vacuum cleaner was created in 1901. However, Dyson didn't start working with them until the 1980s. Seventy odd years after the market's inception, consumers are finally getting what they really wanted all along; a clog free, bag-less vacuum. What is ironic is that this problem was well defined long before Dyson came along. Companies like Oreck and Hoover should have seen it coming. However, the design innovation that is so popular today wasn't brought about by these established firms. Instead, it took a toiling inventor to realize the need for a new design. It took Dyson fourteen years to perfect his vacuum cleaner design and bring it to market. In the process he went from being nearly bankrupt from patent lawsuits to becoming a billionaire. Dyson took an idea based on the ideal consumer solution and worked tirelessly to make it happen. Names like Hoover and Oreck, who have been at the game for decades, were left in the dust. (no pun intended) This example just goes to show the power that can be had from properly understanding the concept of design. The next James Dyson is out there somewhere, it could be

---

44 www.dyson.com

you.

The problem with design is that there is no quick and easy way to conceptualize it. If you are like me and don't know a whole lot about the topic going into your research, gathering information on the topic can be pretty tricky. For instance, you can't just go out on any given search engine and type in "design basics" or "the elements of design" and expect to find a bulleted list of concepts that everybody agrees on. The topic of design is not like the 4 Ps of marketing or the 5 steps to whatever. In fact, it seems to me that there is a lot of disagreement on exactly what design "is." For one, the concept is still evolving. Much like the concept of "innovation" and how to create innovative ideas, the concept of "design" is still taking shape. The great design thinkers are still hammering out what all is encompassed by the practice and how to go about helping people understand it. Secondly, design means different things to different people. Design takes on different meanings for the artist, the webpage designer and the business person. Much in the same way that creativity has unique applications for each profession, so too does design. So for this chapter and developing a framework around design, I am going to present my take on the topic and its relevance to the business population. The beauty and difficulty of doing so is that there is no right or wrong answer. The concept is still a bit fuzzy.

In order to start utilizing design as a source of innovation, we first need to discuss the various reasons that people employ design in the first place from a business perspective. What do we seek to accomplish for the consumer? What do we seek to accomplish for the firm? If design is more than just a new color or a new feature, we have to look at all of the possible reasons an entrepreneur might employ this source. When you start to understand all the elements in play and what else is out there, you can then begin to uncover opportunities to use this source. Having a multitude of design concepts at your fingertips is a way to see how industries operate and how they can change. For that reason I am going to lay out a few of the basic design elements and what they accomplish. We are also going to look at some of the ideal end products of good design. Read them, understand them and then look at the alternative design focuses to understand where industries could head in the future. At the same time, you need to supplement this knowledge with further research. I was not a design major and this is not a textbook. Fully understanding all the possibilities that design affords is on you, the reader.

As you read through these, reference the idea of an equalizer that is talked about in the chapter on "consumer appeal levels." Every product or service is going to have multiple aspects of design in play, some to a greater extent than others. Creating new products and services is not about focusing on just one type of design over another. Redesigning products is about altering the degrees to which each is present. As an entrepreneur you are changing the equalizer settings, not necessarily eliminating or introducing elements of design entirely. An innovative idea simply changes the emphasis, it doesn't have to be the complete opposite of what is currently being done.

Elements of Designing the Physical Product:[45]

Form:

Designing for form is about creating a product based on the way you want it to look and feel. The shape, size and texture of a product are all elements of its form. The mixture of these elements stems from what you believe it will accomplish when the customer observes or handles the product. Will they find it eye catching or modest? Rugged or delicate? Whatever you want the consumer to feel when they see a product should be captured by the form you have designed for it. The form that products come in speaks volumes to customers about what they are buying. The form of a product is the embodiment of the message you want consumers to get when they use your product.

As a generic example, the "chair" industry is a good place to look at how firms seek to convey messages through form. (For some reason, almost every design awards competition list always features a new take on the modern chair) The idea of the chair is always the same; someplace for humans to sit. However, you can see the variance of forms across every type of chair. From the fold out chair and the recliner, to the ergonomic desk chairs and chairs as an art form, each one that you see speaks to you about how you will feel owning the chair and sitting in it. We can see the benefits of comfort, convenience and art appeal all in one mundane category. This concept of form is captured in many different manifestations. As an entrepreneur we need to look at how products like this are being presented to the consumer. Is your industry as diverse in its take on form as the chair industry? Are there benefits of a product that aren't

---

45 Some portions of Design Principles influenced by :http://www-03.ibm.com/easy/page/6

being conveyed to a consumer when they look at your industry? How can form achieve the right message and stand out from the rest? What other forms could your product of choice take on?

Function:

Designing for function is about designing a product or service for the specific purpose for which it will be employed. This means taking into account the necessary product features to accomplish the task at hand and also the situation in which the user will find themselves while utilizing the product. A combination of these factors will determine the overall functionality of a design. Sometimes firms forget the delicate balance of features and situation. Designing a product with the right features for the task at hand is pointless if you do not also take into consideration the situation in which the consumer is going to be using your product. At the same time, designing solely for the situation the product will be used in is pointless if the product lacks the necessary features to get the job done.

Take "squirt bottle" products as an example. For as long as I can remember, my shampoo bottle, ketchup bottle and many other "squirtable" products had been sitting upside-down in their respective areas around my house.[46] Bottles teetered awkwardly around the refrigerator and in the bathroom. Product used to spill and hardened around the cap area. The products themselves were perfectly fine feature-wise, but firms were not taking into consideration the situations in which their products were being used. It was not until recently that this has changed. Nowadays, my "squirtable" products have been designed to exactly meet their functionality in my home. Most of the products now have a wide base for sitting upside down. They also have spill resistant caps and their design allows me to squeeze out every last ounce. When you cater a new product by designing to the functional use of consumers, you have a relatively simple way to set your product apart from the rest. Understanding the balance of features and situation is crucial to a well thought out design. Do the competitors in your industry understand this? Do the products on the market now have the ideal functionality the consumer is seeking?

I'm going to briefly interrupt here. The reason is that once

---

46 Influenced by: Hamner, Susana. "Packaging that Pays." Business 2.0. Jul. 2006, pp. 68-69.

I have explained the idea of form and function, things start to get a little murky again. You see, the rest of the design principles for business that I am about to lay out are not separate from "form" and "function." I cannot just keep listing them as though they are on the same level. It is my understanding that the rest of the reasons to design something are a mixture of form and function. It is as though form and function are the two main principles of the topic and everything else follows. At the same time, I also cannot see putting the rest of the design ideas as sub-categories of form or function either. Although some may lean more towards one or the other, none of them are strictly subcategories. They are desirable outcomes that businesses seek by employing design, but they are not separate design categories. Each of the categories is an "equalizer" setting if you want to think of it that way. Both form and function play a role, and even though one aspect may be emphasized, the other still exists. Before I digress too far, here are some of the common goals of design that are derived by properly mixing form and function.

Common Goals of Design: Designing for the goals of the firm

Design for Production:

The design for your product should not only appeal to consumers, it should also be a way in which a company can directly benefit. Designing for how a product is going to be produced is a way in which firms can reap the benefits of design. This idea might be as basic as redefining a manufacturing process to increase efficiency, or it might be as complex as revolutionizing the way a product is produced. As entrepreneurs, we need to take stock of how things are currently being done in our industry. If the product designs that already exist are not focused on maximizing production efficiencies, why not? What are they designed around? In designing with the production process in mind, we get a whole new sense of how things can be created. Designing for production can take on many forms. Can we change the way an industry creates its products? Can we return money to the bottom line? Can we boost convenience or replacement ease? What are the most desirable traits of a product in our industry, and how do we formulate a production design to achieve them?

Think of Henry Ford's assembly line or Eli Whitney's interchangeable gun parts. These new design tactics for streamlining

production and construction revolutionized their respective
markets. The production of everything from guns to cars and
houses has been revolutionized by thinking about producing
standard, interchangeable parts. The resulting benefits from such
thinking drastically reduced production and replacement costs.
That is the idea behind designing for production. New ideas about
how products can be produced can create entirely new markets
of opportunity. When you look at your industry of focus, are the
competitors reinventing the production process or doing business as
usual? Is there a need for a better production process? What value
could be derived if we framed production in a new light?

Design for Distribution:

For many of the same reasons as designing for production,
firms must also take into consideration the distribution of their
product. The packaging, materials and specific distribution channels
need to be chosen carefully when launching a new product. The
wrong strategy can make or break a firm. Packaging keeps the
product safe and contributes to the marketing effort. The materials
used for distribution enhance or hinder the ease of which the
product flows to market. Also, the chosen distribution channel is
an element in designing the entire product offering. Entrepreneurs
who are successful at launching a product understand each of these
considerations. Designing for distribution is about putting your
product in the right place, with the right message and in a cost
efficient manner. Designing a distribution plan to accomplish all of
this is difficult but essential.

I was recently reading Business 2.0 about the evolution of the
Netflix DVD mailer, and I think it illustrates the idea of designing
for distribution quite well. Since the inception of the entrepreneurial
venture, the mailer that the Netflix DVDs travel around in has been
changed over ten times.[47] The design of the mailer is crucial because
it is one of the major cost centers in the business model. The mailer
not only has to protect the DVDs while in transit, but it must also be
as lightweight as possible to reduce shipping costs. Along the way
they have experimented with top loading, side loading, cardboard,
paper, plastic, adding airholes, adding foam, removing foam,
stickers, barcoded mailers and non-barcoded mailers. The design
of something that seems so simple can literally make or break the
company. When entrepreneurs understand this concept, it sheds light

47 Zachary, G. "Evolution of an Envelope." Business 2.0. Apr. 2006.

on distribution in our own areas of focus. What are the distribution strategies? Are they working? What could be done to change the way products and services are disseminated out into the marketplace? What are other distribution possibilities?

Common Goals of Design: Designing for the consumer's needs.

Designing for Ease of Use:

This goal of design is pretty self explanatory. When firms undertake the design of a new product or service, a key thing to keep in mind is how easy or difficult it is for users to adopt and use their product. Being able to incorporate all of the necessary features while maintaining the correct level of usability is a double edged sword. The firms who win out in the marketplace often understand this delicate balance the best. Knowing when to add and subtract features and how to present them in a product form is challenging. As entrepreneurs, it is your opportunity to spot markets where this ideal balance has not yet been found. If there is not a definitive answer as to what the best solution is on the market, chances are it doesn't exist yet. Understanding how to redesign products to achieve the right level of ease of use can be the determining factor in many purchase decisions.

Take for example the mp3 player market. The first mp3 player was developed in 1997. The technology to transfer music to these players was prevalent. The programs for downloading music over the internet and burning CDs from mp3s were also well known. There were many electronic companies who made small, lightweight and desirable mp3 players. Yet in the late 1990s and early 2000's you would have had a hard time naming two or three dominant players in the market. It was a fragmented market space. Flash forward to today and the the industry leader is a no brainer. The word iPod is almost synonymous with mp3 player. The iPod is no longer even just an mp3 player. It is a fashion statement and a must have accessory. So how did this all occur? Apple was not the first mover in the mp3 market. Many factors contributed to Apple's success, but it is an excellent example of the power of great design. Just looking at an iPod design screams ease of use to the potential consumer. One spinning, touch-sensitive wheel and a button to accomplish so many tasks that media users love. Without even knowing about an iPod, clueless consumers can tell you that the iPod is sleek, stylish and easy to use just by the physical traits of the product. Among others, designing for ease of use is one way that Apple succeeded in running away with the mp3 player market. Are the competitors in your market constantly innovating to achieve the proper balance of features and ease of use? Could specific subsets of consumers use a new design? How could you enhance the overall ease of adoption of a product?

Design for Aesthetics:

Another use of design comes from catering to the aesthetic needs of the consumer. This area of design may not be as practical or necessary as the others, however it does provide another point of differentiation in the minds of consumers. When we focus on the aesthetics of a product, we are talking about the visual appearance and emotional appeal to consumers. The inclusion of art or designing a product to be considered art in itself is one common use of aesthetics. If two products are essentially the same, yet one offers a more aesthetically pleasing appearance, chances are the consumers will opt for the aesthetically pleasing product. Designing for aesthetics goes above and beyond the features or necessary elements to solve the problem at hand. Designing for aesthetics is about enhancing the overall experience and creating a point of uniqueness in your product line.

Take for example the Kleenex brand oval box. The most recent addition to their line of products is the addition of Kleenex packaging that complements the décor of a dwelling.[48] The boxes are oval in shape and the art on the outside reflects the season of the year. Not only did the new design replace the common rectangular form, but it also introduced colors that add the emotional appeal of the time of year. The incorporation of art into the packaging did not affect the fundamental use of the product, however it did help to double sales according to Business 2.0 magazine. Designing for art's sake or for the "experience" is what allows many firms to set their products apart from the competition when put side by side. By using the power of aesthetics, entrepreneurs can take bland product lines and commoditized options and set them apart. Does your industry take aesthetics into consideration? Should it?

---

48 Hamner, Susana. "Packaging that Pays." <u>Business 2.0</u>. Jul. 2006, pp. 68-69.

Other Design Considerations in Business:

Safety:
Minimize the potential risks associated with a product or service. Design a physical product that reduces risk to consumers and legal concerns for firms.49

Reliability:
Products are designed so that they work properly over the intended lifespan of the product. Set your product apart by being more reliable than the competition.

Versatility:
Designing products so that they can adapt to the changing needs of the firm and the consumer over time.

Customization:
Producing products and services that are adaptable to the specific needs of the end user and the firm.

Systems Focus:
Designing a product or service to fit into the context of the entire system of the firm or the end user. A systems focus does not necessarily optimize the specific element of a product or service in and of itself. Instead, designing for systems is about optimizing the entire process you are looking at, whether it be production, distribution, ease of use, et cetera.

User Centered Design:
Designing a product around the specific needs, desires and limitations of your customer base.

So I have presented you with some of the main things that are taken into consideration when we seek to design new product and service offerings. I have undoubtedly left some design concepts out, and I probably have a slightly different take on the topic than you might have. The whole point of the chapter is not to be

---

49 http://www.prosci.com/prp2.htm

academically correct, the point is to get your mind going about all
of the possibilities that the concept of design offers to entrepreneurs.
When we look at all of the possible reasons people design products
and services the way they do, we begin to see what else is available
to us. By understanding how an industry currently treats design, we
can then start thinking about ways to incorporate new and different
design ideas that do not currently take precedence in an industry. By
recognizing this, and subsequently implementing a new design focus,
we have the opportunity to take industries in entirely new directions.
Entrepreneurs can redesign the way things are currently being done
and spark innovation in places where it may not have existed prior.

I'd like to finish this chapter by looking at some of the
circumstances in which I believe a new design can have the most
impact in an industry. While new and unique designs are always a
good thing to consider, I think that specific times in product lifecycles
can be focused on by entrepreneurs to have the most impact.

The first time period I want to talk about is the introductory
stages of a product's lifecycle. When a market is just starting out and
the first set of competitors are lining up, chances are the products
being offered are rudimentary compared to where the market will
eventually go down the road. Chances are that the early-adopting
consumers are just entering the market as well. What this all adds up
to is a scenario with incomplete solutions. Consumers haven't figured
out exactly what they want in a product, and firms haven't figured
out exactly how to create the ideal product. Entrepreneurs can focus
in on these industries because there are obvious needs for product
design innovation. When we see solutions that are far from ideal, we
have the chance to develop them. We have the opportunity to try and
shape markets by offering up our own unique solutions.

So how do you recognize these fledgling markets? I think
Richard White had some interesting thoughts on this. He suggests
that you start by researching what sort of start-ups are being funded.
What are the growth industries that banks, venture capitalists and
private equity firms are giving money to?[50] By identifying these
industries, you see where important markets are beginning to form,
usually without a clearly dominant firm or product. You can also
use your observation skills to see where fragmented markets exist.
Industries that have been playing out for some time without a clear
product leader in the category are a good place to find inspiration.

---

50 White, Richard M. The Entrepreneur's Manual. Radnor, PA. Chilton Book Company, 1977,
pp. 50-51.

The second time period where I believe design can have the most impact in a product lifecycle is in the complete opposite scenario of what we just talked about. While the nascent stages of a market provide entrepreneurs with a definition problem, the mature stage and decline stage of a market provide them with a redefinition problem. The reason is that product designs within an industry tend to get cemented as time passes. Once a market has hit maturity, most of the product offerings in an industry are similar in looks and features. Firms within the industry are generally schlepping along the way things have always been done. It is in a mature stage that entrepreneurs have the ability to use design to redefine the way things are done. It is your opportunity to reexamine the situation and see if mature industries might be in need of an overhaul. Things change, products evolve and consumers are willing to pay for product designs that set themselves apart. The goal of entrepreneurs focusing on mature markets is to start a new growth curve. Product design innovation is one way to accomplish that.

So whatever industry you choose to innovate within, start taking note of the design focus of the products available. Are they meeting the ideal solutions of the target market? Are they meeting the ideal goals of the firm? Could you utilize a new design focus to change the way things are being done in the market? You have the capability to define new markets and redefine old ones. You have the ability to determine where industries head for the future. You are already ahead of the curve with this information, as most people are just starting to understand what "design" really means. Now it is up to you to exploit that knowledge and create your opportunity.

Consumer Based Strategies

Chapter 20:
Consumer Appeal Levels

"It was never what I wanted to buy that held my heart's hope. It was what I wanted to be."

- Lois McMaster Bujold

Consumers do not buy products just to own that particular object. Consumers buy a product for what it can do for them or make them become. Lucky for us entrepreneurs, consumers want to be a lot of different things at many different times. For instance, when a consumer needs a cheap pick-me-up coffee they probably go to McDonald's. When they are looking to supplement breakfast they might pick up some coffee from Dunkin' Donuts. When they want top of the line quality or to treat themselves, they might go to Starbucks. Consumers are constantly trading between functional product levels. Consumers will trade up or down on certain qualities of a product category depending on the desired outcome and timing of the purchase.51 They are purchasing based on the situation the product will be used in, and they are purchasing based on what they want to be at a certain point in time; thrifty, classy, comfortable, et cetera. These varying levels of consumer needs represent different niches that need to be filled in the marketplace. You as an entrepreneur have the opportunity to recognize and exploit these niches. Consumers' desire to trade up, down and between product categories at different times and in different situations provide a great source for innovative products, services and ideas.

Coffee is a good example, because the range of consumer needs is pretty much covered. However, this is not necessarily true for all products. We do not have to travel back very far in the past to see this in the example we just used. Before Starbucks, who would have known that consumers would be willing to pay $4 for a cup of coffee? The only place to get a $4 cup of coffee might have been at an upscale dining establishment. These establishments are neither convenient nor accessible for most consumers on the go. In fact, consumers probably did not even know they were willing to pay $4 for a cup of coffee. Many of Starbucks current customers probably would have voiced opposition to the pricing if you had asked them

---

51 First paragraph based on discussions of customer appeal levels in marketing class at Ohio State University with Professor Leslie Fine.

before Starbucks existed. Consumers will not understand paying $4 until an entrepreneur can show them at least $4 worth of value. Consumers will not understand $4 for a coffee until you can prove to them that the money is worth what they are trying to attain at a certain point in time. This is where entrepreneurs like Starbucks creator Howard Schultz can thrive. Showing consumers new and different functional levels of products can be a huge opportunity for entrepreneurs if we can figure out how to locate or create such opportunities in the marketplace.

As the entrepreneur, it is your opportunity to understand where, when and why consumers trade between different functional levels of a product. Understanding the potential market and researching consumer trends are keys to identifying untapped areas of the marketplace. When purchasing, do consumers look for the most practical option? Will they trade up to a mid-range price or will they opt for the highest quality level and the "experience?" Some consumers may never trade out of one level, but multiple levels will exist. Twenty years ago, few people would have believed that people would be willing to pay for bottled water and use it in their homes right next to the virtually free tap water. The first companies into this marketplace were taking a bold step. Few people would also have envisioned paying $3.99 for a cup of premium coffee or $60 for a bottle of ultra-premium liquor. In the not so distant past, paying these kinds of prices for a product would have been seen as a ludicrous notion. Also, had you asked consumers, most would have vehemently opposed ever paying such high prices for these items. However, entrepreneurs such as Sidney Frank and Howard Schultz recognized that consumers would be willing to pay it if you could show them the equivalent value proposition for the money. Since even most consumers would have been opposed prior to the product's release, these entrepreneurs had to create a new consumer demand. Consumers were willing to pay for more than just the average benefits of a product, but they didn't even know it themselves. Now they are more than willing to pay for the "experience," or a perceived level of quality that a product brings to the table. The branding of companies such as Starbucks has not only delivered above the line on quality, but they have surrounded the products with an upscale, personalized experience. America found out very quickly that the average consumer was more than willing to partake in a new consumer appeal level once they realized it fulfilled an unmet desire.

The trick to innovating within the realm of consumer appeal

levels is multi-faceted. The framework begins by understanding what "levels" of products and services exist across industries. It is also about understanding what levels currently exist in the market you are targeting. So the first step, as usual, is to start learning, analyzing and observing consumer options in the market you are passionate about. When you first begin to look at them, they might seem vague. It is not about having strict categorization like a "low," "middle" and "high" attribute scale. However you decide to categorize the levels and spectrums of need is fine. For the purposes of this chapter, I am going to lay out how I categorize levels of need and the functional levels of products that work for me. Use them or make your own, but I have to insert my own thoughts here in order for the chapter to continue. In my opinion there are at least three to four spectrums or levels that consumers trade both up, down and inbetween. The following paragraphs describe these spectrums that work for me.

Price:

One of the most obvious spectrums in which consumers trade up and down is the spectrum of price. Consumers choose products at various levels based on the almighty dollar. They trade between price ranges constantly, depending on the situation. Make sure each demographic that is currently being targeted, and that you could possibly target, are all taken into consideration. Understand how each demographic would react to various prices and how they currently react. What constitutes a low price to one person may seem unattainable for others. Price will be just one attribute that will be considered, but it is a big one. Each consumer will consciously or subconsciously decide on a price point for each situation in which they encounter a product or service. Knowing what price levels are cutoffs for which situation and to whom they are relevant is key. Price is a very basic and obvious way to establish levels of need in a market, but it can be crucial. Many entrepreneurs have found profitable business at all levels of the price spectrum. Keep this in mind as you start to look for opportunities and levels of consumer needs.

Function:

The second spectrum I formed for my mindset is the spectrum of functionality. Functionality is the purpose or use that the consumer has for a product.52 While each product and service grouped in a market generally accomplishes the same core utility, there are still usually numerous brands, makes and models that offer hundreds of different features and options. Each one will provide different levels of functionality. The process of deciding on a product will vary depending on how much functionality consumers want to incorporate. In some industries you are the consumer equivalent of a caveman, and in others you are the equivalent of a rocket scientist. For doing the lawn work around the house you may just need the core basics, whereas when you buy computers you want all the bells and whistles. A spectrum starts with the most basic, core product and extends out to the extreme, specific functions. Another example is a knife. You can buy a regular pocket knife with one blade, or you could invest in a 37-in-one Swiss Army knife. Each knife cuts things, but the two options are on completely different ends of the spectrum of functionality. Likewise, each market ranges from the most basic to the most extraordinary functionality levels for attaining the same core utility. Depending on the situation in which the utility needs to be accomplished, consumers will trade along the spectrum. Understand why, when and who trades between functionality levels when you begin looking for opportunities for consumer's levels of needs.

Experience:

A third spectrum that exists, in my opinion, is the experience spectrum. Each consumer has an experience when they utilize a product. It may be bad, good or extraordinary. It also may be conscious, or it may be subconscious. The past experiences or perceived experiences that consumers could attain cause them to trade between different products within a market. The importance of repeating or not wanting to repeat a certain experience is reason for consumers to trade up or down within the spectrum. Many consumers go back to a brand or a specific product because it delivers exactly the right experience. Other times, consumers experience something and believe that they could use more or less of a product experience to be content. Either way, each time we encounter a product or service, we are judging the experience and will trade up or down until we have found the desired level on the spectrum for each situation we encounter.

---

52 Loosely based on Merriam-Webster's College Dictionary, tenth edition

Status:

A fourth spectrum that I think is important, but maybe more obscure, is the spectrum of what I will call "status." Whether we intend to or not, humans form opinions of each other within seconds of seeing and meeting each other. We are keenly aware that we do it. We are keenly aware that other humans are doing it right back at us. Therefore, consumers trade up and down among products and services depending on how they want others to perceive them when they are seen using a product or service. A "status" spectrum might range from "other people will never see me consuming this" to "everyone is going to see me using this." Each product or service category has an importance level relative to the consumer. Depending on the activities and status quos of the groups that consumers associate with, a product will have relative importance. A model might be highly concerned with her fashion but couldn't care less about the computer she purchases. On the other hand, a devout video gamer might be highly concerned about the advanced technology he purchases in a computer and put fashion at a relatively low status importance level. Either way, consumers are constantly taking status into consideration with each purchase, and it is something to be aware of when you begin thinking of innovation.

There may be more spectrums by your understanding, or there may be fewer. You're smart enough. You'll figure out how it makes sense in your own mind. The key is having some framework to go off of. It is important because rarely will consumers consider product offerings strictly within one spectrum of need or want. Most often, all of the spectrums are present. You might think of these spectrums as being similar to equalizer bars for music. You increase one or decrease another. You keep some the same or turn them all to the extremes. A purchase decision usually begins with the price a consumer can afford to pay. Based on their own finances and needs, they will decide on a price point, usually pre-purchase. It is then up to the product offering to cater to the other spectrums. Can I get the functionality I need within my price range? Do the products available in my price range give me a good enough experience? Then, finally, if I have found a product that meets my requirements, does it communicate the status I want when others see me using the product? Consumers make tradeoff decisions among the spectrums and they play off of each other. A consumer will trade up and down until a decision is made whether or not the product works to satisfy their overall need. It is important to understand the target consumers and approximately where their resources, needs and wants fall along the spectrum of each of these metrics. It allows you to see why the current consumer need levels exist and then, ultimately, where you can innovate to create your own solutions to fulfill their needs.

Once you are consciously aware of the consumer need levels in an industry, you can start posing questions and theorizing possibilities about them. You can start looking at industries and figuring out the current playing field. What are the consumer appeal levels that are already out there? Sometimes all of the levels appear to have a solution, and other times it will be the case that a price point or quality level just doesn't exist. Recognizing that a consumer need level doesn't exist can be one of the easiest problems to identify. It is now a case of problem solving. How can we pull it off? What has to be implemented? Is it feasible? When the problem is as basic as simple omission, the solution is most likely just as easy. A good example is where only one need level is being addressed. For example, cheap or low quality is the only option. Why is that? How can you change that actually or perceptually? How do you create product attributes that boost the value proposition and allow you to charge more? On the other hand, lets say that something has always been of ultra high quality and expensive. How could you maintain that quality (actually or perceptually) while tweaking the attributes and processes to lower the cost and bring the product to a new group of consumers? You can go both ways with mid-range items. How do you go up and how do you go down? It is up to you the entrepreneur to find product and service categories that do not exist, could be tweaked or need to be created where the consumer would never even think to ask for it.

Let's look at an example of a need level being omitted. Consider the following. The May 2006 edition of Business 2.0 included an article about a Japanese fisherman that turned around the consumer's notions of what was once of the lowliest fish in the sea. The mackerel was always seen as an exceptionally oily fish that spoiled almost instantly upon death. This made eating the fish generally unpleasant without a lot of doctoring. For that reason, it was relegated to the lowest price point and quality tier of the fish market. However, Kishichiro Okamoto found a way to change that. The spoilage of the fish was due to the way that they were being harvested, killed and handled excessively. By minimizing handling, draining the blood immediately and choosing only certain fishing grounds, Okamoto was able to drastically improve the quality of the fish. The resulting fish has lost its oily taste and is a sought after brand of mackerel. Where regular mackerel might fetch $10 a head, Okamoto's fetch $60.[53] The mackerel isn't just good; upscale Japanese restaurants are offering it now as sushi grade, something that would seem preposterous five years ago. This example illustrates the filling of a consumer need level that had simply been ignored. Why should Mackerel have always been a lowly fish in the sea? It didn't have to, and one entrepreneur is now profiting for realizing the potential for it.

Opportunities that exist when a consumer need level has been omitted are the easiest and most obvious to spot. Unfortunately, most of the time it is not that easy. The real challenge to the entrepreneur is to get beyond assigning every product with a low, medium and high level of quality. The opportunity lies in your ability to expand beyond those generic levels in an innovative fashion; to mix, match and overlap levels of consumer needs to create something completely new and innovative.

More often than omitting consumer appeal levels, they will exist but at low levels of representation and accessibility to sizable target markets. For instance, before Starbucks you *could* have purchased a cup of $4 coffee. The problem was that you had to buy it at an upscale restaurant or other select outlets. For consumers, that would involve traveling to a limited number of locations around town and having to sit down to drink in a restaurant style environment. This was neither economical nor practical for the average consumer. The innovative aspect of Starbucks was not recognizing that people would pay $4 and then charging $4. The innovative aspect of Starbucks is that they realized that everyday average consumers would pay $4 for a cup of coffee if you surrounded $4 quality with the right atmosphere and convenience. In order for Starbucks to be successful, they had to be able to deliver this atmosphere and quality at approximately the same amount of time investment associated with the other quality levels. It wasn't simply an omission of high priced coffee. They catered their product to two different consumer appeal levels in order to bring out a combination that did not previously exist, high quality with a low time investment. It is this overlapping and original combination of elements that lends consumer need levels to being a source for innovation. You can see trends in ideas that seem to work across industries. By using Starbucks' success as a thought stream you might wonder; What other industries have consumers at the fringe of their product offerings? How do you bring

---

53 Mikami, Mariko. "The Moet of Mackerel." <u>Business 2.0</u> May 2006, pp. 84.

those consumers into the marketplace? Why aren't they purchasing certain levels of a product category? Why weren't they able to consume before? Projecting successful innovations with consumer need levels onto other industries can produce some interesting insights.

The flip side of the previous example could be replicating high end quality at a low price point. The auto industry is a perfect example of how Japanese companies have been able to steal substantial market share away from American auto producers. The foreign producers are able to make cars of the same, or better, quality as American cars and at much lower price points. The Japanese have exploited cost cutting avenues while continually improving their processes to produce cars that rival or beat American brands. The Japanese auto manufacturers have brought a high level of perceived and actual quality to a group of consumers who previously would not have been able to afford it. This is powerful to entrepreneurs. The Japanese auto manufacturers did not simply recognize that there were insufficient levels of cheap cars in America and then make cheap cars to sell to Americans. The innovation was finding a business model that produced cheap cars while maintaining the quality level of higher end American models. They got Americans the price point they desired while at the same time rivaling the quality of cars two and three times their prices. It is the idea of playing between consumer need levels as in this example where innovation can really run. In this example, they employed price and quality playing off of each other. Usually, price is an indicator of quality. The innovation is that this doesn't have to be true. The Japanese have proven that they can provide high quality at low prices and have surpassed many American car manufacturers in the process. The point of the past two paragraphs and the power of this source of innovation is to learn to mix, match and overlap the consumer levels of needs. Breaking down the traditional levels of product categories is a powerful way to be entrepreneurial.

A final thing I wanted to add to the framework is an understanding of how we can utilize this source when looking at specific types of markets. Fragmented markets and the introductory stages of an industry can be a great place to utilize consumer need levels as a source. Many times when a product category or industry is in the introductory and growth stages, entrepreneurs are taking their best guess at consumer wants and needs. Products, services and ideas in the nascent stages are generally focusing only on one or two of the spectrums in consumer decision making. For instance, new technology at the outset is usually focused on functionality. What do we need to do to get this technology to the functional level needed for consumers to purchase it? The focus has to be on that. Concentrating on dropping the price, making it stylish or providing the consumer with the perfect experience is not the goal, or at least not until the technology is advanced enough to warrant the purchase in the first place. This is something that the entrepreneur should be watching. Many people will fail during the nascent stages. Many others will never redirect their focus once the technology is "good enough." Industries can be won out by entrepreneurs who realize the total solution that consumers are looking for. One company can shoot out of a million fragments if they truly figure out how to meet the multiple levels of needs of consumers. Look at Apple and the iPod in the mp3 player market if you need any proof. If the other players in a market are defining their offering by only one or two spectrum metrics, the opportunity for innovation exists to enter and take market share.

So we've said a whole lot about what seems on the surface to be a very basic idea. Come back and read through this chapter again if you didn't catch it all. The problem is that innovation can be pretty simple stuff, so simple in fact that many people never think twice about it. However, the reality of it is that simple concepts that do not get articulated get ignored and go unused. Understanding how to exploit consumer need levels is an example of that. Consumer appeal levels can be tricky and the need levels of the consumer come in all types of combinations and "equalizer" settings. It is up to you to master the information and think about it on a regular basis. It is up to you to search out omissions. It is up to you to pose questions and recreate industries. Uncovering and creating new levels can be a task for you to systematically consider each and every day for locating your opportunity.

Chapter 21:
Shifting Demographics

"If you don't pay attention to the periphery, the periphery changes and the first thing you know the periphery is the center."
- Dean Rusk

At any point in time the world is made up of billions of consumers. Companies around the world are targeting their products to these consumers by segmenting, or breaking down the aggregate consumer base into smaller subsets. These segmentations often come with demographics as the basis. Demographics refer to any characteristic that a group may have in common. Values, age, race, culture and attitudes are just some examples of what commonalities might be grouped together. Companies are constantly analyzing these commonalities. Who are our consumers? What are their demographics? What do they value in a product or service? They do this because they realize the economic potential that their target demographic represents to their business. Their attitudes, values and changing preferences determine whether a firm is in a position to sell to them or if they are not. When the attitudes or values of consumers change, so too must the product offerings of the firms that sell to them. Failure to do so may mean obsolescence for those firms. This idea is a valuable concept for the entrepreneur to understand. Sizable demographics have the power to influence and change the way industries operate. When the rules of an industry change, entrepreneurs should be there to lead the charge with innovative new products and services.

The concepts of demographics and segmentation are well documented and taught extensively in business school. For this reason, many of you will be familiar with the concept. However, the idea had never been given the conceptual lens that entrepreneurs needed until Peter Drucker came along. The idea that shifting demographics could be a source of innovation was first articulated in Drucker's book, <u>Innovation and Entrepreneurship</u>.54 Recognizing a shift in demographics is not an end in itself, but rather an indicator that change is brewing. You can see it in census data on government websites. You can see it when you analyze the changing attitudes of consumers. Shifting demographics is really just an indicator that

---

54 Drucker, Peter. <u>Innovation and Entrepreneurship</u>. New York, NY: HarperBusiness, 1993.

there is going to be a problem in the future. It is the "most basic answer" before it happens. This concept is powerful because many industry players are going to miss the boat to change their business model to cater to the changing consumer preferences. Many times existing companies find out there is a problem with their product offering after it's way too late to do something about it. By the time they realize it, entrepreneurs like you have swooped in and stolen large portions of the new market. Even more often, companies ignore the problem because they do not feel that it actually exists. Their ideas for where markets are headed and the actuality of what happens can be vastly different. Their failure to act and myopic views of their industry is your chance as an entrepreneur. It is your opportunity to better understand where consumer preferences and markets are heading down the road. When entrepreneurs are more adept at recognizing the changing needs of consumers and framing new ventures accordingly, they often beat out the existing competition. The faster the target demographics are changing, the faster those industries are going to need innovative solutions to their problems. Understanding the changing consumer landscape and what it will mean for the future is your opportunity to be ahead of the curve.

I've mentioned shifting demographics numerous times without really diving into how they can indicate where problems and needs will be in the future. What I am referring to is interpreting and expanding on the data regarding demographics. What are the implications of rising birth rates and expanding waistlines? What happens to markets as consumers start to prefer online media as opposed to traditional TV and radio? The great thing about it is that data on demographics is extremely prevalent. The indicators are all over the place. The census bureau can be your first stop to see how the demographics of the United States have changed over the years and where they are trending for the future. Similar statistics abound from various agencies tracking consumers around the world. Fast Company's March 2006 edition of their magazine provides a plethora of demographic information and which companies are exploiting it. What we need to do to use demographics is extrapolate on the data that is available to us. For instance, the growth of the Hispanic population is outpacing any other minority in the United States. Baby boomers are aging and large numbers of them will soon be considered senior citizens (but don't call them senior citizens or you've lost them). American waistlines are expanding exponentially year after year. These are just three demographic trends currently affecting the

United States, let alone the hundreds that are affecting people around the world. What we need to do is theorize the effects of these trends and others. What industries will change and why? What industries that were once niche markets will now become mainstream? Are firms in those industries prepared to cater to these trends? What opportunities do these trends bring? How can we exploit the trends? Using shifting demographics as a source of innovation is about interpreting data of trends and planning businesses around the trends. It is about interpretation in order to exploit the potential problems that demographic change presents to entrepreneurs. To use demographics as a source of innovation, you are pitting your vision of what the future will bring versus what others believe it will bring. Digesting and interpreting the data that is relevant to your industry of choice can be a great way to see change coming and how it will affect markets. The change that will ensue brings the necessity for new solutions. You, the entrepreneur, are the person who needs to implement those new solutions.

It would seem that with all this data, everyone will be in a position to exploit the same problems that you see. However, this isn't necessarily the case. Incumbents who have been doing things the same way for years are going to be susceptible to ousting. Why? Quite simply because most individuals and organizations resist change. They do not realize or believe that the way things have always been done just won't work for the future. Some market players will see it coming and choose not to change out of ignorance or stupidity. Some won't even see it coming. Other times it will be a matter of companies being so committed and entrenched to a certain way of doing business that they can't change. Either way, this presents a huge opportunity to the nimble and flexible entrepreneur. Keeping an eye on demographic trends and the markets that those trends affect can have big implications for new ways of doing business. New target segments are going to demand new solutions to old problems. A shift in demographics usually means that the products and services available are going to have to change to cater to the new customers. Entrepreneurs who understand the makeup of the shifting demographics and the makeup of certain industries are privy to understanding how to change and evolve product offerings to gain the purchasing power of the new demographic. Incumbents would rather things stayed the same as usual. They enjoy the current level of profits and the status quo. They believe that what has been working in the past will work in the future. Whether they choose to change or not, they can't stop the shifting. Someone will rise to the occasion of pleasing the new demographic status. It could be you.

Just to illustrate the importance of shifting consumer demographics, I thought it was important to incorporate an example. We are currently experiencing what some call the "greening" of America. Basically, our attitudes and values are changing towards our environment around us. Businesses and individuals around the nation are clamoring to develop green technologies and products that do less harm to our world. The president is calling for a reduction in our dependency on fossil fuels. Governors and citizens are enacting plans to require environmental standards of corporations and the products and services they provide. Movies such as "An Inconvenient Truth" are no longer offbeat independent films, but rather nationwide major releases.[55] There is a fundamental shift in viewpoint and attitude in a sizable demographic in the United States regarding our environment. In the past this "periphery" demographic was considered tree-hugging environmentalists. Now those same viewpoints are gaining traction in the minds of the majority. In the past, most people shrugged off helping the environment as a nice ideal and a passing thought. Now we are realizing that things are going to have to change or else we will suffer some harsh consequences. In any event, this fundamental shift has been a long time coming. As we mentioned, the periphery has been changing for some time now. Environmental concerns have been gaining traction with a larger segment of the population and corporations in recent years. The shifting perception of the demographic could be seen evolving over time. The point is that this presents huge opportunities for entrepreneurs. The periphery is not yet the center. We are on the cusp of some serious innovations in the realm of environmentalism, but we aren't there yet. What opportunities does this present to you the entrepreneur? How could you exploit the changing norms in America regarding the environment? People have an idea of what the future will hold for our "green" America, but are they on the right track? Do you see a better solution? I hope you do. This shift and others in our world present huge opportunities for entrepreneurs looking for new ideas for ventures.

Look around you, read updated census material, talk to consumers, read about trends. One thing about shifting demographics is that you do not lack the necessary data needed to theorize business ideas. The data tells the story of where we

---

55 http://www.climatecrisis.net/

are and where we are headed. In doing this, you begin to see how demographics shift over time. Americans are getting fatter. The Hispanic population in the United States is on the rise.56 China and India are fast becoming economic powerhouses. All of these shifts are opportunities to redefine how industries will operate and potential areas for innovation. It is no wonder that companies are popping up left and right to cater to our expanding waistlines. It is no wonder that sales for tortilla producers are growing exponentially and sales of white bread are decreasing.57 It is no wonder that companies are looking East to booming economies with expendable income. All of these demographic shifts represent a potential for change. Change represents an opportunity for you, the entrepreneur. Digest the data, recognize where shifts in demographics will alter the competitive marketplace, take the opportunity to better serve the new demographic. It is up to you to figure out how to upend the incumbents and create the business landscape of tomorrow.

56 http://www.census.gov/population/socdemo/hispanic/ppl-172/tab01-1.pdf (2001)

57 Zolli, Andrew. "Demographics; The population Hourglass." Fast Company. Mar. 2006: pp. 57 – 63.

Chapter 22:
Consumer Targeting

"When one door closes, another opens. But we often look so regretfully upon the closed door that we don't see the one which has opened for us."

- Alexander Graham Bell

Even in a world of one-size fits all product lines and mass market conglomerates, some consumers are still left feeling empty with the products that corporate America churns out. In some circumstances, that person may even be you. Think about what happens when corporations do their job well. A market emerges and the competitors line up. Each of them scours the demographic landscape with a fine-tooth comb. Who wants our product? What do they want? How do we create it? How do we market it? In the process they are filtering. They are filtering out the most profitable consumers and determining how to cater to their needs. This is normal and good. However, what happens when you are one of the people caught in the filter? Often times you are left with products that fit the needs of others well, but not your needs. You have been a victim of "consumer targeting" as I will call it. Consumer targeting is a good source of innovation because it points you to a problem. Somewhere in the process of filtering, segmenting and marketing products, corporations have purposefully chosen not to cater to a large portion of society. They are going after the consumers they believe will be the most profitable and crucial to their business. In the process they have left a lot of target markets behind. This is where you can come in. Clayton Christensen described the categories of people left behind as overshot by product capabilities, undershot by product capabilities and non-consumers.[58] A source of innovation exists in recognizing these consumers and catering to their needs that other players have chosen to ignore.

We're going to take a look at each of the three categories I just mentioned, one at a time. The first problem I want to discuss is when the products available to consumers overshoot their needs. Essentially, the available options have too many capabilities for the task the consumer is trying to accomplish. This would be the

---

58 Generalized from Clayton Christensen's three books: The Innovator's Dilemma, The Innovator's Solution and Seeing What's Next

equivalent of buying a John Deere riding mower to mow three square feet of grass in front of your apartment. For the individual consumer, the products are overkill. Often times the consumer is left with the option of not consuming or buying way more capabilities than they require. This is often costly in both cases. One solution has them paying a premium price for products they cannot fully utilize and the other leaves them with unsolved needs. If you can recognize situations where this is occurring, you are being pointed to the source of a problem. Let's look at an example.

A recent hit business model that illustrates our point well occurred in the realm of physical fitness. The company called "Curves" is a fairly recognizable name by now. Curves offers physical fitness solutions for the average woman across the nation. One way to look at the way Curves framed their business is that they have catered fitness to women who are overshot by other fitness solutions, namely paid membership gyms. If you think about traditional membership gyms, and then think about individual needs of the people who go there, you can see my point. In a typical gym you pay upwards of $50 or more a month for membership. Once you are in, many people are only utilizing a fraction of the equipment and resources available. This is especially true for the average woman. I can't recall the last time I saw a woman spending time bench pressing or hitting the basketball courts at my fitness center. Likewise, many women found it hard to find time to utilize all of these extra amenities with their busy schedule. However, they were still paying for all of these things. On top of that, many women felt the traditional gym was intimidating.59 Researching their needs and understanding their desires revealed that they actually don't want to be seen working out, especially in front of men. Then along came Curves. What Curves did was to recognize a large consumer market that was being overshot by the products available to them. They recognized that many women went without consuming. Women either planned on working out from home and never did, or they bought a costly gym membership that they couldn't fully utilize. In both cases, a need existed that was being poorly solved. The consumer was being overshot. What Gary Heavin and his wife Diane did with Curves was eliminate the excess and amplify the elements of fitness that women most desired. The environment is specifically catered to women. The equipment and diet plans are specific to women. The time commitment is low and the membership fees are

59 http://www.curveshealthinformation.com/page4.html

a fraction of traditional gyms. By doing this they have eliminated a lot of the things that their specific target market does not need and improved on the things they do need. Essentially, Curves got rid of the overkill. After identifying the overshot consumer, Curves came up with a better solution. Now the target consumer has the perfect solution. For their efforts the entrepreneurs who founded Curves have a company that is now worth over a billion dollars. It just goes to show how some of the most lucrative businesses are often founded on easily identifiable premises. Targeting overshot consumers can be a powerful source when you have a group of consumers with no product to identify with and a strong desire to change that.

It is examples like Curves that point the entrepreneur in the direction of where to look. When the product capabilities of a market overshoot the consumer, what are they doing to solve their problem? In most cases they go without consuming or they end up paying a premium. This is a huge opportunity considering people have a need and are willing to pay for the proper solution. Entrepreneurs should recognize that money is being left on the table. If we can identify where overshot customers exist, it often times is not hard to tweak the current solutions to better cater to their needs. So when you look at the industries you would like to innovate in, start analyzing the consumer base. Who is the target market? For this source, throw that market out. Now, who is left? Are they consuming the product? Do they have a motivation to consume the product? If you find that there are non-consumers who would like to consume, you have found a source to target for a venture. Likewise, if you can find consumers who believe they are paying too much to use too few of the capabilities of a product, you also have an opportunity. The traditional consumer targeting process leaves market segments with poor solutions all the time. Systematically looking to places where consumers might be overshot can give us a great insight into areas that are in need of some better solutions that can lead to new venture opportunities.

Clayton Christensen, who first articulated overshot customers in detail in The Innovator's Dilemma series, has some excellent material for your research. If you want to truly understand how to locate them and what types of solutions they desire, you should definitely check out his books. One of the key things that Christensen touches on is that overshot customers are willing to pay less for products that are not quite ideal instead of paying more for products that way overshoot their needs. If you can reach the people who chose to be non-consumers instead of overpaying, you have tapped into an entirely new market. Likewise, even if a product is not exactly what an overshot customer is looking for, they are usually more than happy to switch to an inferior solution if the price is right relative to their needs. Figure out who these people are and start looking at markets to see where you might be able to exploit this source of innovation.

Much in the same way that consumers can be overshot, many targeting techniques leave consumers wanting more from available product lines and therefore have individuals who are undershot. To keep with the lawn care examples, this is like buying a pair of scissors to trim four acres of grass. If the target market for a product is well below the capability needs of some consumers, then the same thing occurs as when there are overshot consumers. The people who are left wanting more from a solution can either choose not to consume or to consume at a level that undershoots their needs. In both cases, again, we have a problem. I won't prolong the chapter by providing an example. I think you can figure this out on your own. Using the same techniques for analyzing consumer needs that we talked about above, we can start to identify where current solutions fall short of the needs of some consumers in a market. Once we have thrown out the target market and figured out who is left, we can start to define the total solution they are seeking. What prevents them from achieving it? What kind of money is being left on the table? How can we cater a new venture idea to the needs of these consumers? Again, often we can tweak and expand on the current solutions in an industry to find solutions that better suit the needs of markets outside of the mainstream target. Start looking for where these people are. Figure out what can be done to help them solve their problems.

One caveat to the undershot consumer that Clayton Christensen touches on is the fact that established firms are more likely to move up market to cater to their needs. Essentially, that means they are more likely to try and kill your firm and protect their market space. Upmarket and more demanding customers generally provide higher margins and a source of high dollar revenue.[60] It makes sense that the entrenched firms would want to capture these customers and keep them. To the established firm, moving up market and gradually producing better and better products comes pretty naturally. Therefore, we have to be very careful pursuing

60 Generalized from Clayton Christensen's three books: The Innovator's Dilemma, The Innovator's Solution and Seeing What's Next

opportunities where customers are undershot. It is only under the right conditions that this should be attempted. For instance, being a product leader in a fragmented market could be one scenario. If noone has taken control of a market, then it is probable that noone has properly defined the needs of the consumer. If noone has successfully catered to them to begin with, it would be difficult for them to move upmarket anyways. However, just blindly entering a battle with simple ideas versus a larger firm is not a good idea. So be careful. Read Christensen's books and decide when entering a battle against larger firms is a good idea and when we should steer clear.

At the same time that Christensen points out why we should often steer clear of undershot consumers, he also gives us the reason why overshot consumers are such high potential for firms to target. It is completely the opposite of the undershot logic. Basically, when we cater to overshot customers, we are introducing products that are less technically advanced, are not as good as some of the other solutions out there and have less revenue and profit margins associated with them. Why would the incumbents want to pursue those markets? Diluting their product line and their revenue doesn't make much sense to them. In this scenario, instead of defending that space, the established firms are more likely to ignore overshot customers. The reason that it is such a great opportunity for the entrepreneur is that we do not have the same frame of reference as the established firms. What might look like an inconsequential market to the established giants of an industry might be a highly profitable niche for the smaller, just starting entrepreneur. This is the reasoning behind overshot customers. Understanding this and exploiting the motivations of all parties leaves the potential for highly innovative ideas to come forth.

The last thing I want to touch on is the idea of someone choosing not to consume at all. They are all of the people who choose not to purchase products and services within a marketplace. The issue of the non-consumer, however, is not always black and white. They are not necessarily choosing not to consume because they lack the desire. Many of them would like to consume. However, for a variety of reasons that we will talk about in a minute, they are unable to do so. This phenomenon points us in the direction of a problem. We have a group of consumers with the desire to purchase but who cannot or choose not to under the current industry conditions. Identifying these consumers and subsequently finding a way to service their needs is a powerful source and director of business ideas.

The reasons that people have for being non-consumers are mostly common sense. As we touched on above, the product capabilities may undershoot or overshoot their needs. On the other hand, the product or service may be out of their price range. It may also be the case that the consumer does not have the skills or requisite knowledge needed in order to utilize the product. Sometimes the necessary product does not exist. Whatever the reason may be, consumers will flat out ignore the need if the necessary solution is not readily available or accessible to them. The focus then becomes "why?" What are the underlying causes of people choosing not to consume. If we can uncover why people are motivated not to consume, we identify a direction for our thoughts. When you get to the core of their reasoning, your efforts can be directed to remove the barriers to their consumption. Turning non-consumers into consumers unlocks entirely new markets that often have few competitors.

The first element of figuring out how to innovate with this source is finding out who the non-consumers are. Who are the outlying individuals that the industry chooses not to focus on? In many cases the answer is obvious. Industry players and the way in which they are presenting their products should paint a relatively clear picture of whom they are targeting. Dissecting their marketing messages, product placement and advertising efforts gives you a clear picture of the intents of the firm. The approximate demographic they are seeking is usually right out in the open for you to see. Once you have looked at who is being targeted by the firms in a market, you should have a pretty good idea of who is being left out. At that point, start figuring out why the non-consumers exist. By interviewing consumers, reading about markets and doing some general research you should be able to identify if you have a potential problem to solve.

The innovative mind should see non-consumers as a challenge. If consumers have the motivation to purchase but lack the resources, there is a problem that exists. Whatever the barrier may be, revenue is being lost because the existing firms in place cannot deliver to the consumers who would like to buy. This idea sort of spans the boundaries of where it can be applied. Sometimes you need process innovation to provide access. Other times you need product innovation to cut costs. The idea can be applied across a multitude of categories. The idea of non-consumers is a starting point of where to look in an industry. It is a source of where to focus in. If we take out the current demographic of who is consuming, we are left with a pretty large chunk of people who are not. Why? How can you change that? You are not going to be able to satisfy everyone who wants in on the action, but what if you could break down a barrier that would allow for the next 10% of people on the fringe of markets to buy? Catering to non-consumers is about identifying the barriers and then breaking them down. Removing the obstacles to a market or product that people desire to consume can become a very profitable niche and source of innovative thought.

So no matter what market space you are looking at or product line you are considering, out there in the marketplace there are vast numbers of consumers who are poorly represented by the solutions available. Whether they are overshot, undershot or non-consumers, the idea of consumers that lie outside of target markets is a powerful source of innovation. Money is being left on the table and ideas for new ventures are up for grabs. It is up to you to identify these consumers. It is up to the entrepreneur to frame and solve the problems so as to exploit the motivations of all parties involved.

Chapter 23:
Specialization and Niche Markets

"Our culture and economy are increasingly shifting away from a focus on a relatively small number of [mainstream products and markets] at the head of the demand curve, and moving toward a huge number of niches in the tail."

- Chris Anderson

Finding or creating a niche market to serve has long gone hand in hand with creating entrepreneurial ventures. These niche markets cater to a smaller, more specific group of consumers within the overall marketplace. A niche market lends itself to entrepreneurship because, generally speaking, entrepreneurs can create customized solutions that better suit the needs of their target consumers, as opposed to the one-size-fits-all solutions offered by larger firms. You might think of a niche market as another way of saying that an entrepreneur specializes at a certain product offering, hence my title for the chapter. Entrepreneurs can get away with stealing these niche markets because niches are often too small for the larger competitors to concentrate on defending. The profits that are lost to niches usually go unnoticed by giant corporations. This chapter is going to show you how we can exploit this source and why specializing and creating niche markets can be a great source of innovative opportunities.

Generally, when people discuss niche markets they are referring to small, specific groups of consumers that are segmented out of the larger pool, primarily on the basis of demographics. Demographics are a way to break down large groups based on their common characteristics. Some of the most common factors used for segmentation are; gender, age, race, culture and values. Demographics serve as a convenient way to identify smaller homogeneous groups of consumers within the larger scheme of the market. Demographics, however, are limiting when thinking entrepreneurially. It is not necessarily entrepreneurial to look at a large population, decide that a certain age range or gender needs their own product line and then start a company. You could do it that way, but then you are just doing the same thing every other firm is trying to do. Rather, specializing and niche market creation can be much more innovative than these traditional methods.

One of the more interesting niche businesses that I read

about recently comes from the world of golf. The featured company
in the article, TopGolf, has found a new niche within the golfing
community and a way to play off of the sport's popularity.61 Once
I explain their venture, like many entrepreneurial innovations, their
product seems obvious and it is an opportunity that has been staring
golfers in the face for many years. TopGolf has done for the driving
range what thousands of entrepreneurs have done with the putting
green in the past. Like putt-putt, TopGolf has redefined the driving
range to make it an entire game in itself. TopGolf has developed
a system whereby golfers, at their specialized ranges, can compete
against each other while they practice. The once low-tech yard
markers and far away pins are now likened to a dart board. Players
hit specially designed golf balls equipped with tracking devices
towards their target pin, which is surrounded by a series of circular
openings.62 Each opening represents a point value and the closer
you are to the pin, the higher the point total. The GPS system and
specialized retrieval grid record how close to the pin a golfer actually
comes and records their score. Players compete in special sheltered
enclosures equipped with computers to record the scores and where
their balls landed on the target. With all of these tweaks at the driving
range, TopGolf has created an entirely new game within the overall
game of golf. Avid golfers and casual fans alike can now compete
in a whole new way. TopGolf has stretched the idea of a niche by
segmenting out a process within the game of golf, as opposed to
specific consumers. The founders can only hope their innovations
will be as popular as its miniature golf counterparts.

        The TopGolf example may not strike you as a traditional way
to look at a niche market, but isn't that the point of innovation? When
we can stop thinking linearly along demographics and standard
business metrics, we start seeing where stretching ideas allow
innovation to come forth. Instead of segmenting the consumer base,
TopGolf's idea segmented out one of the smaller subsets of the game
of golf itself. Specializing and creating niche products can just as
easily be about a subset of a game or a firm or a market as it can be a
subset of consumers. Use this example to start thinking about how
else we can frame the idea of a niche market and specializing. What
other implications does it have beyond demographics? How else can
we exploit this concept?

        If you can't think of any ideas beyond what I have already

61 Feldmeier, Julia. "Driving for Dollars." Business 2.0. Aug. 2006: pp. 62-64. (TopGolf)
62 Feldmeier, Julia. "Driving for Dollars." Business 2.0. Aug. 2006: pp. 62-64. (TopGolf)

presented, here is another example to get your mind going. Echo Mountain, a company in Denver, CO opened a few years back with a radically different way of presenting a ski resort. In fact, it's not a ski resort at all. Instead of buying up hundreds of acres of land and developing astounding lodges with miles of groomed slopes, the founders of Echo bought just 50 acres.[63] Their aim was not to appeal to the Vail or Aspen jet set community, but rather to focus on an often overlooked niche. That niche was extreme skiers and snowboarders. The mountain is much less of a resort and much more akin to an extensive snow park. It caters to snowboarders and skiers who would rather watch their buddies carve up the half pipe or hit the grind rails as opposed to tackling endless miles of powder. Instead of gourmet meals and wine, the lodge offers microwaveable burritos and a video game room.[64] Instead of snowboarders and extreme skiers being the bane of the mountain, they are the focus. Lift tickets at some of the more popular ski resorts in Colorado might run you upwards of $100, but at Echo they charge $25. The founders of Echo Mountain figured out that boarders and extreme skiers did not need or want all of the perks of traditional resorts. They did not need neatly groomed powder or heated gondolas that skyrocket the cost to ski or board. Their niche consumers needed something affordable without cutting out the attractions they sought. Snowboarders and extreme skiers also needed a place where they fit in. Echo Mountain created that place. In fact, the park has been so successful that they are looking to expand their winning formula into other parts of the country. Why is it working so well? It works because the founders recognized a subgroup of an industry that was not being catered to. They built a solution to fit the specialized needs of an overlooked niche. However, you wouldn't have uncovered this niche by combing the demographics of traditional ski resorts. These consumers didn't need more within the confines of what existed, they needed a completely new solution spun out of the concept of a ski resort. Echo Mountain is about expanding the idea of a niche and what it means to specialize. The formula has been paying off and it is just one more innovative way to look at this topic.

Echo Mountain is yet another example of not thinking in a linear fashion. Before we get into setting up a framework for emulating their success, it is worth noting that this concept not only applies to this chapter, but it applies to innovation in general. Peter

---

63 http://www.echomountainpark.com/echo_facts.php

64 http://www.echomountainpark.com/echo_press.php

Drucker once commented that when he tried to lock innovation
into specific categories or sources, it was impossible. Innovation is
innovative precisely because it is freeform. It overlaps, it incorporates,
it transforms in many different ways. Pinning down innovation will
never be about locking it into a definition or giving boundaries. (much
in the same way that I am asking you not to pin niche markets or
specialization down to a specific definition) Pinning down sources
of innovation is more about creating the spark for the imagination.
You could put TopGolf into so many categories. You could call it
the merger of alternatives between golf and darts. You could call it a
copy cat of the putt-putt innovation projected onto a driving range.
You could call it a new spin on non-innovators and mature markets.
Or, like I have done here, you could call it a niche market within golf
or a specialization. The purpose of innovation and this book is not to
pin down which category it falls into, the purpose of pinning down
sources of innovation is to create multiple angles to think through.
We do this in order to get your mind thinking in new and different
ways. It doesn't matter which way you looked at the opportunity.
You could have arrived at the same type of business from many
different angles. The key is that you have all of those angles at your
disposal, and your mind thinks beyond categorical classifications with
this source and others. The key to thinking about all of these sources
is to be keenly aware of all of them, mix and match them and let them
flow over into each other. That is the essence of innovation. That is
how it occurs. Not falling into a category is precisely why it probably
hasn't been thought of or done before.

So now that I have hammered this idea into your mind with
examples, I want to put a basic framework around creating successful
niche business ideas. We'll build off of what we see in the previous
examples and also add to those concepts by incorporating some
traditional strategy.

The first order of business is breaking down the larger
industry, product or process that you are going to be pulling from.
Specializing and creating a business from a niche is about any angle
you can take on a smaller subset of a larger whole. Figure out all
of the inputs that make up the whole or the experience that you are
focusing on. Consider the consumers, the processes, the products
and the existing firms that are out there. Each input and each entity
can be analyzed as a possible way to spin off another product, service
or industry. What are the solutions the customer is seeking and how
are firms catering to it? Are there sub-levels of needs that consumers

seek within the overall solutions?   Sub-level processes? Sub-level products? Each thing that makes up a larger whole is something that could possibly be expanded and built upon. The good news for entrepreneurs is that America and its corporations love to churn out one-size-fits-all products that cater to everyone. With that in mind, there should be plenty of opportunities at the tail of the demand curve to uncover business opportunities. Consumers often do not question the validity of such an offering because it does solve their problem somewhat. Consumers often won't ask for new solutions because they have a half-baked way of solving their problems already. It is up to the entrepreneur to question that. It is up to the entrepreneur to creatively spin off an input in a way no one had thought of before.

A second step to the framework is what we have already harped on; use words like "niche" and "specialize" in a loose, innovative fashion. Too often these words are associated with tweaking existing solutions. Many business people incorrectly equate uncovering niche markets with doing more within the confines of what already exists. As you can see from the examples above, I chose them specifically because they are not tweaks of existing solutions. TopGolf isn't trying to create golf courses that incorporate technology or high tech scoring systems. They aren't forcing their idea into the realm of the existing game of golf. Echo Mountain is not trying to create a ski resort with more perks for snowboarders. They created an entirely new solution for them. Both of these examples took a niche element and spun it into completely separate entities that aren't trying to compete with the "whole" that they were extracted from. Other people aren't in their market space because they took an angle on the "niche" that isn't taught in business school. Once you put aside your preconceived notions of a niche, put your own spin on specializing and creating niches. Your solution to consumers' needs doesn't have to accomplish the same task as the original whole that you are borrowing from. It can spin out from a product feature, a nested process, a consumer subset, a set of attitudes, et cetera. It doesn't matter. Just be innovative in your approach.

Finally, now that you have your own unique way of looking at niches and your subset of a larger whole, execution becomes critical. Too often firms who have innovative ideas revert back to traditional methods of thinking when they go to implement the idea. Clayton Christensen talks extensively about this in his series of books on disruptive innovations. Your new "niche" is going to have to be something that is built up in a completely new way from what has been done in the past. You have to avoid letting the status quos and social norms of the larger whole that you extracted your idea from affect the way that the new business will operate. Too often entrepreneurs and firms try to fit an innovative idea back into the way things had always been done in the original industry.65 But that isn't your opportunity. You need to implement your ideas in a unique manner. Your new venture has to be built to cater to the needs and desires of your new consumers, not the ones who are satisfied with the one-size-fits-all solution. Your execution of a niche will be key to your success. Attempting to push the idea back into the realm of the original industry will satisfy neither the existing customers nor the ones you hoped to pull out of it.

If you haven't already, go back and read chapters 7 and 8. As you begin to go through the process of focusing your ideas and peeling back the layers of industries you will see all the "niches" that you could possibly exploit. The chapters illustrate how to break down each industry you might consider. Each input and process can be viewed as a niche from which to create an entrepreneurial firm. Each area of an industry is a chance to specialize and differentiate. You have literally millions of options for niche markets in the world. Whether you use traditional demographics or choose to use the tactics from this chapter, the chance to start a proactive search for niche markets begins today.

---

65 Generalized from Clayton Christensen's three books: The Innovator's Dilemma, The Innovator's Solution and Seeing What's Next

Chapter 24:
Outsourcing

"The perspective on outsourcing must shift from a focus on cost arbitrage to one encompassing a global search for resources and methodologies for leveraging resources. That's the new basis for innovation."

- C.K. Prahalad

The term outsourcing has become a buzz word within the American economy. The most heated of debates center on the outsourcing of American jobs to foreign nations and the downsizing of American employers. However, there is much more to outsourcing than sending jobs overseas or finding cheap labor sources. Too often outsourcing and "offshoring" are used interchangeably. While offshoring does mean sending jobs overseas, outsourcing simply means that we shift some of the inputs of a business to a person or company who is outside of our firm. This can happen domestically or internationally. It could be sourcing out to your neighbor Larry. The tasks we choose to outsource do not necessarily imply labor sources either. Companies are outsourcing advertising, sales, web design and any facet of the business that is not their area of focus or core expertise. The resulting mix of in-house and outsourced operations creates a combination of inputs that represents your business model. Any new combination that differs from the other firms competing in an industry has the capacity to create value beyond their solutions. Since it is the job of the entrepreneur to create new ventures by recombining these business model inputs, it is easy to see how outsourcing can be a great source of innovative thought.

The term "functional shiftability" may be a more appropriate way of thinking about outsourcing. When companies outsource they simply shift a function of their business to someone else.[66] They shift functions that are not their specialty that people pay them to do. For instance, if my company is formed in order to provide public relations and event planning, I might outsource such tasks as payroll, taxes and web design to other firms who specialize in those areas. My event planning firm would be highly inefficient at doing web design or some other unfamiliar task. The more you do something, practice something or create something, the better you become at it.

---

66 Based on class discussion, Marketing 650, Professor Roger Blackwell

In this case I would excel at public relations. Becoming more efficient should then translate into less time, money and physical resources you waste. Ultimately, your efficiency equates into monetary savings and value. That is why people specialize at certain tasks. When the maximum value can be squeezed out of a resource, especially money and time, everybody benefits. Thus the right combination of in-house and outsourced operations creates a system whereby the maximum potential is being created from the time and money available. Entrepreneurs can shape this as a competitive advantage against firms who do not operate in such an efficient manner. Businesses and ideas can be generated both by being the outsourcer and the outsourcee.

Let's take, for instance, outsourcing a task to someone else as being entrepreneurial. Whatever market space you envision your venture to be in, you are competing against other business owners who have developed solutions to the same problem. How you position and utilize the inputs available to you will determine the success of your company against the competing solutions. You have the option to produce all the inputs yourself or you can source them out. In most circumstances it will be a mix of the two. Outsourcing as a source of innovation is relevant when the entrepreneur understands what inputs currently performed in house could or should be outsourced. This happens when they see more productive entities to outsource to. Products and services are not outsourced without good reason, rather, entrepreneurs recognize outsourcing as an opportunity to save resources. When you can save money, time or effort you reduce the cost of inputs and drive the value up if all else remains equal. When you see businesses or markets that are performing tasks that are not their core competence, then there is probably a place in the market for an improved solution. Start looking around at the markets that interest you. Analyze all of the inputs that go into making the products or services in that industry. Are the suppliers making the most efficient use of the inputs they employ? Could things be done better? Are there better solutions or combinations of solutions out there that could save resources? How could you capitalize on competitors who have an inefficient solution to the problem at hand? Outsourcing is a great source of innovation when you can use it to craft better solutions to the problems at hand than does the competition.

Instead of providing one simplified example of outsourcing, I want to look at a theoretical situation. I have always been fascinated at the idea of outsourcing everything in a business except the founder.

In today's day and age we can literally outsource almost any input that we would need to comprise a business venture. Manufacturing, sales, taxes, you name it and you can outsource it. The implications for the entrepreneur are huge. Essentially you can form a loose network of 3rd party firms that can be formed and disbanded in a short amount of time. If you manifest this theoretical situation, you are the most flexible business entity in the marketplace. Product obsolescence, changing consumer preferences or anything else that can turn the tides against a firm are hedged against by not being wholly invested in any one aspect of your venture offering. One of the strengths of entrepreneurs is being able to respond to changing market conditions. When you utilize outsourcing to any extent you leverage your ability to do that. You can hire, fire and disband entire operations or competencies at a moment's notice and change to fit the new market. When you are competing against firms who do not have this flexibility, you potentially have a competitive advantage. Your ability to do this can mean your survival and their demise. So while this theoretical situation of outsourcing may not be the most cost effective or practical way to run a venture, it does illustrate the opportunity that outsourcing presents to the entrepreneur. With outsourcing you are able to frame a business in a manner that will better cater to or respond to the changing needs in the market. Outsourcing and leveraging your flexibility can be key in competing in the fast paced global economy of today. Framing a business venture with the right mix of in-house and outsourced operations is crucial to the current and future success of a proposed venture.

Before we move on to being the outsourcee, I want to point out that outsourcing levels the playing field for entrepreneurs in business. Functional shiftability is a tool for an entrepreneur because it allows access to resources that might otherwise have taken years to produce themselves. Entrepreneurs can use third parties that offer products or services to instantly compete on the same level as other firms in the market. You can purchase or hire everything from consultants to marketing firms and payroll services to sales representatives. Outsourcing gives entrepreneurs the power to employ the best products and services while focusing on what it is that they do best and allows them to compete in the marketplace. When you get ready to start your business, just remember the concept of functional shiftability as a way to level the playing field to compete and win in the marketplace.

The second aspect of outsourcing that I wanted to touch on

was the idea of being the person or firm to whom other individuals or firms outsource. When you look at any business model or market you should be able to observe what the firms do well and what it is that they do poorly. The opportunity to be an outsourcee lies in specializing in and making more efficient those tasks that they do poorly. Labor markets are the most common example of this. If you only have to pay a foreign source of labor 1/3 of what you will pay domestic workers for the same quality, then you are getting the same output at a much better price. Beyond labor costs, what else can be outsourced? If you see some product or service that is done poorly or at a very high cost, how could you create a firm to reduce the cost or improve the outputs? Any function of a market can be shifted to the most efficient party. Why don't you become that party? You could base a firm off of more efficient processes or more efficient inputs. Just look around and you will probably see many problems being solved very poorly. Recognize that opportunity to create a firm that solves the problem by being more efficient.

Let's look at an example of becoming the firm to whom other companies will outsource. The May 2007 issue of Fast Company featured a company called Shiftwise that illustrates this idea well. Shiftwise is in the process of transforming the "temporary nursing services" industry. The problem was, and still is, that there is a shortage of nurses in the United States. Hospitals are often faced with being understaffed at peak times and have a need to hire on temporary nurses to help fill the void. However, bringing on specialized employees requires the hospitals to go through extensive legwork to confirm the qualifications and certifications of the temporary staff. On top of that, scheduling the temps and their shifts was a huge hassle. One of the healthcare facilities that staffed with temporary nurses reported using 22 different staffing agencies to fill the gaps across their 43 clinics.[67] Staffing requests were different across agencies, with some relying on phone, some on fax and some on e-mail. This all equated to an extensive investment of time and money, drawing away from the core job of the hospital, just to keep up with staffing requirements. This was a big drain on the hospital's resources, but also a necessity. Then along came Shiftwise. Shiftwise is an online application that allows hospitals to schedule nurse temps as easily as you or I would be able to go online to book a flight or rental car. It eliminated the paperwork by consolidating it in the virtual world and reduced the man hours necessary in tracking down

---

67 Borzo, Jeanette. "Nurses on Demand." <u>Fast Company</u>. May 2007, pp. 40.

temps by offering a one-stop shop. Essentially, Shiftwise streamlined the entire process by allowing hospitals to shift unwanted scheduling duties out to their 3rd party firm. Shiftwise was employed to bear the burden of temporary staffing and the hospitals were left to do what they do best, saving peoples' lives. The result? Oakwood Healthcare, the featured hospital utilizing 22 temp agencies, implemented Switchwise and realized cost savings of $1.2 million dollars in a one year period. On top of the cost benefits, Oakwood saved themselves the headaches of dealing with 22 firms, allowing them to re-concentrate their efforts elsewhere. In the end both parties benefit; firms like Oakwood realize extensive efficiency savings and Shiftwise gets paid a tidy fee for their efforts. Both parties are left alone to concentrate on what they do best and Shiftwise is in the process of transforming an entire industry. It is your opportunity to replicate a success like this elsewhere. Uncover the process problems in a firm or an industry and become a specialized "outsourcee" to change the way things operate.

Finally, we come to the point of putting a framework around innovating using the concept of outsourcing. The examples should give you a pretty good picture of the scenarios you are looking for, but just in case, we're going to lay out the situations where outsourcing makes good business sense. The following are some of the key characteristics of when and why firms are looking to outsource.

1. Reduce Operating Costs

As I have mentioned before, reducing the cost of an input goes directly to the bottom line of a company. When outside firms can produce at a lower cost than producing in house, you have an option to outsource. In order to recognize opportunities for outsourcing, write down all the costs involved in the production of a product or service. Any reduction in cost, assuming all else being equal, is an increase in value. Costs could be monetary, time based, opportunity costs, et cetera. Understand which costs are low due to the core competencies of players. Low costs are characterized usually when a company focuses on or excels at a specific task. High costs, on the other hand, are costs that are necessary to business but not the specialty of the firm. These high costs are usually activities that companies have little experience with. Analyze a market or industry. Know the costs incurred at each step and begin to analyze whether an opportunity exists that firms are not taking advantage of. This could mean starting a similar firm with improved, outsourced inputs or it could mean simply becoming the outsourcee.

2. Improve Your Focus On Your Core Competencies

Any ancillary activity that distracts a firm from the way that they create value is a reason to outsource that activity. Your firm is only able to exist if you continue to create value and deliver on core competencies. If a company or an industry is spending money in excess away from their core competence, it most likely could be outsourced. The entrepreneur should be looking for these situations. If an industry is overspending on a process, product or service that could be done cheaper by a third party, then there is opportunity. Recognize, analyze and exploit these situations.

3. Third Parties Are More Advanced Than You

It is pretty obvious that the more you focus on a specific competence, the more you practice it and the more resources you devote to it, the better you become at it. Many times, third parties are cheaper and usually are more advanced than your firm could ever be. It is also obvious that since companies and industries are really only focusing on a couple core competencies in depth, they fall behind in the practice of the ancillary activities. You as the entrepreneur should be able to look at an industry, knowing their competencies and how they make their money, and see opportunities where practices, products and services not related to the core have fallen by the wayside. You have the opportunity to be the person to revinvigorate those inputs. If a firm has been operating the same way for ten years, most likely their processes for completing a task are outdated. The costs are probably high and the result is most likely inefficient. Simply by offering up-to-date knowledge as a third party provider is going to save money and provide a more efficient output.

4. Desire To Change Quickly

We've talked about the incumbents, the giant empires you target for disruption. Many times, the massive amount of resources at their disposal is daunting and threatening to the entrepreneur. You may see an opportunity but not be able to exploit it because of the ease with which they could force you out of their market space. The good news is that it works in the opposite way as well. Their massive resources can also be a liability. Incumbents' entrenchment in a certain space and market gives them power within that market. At the same time, those same investments keep them from being mobile when things change. One of the reasons people outsource is to stay agile and be able to adjust to the changing marketplace. If you substitute a monthly fee for a product or service versus massive cash outlays to produce it yourself, you have the chance to be quick to change with the market. People outsource because they can hire and fire third parties as easily as employees. You cannot as easily liquidate and divest out of activities you have decided to do on your own. Creating a more flexible, changing firm can oust the competition quickly when the tides of an industry are changing.

5. Free Up Internal Resources

The amount of inputs that a company can purchase at any one time is finite. Every day decisions are made to allocate funds across many facets of a business. Going back to the ancillary activities that support the core, companies have to shift money away from those practices that allow them to survive in order to do everything involved in running a business. Often, outsourcing is used as a way to reallocate those internal resources. If firms can shift functions from a high cost internal source to a lower cost third party, this frees up resources. Now the finite amount of resources that they had at their disposal has effectively increased. Firms can shift more funds and more focus onto what it is that makes them profitable and away from cost centers that detract from the mission of the firm. As you analyze the costs associated with an industry, remember that as an entrepreneur you can provide value by allowing industry players to reallocate their own resources. If you can give them substantial value increases from what they are currently doing, you are likely to earn their business by allowing them to focus on their core.

6. Fixed Expenses Become Monthly Expenditures

Markets and industries can be volatile. Consumer preferences change, competition changes and the industry landscape can shift before players have time to react. Another reason to outsource is to change large fixed expenses to monthly bills. The logic in business is similar to the reasons people rent instead of buy. You do not generally buy a house until you are certain you have a future in an area deserving of such an investment. You rent because you can move out on a whim for whatever reason that might present itself. The same is true in business. Companies make massive expenditures in areas they deem will have a permanent or long term fixture in a marketplace. On the other hand, especially in volatile and changing markets, it is easier to rent a solution while the industry works itself out. Third party providers, or outsourcees, are the firms that provide that luxury. Whether you decide to build a firm with a loose network of "monthly payment" solutions to challenge the competitors or you choose to be the "monthly payment" product or service, you have the opportunity to exploit such situations.

These are basic signs of opportunities for outsourcing, but they provide us a framework of where to start looking for opportunities to outsource. Keep in mind that most often your passions are going to be the areas in which you can really take advantage of these indicators. Your passions are inherently your core competencies and what you possess to beat the rival firms in a market. Look for markets where your passions are the ancillary activities and one of the cost centers that firms would rather not have to deal with. It is up to you to spot where you can exploit these situations.

The main point of this chapter is to produce a mindset where every input in a business model is considered as an element to outsource. Subsequently, start using that mindset to break down industries and play with different mixes of in-house and outsourced capabilities. Where are the firms in your industry of interest wasting time and money? Whether you are the person to outsource or the person to whom a task is being outsourced, the end goal is to raise the value proposition. It can be through decreased cost or through increased efficiency. So start looking around you. Exploit this knowledge of functional shiftability and outsourcing where others are failing to.

Chapter 25:
Bases of Competition

"The illiterate of the future are not those who can't read or write but those who cannot learn, unlearn, and re-learn."

- Alvin Toffler

When we seek innovation, one of the key things entrepreneurs must do is challenge everything we know about established industries. Specifically, for this chapter we are seeking to question the established norms for how a firm should compete in an industry. Each industry that you encounter will have both stated and unstated factors that they compete on. These "bases of competition", as they are often referred to, could be anything; price, design, quality, ease of use, et cetera. The standard combination of all these factors suggests a model for how to compete in an industry. Essentially they create an unwritten set of rules for being a player in the market. However, as an entrepreneur you often are striving to be completely different than the standard. The way to be creative and innovative, then, is to first learn all of the rules that the bases of competition imply, then go out and break them. By breaking the rules, you change the way the game is played. It is what changes your venture from a "me-too" firm into an innovative firm. Too many businesses stagnate their growth by framing their business model in the same way as their competitors. If you are looking for places to innovate, start questioning everything about the existing standards for solving consumer problems. One way to become a noteworthy entrepreneur is to employ a different business model than your competition and alter the bases on which an industry competes.

The concept of changing the bases of competition can be a source on its own, but it also encompasses many of the more specific sources mentioned in this book. The reason for the overlap is that many of the more specific sources already inherently change the bases of competition without coming right out and saying what they are doing. In that regard, this chapter is not really necessary. But then I began to think about how we as humans think through innovation. It occurs to me that with such a difficult topic to tackle, every angle that we can be given is that much more helpful. It also occurred to me that we think on different levels at different times. Sometimes it makes more sense to attack innovation from vague angles like looking for an "unmet need" or a "problem." Other times it is more helpful to think on a specific level and look for things like "substitutes" or "consumer appeal levels." In that regard, viewing "bases of competition" as a source in itself can be very helpful. If you are having trouble thinking of specific ways to utilize the sources in this book to change an industry, you have the option to zoom out to a wider lens. Stepping back and analyzing how an industry currently competes and analyzing the way the firms in an industry frame their business models can give you a new perspective on things. Subsequently, you can begin to think through new business models that change those bases. If you can use "bases of competition" as a way to get started, then you can zoom back in to figure out specifically what inputs to alter.

One of the first things to consider when you look to change the bases of competition is the response of the competition. You learn that as an entrepreneur you have few advantages going up against companies that are entrenched in a marketplace. When you take on firms that are motivated to keep the market space that you are trying to steal, it is an uphill battle. As long as you are playing within the boundaries of their rule book, you have little to gain in that space. Therefore, creating a business model that avoids head on conflict makes a lot of sense. As an entrepreneur you need to strive for new solutions and new ways of accomplishing tasks to avoid battles for market share against bigger players. This is true not only for the sake of creating something new, but also for reasons of self-preservation. The first part of utilizing this source then, comes from an understanding of the industry players you are targeting and their system for catering to consumers. You need to understand the underlying factors that motivate firms to behave in certain ways and how they are likely to respond to new competition. First, get a good sense of their model for success, then go out and find ways to creatively break out of their model. If done properly, many times you can frame a business so the companies entrenched in the old ways of doing things ignore your firm or are unable to respond.

The second thing you need to consider to use a source such as "bases of competition" is your knowledge level within the industry. Unless you are directly involved in a specific field and are steeped in experience, chances are you know very little about most industries. Your answers to how you think industries operate, and the bases that they compete on, could be far off base from how things actually work. For this reason, this source and most of the sources in this book demand that you stop your passive search for innovation and start actively pursuing it. Researching, digging and leg work are the only way to understand an industry that you are not associated with or do not have years of experience with. You have to learn the rules. You have to know what industries compete on and the business models they employ before you can change them. Why? Because a change in the bases of competition cannot be arbitrary. It has to be purposeful and it has to be specific.

When I say that a change in the bases of competition cannot be arbitrary, it relates to how people currently think through innovation. If you employ tactics such as the ones I discussed in the chapter about "flash-in-the-pan innovation," chances are that you are going to get arbitrary results. This is because most of the current tactics for generating business ideas are based on randomness. Random inputs beget random outcomes. But consumers do not randomly choose to change. They do not go to purchase a product or service one day feverishly searching for new or different products. They go with the intent that they will purchase the same solution that they normally do; it's consistent and it solves their needs. Consumers do not change their product and service preferences just because someone has thrown out some new options. They change only when someone can present to them, and subsequently sway them, that a better or different solution exists. If your reason for changing a product, service or industry is not based on a specific market need or a better solution, they will not change. So when you look at innovation through the lens of "bases of competition," be sure you fully comprehend what the consumer is trying to accomplish. When you are ready to theorize how to change things up, understand the difference in changing just for the hell of it, and changing to better suit the needs of the consumer. You must have a new solution that compels consumers to buy. You must build a different business model than your competition to capture consumers' attention and at the same time it must be a purposeful departure.

The framework for how to employ this source has already been done before. Considering there is no reason to fix something that is not broken, I will summarize a framework based mostly on ideas found in the Blue Ocean Strategy. The Blue Ocean Strategy is over 200 pages of information on ways to purposefully depart from the way things are currently being done in the marketplace. The execution part of this chapter is going to be based on a few of the ideas that Kim and Mauborgne present in their book. However, I could not even begin to replicate the depth of their information in one chapter on which they built an entire book. A true grasp on this topic should be supplemented by a read through of their bestselling book. However, I am going to reproduce some of the key points of the book that are relevant to this chapter. By briefly looking at some of the topics they hit on multiple times in the Blue Ocean Strategy, it gives you an important first step in a framework for creating new business models with this source.

The first task for creating new bases of competition is to lay out how the firms in an industry currently compete. Kim and Maugborne suggest you map out the attributes of an industry and each major firm that competes within it. The authors use what they have dubbed a "strategy canvas" to do this. The strategy canvas is basically a graphical representation of what factors an industry competes on and what each firm looks like visually.68 First, the relevant bases of competition for the industry are put on the horizontal axis of a graph. Second, the vertical axis of the graph depicts the degree to which each base of competition is employed, from a low level to a high level. Finally, you would plot out where each major firm in an industry falls on that graph. (See fig. 1 on the next page for an example) By doing so, you get a visual picture of the current state of an industry. This gives you a good view of where the major competition falls with their business models. This visual should give you a snapshot of how similar or different the major firms of an industry are in their business models. If every firm in an industry has a similar looking plot on the graph, chances are there is room for new solutions. If the firms are all over the board, chances are the winning solution hasn't yet been developed. Either way, this visual map gives you an idea of where you can start changing and tweaking for a new solution. Deciding where consumers would value a varied solution to what exists starts you down the path to new ideas and new models for a business. Take a look at the graph now to better understand this concept and then the next paragraph is the example on which the graph is based.

---

68 Kim, W. Chan and Renee Mauborgne. Blue Ocean Strategy. "How to create uncontested market space and make the competition irrelevant." Boston, MA: Harvard Business School Press, 2005.

Figure 1 - This is my personal opinion on what the strategy canvas of the "video game console" industry might look like. The X axis is the bases of competition. The Y axis is the degree to which each firm employs the X axis category. Then I have plotted the major firms on the graph. The three main competitors I have identified are Sony, Microsoft and Nintendo. Those systems are the Playstation 3, the X-Box 360 and the Nintendo Wii, respectively.

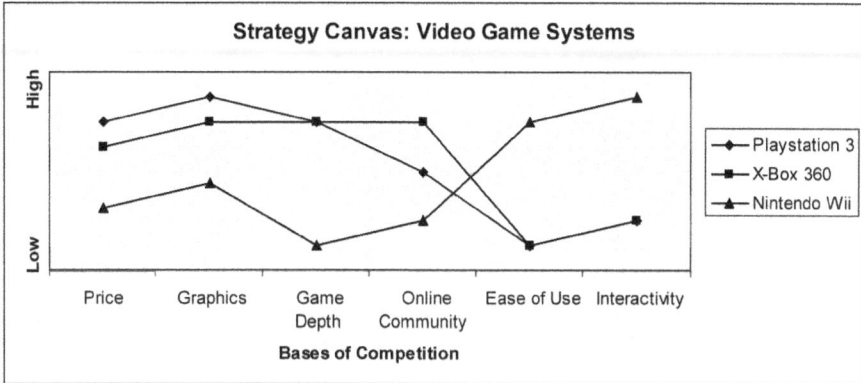

Strategy Canvas: Video Game Systems

For our example, I have chosen the "video game console" industry. The example and the strategy canvas I have presented are my personal interpretations of the industry, not fact. Please keep that in mind if you don't like my interpretation. Also, for those of you who aren't sure what I mean by a "video game console," I am referring to the physical hardware on which video games are played.

For illustration purposes, I have chosen three of the major players in the video game console industry to plot on the strategy canvas; Playstation 3, X-Box 360 and the Nintendo Wii. As you can see in the graph, the bases of competition that I believe the industry competes on are as follows; price, graphics, game depth, online community, ease of use and interactivity. The following is a brief description of each so we are on the same page:

Price - Retail price that consumers pay for the system.

Graphics - Refers to the quality and realism of the images that a game console can produce on the TV screen. Graphics are a result of the hardware and technologies that the manufacturers attempt to incorporate and build games off of.

Game Depth - Refers to the complexity of the story line and the time it takes to beat a game.

Online Community - To what degree the system utilizes the internet to connect gamers. This factor is a combination of allowing gamers to play each other over the internet and also the sense of community.

Ease of Use - Refers to how easy it is to play the games available. This refers to a combination of the controller complexity and the skills necessary to understand how to play.

Interactivity - The degree to which the video game player is physically involved.

The bases of price, graphics and game depth have been around since the early days of the video game industry. These factors have always been part of the equation. Companies have continually tried to balance between pushing the limits of video game console capabilities and maintaining profitability. For the foreseeable future, they will remain critically important bases on which the industry competes. It wasn't until more recently, with the advent of the internet, that the idea of online gaming and having an online community has been added as a factor worth competing on. The market players are now forced to not only develop games and console capabilities, but also to see how far they can push the idea of a community and a marketplace online. For that reason, I added this to the graph. Finally, the idea of interactivity and ease of use has seen some significance in the past but had not become a major element of the equation until recently. Sure, Nintendo and Atari were simple and easy to use when they first came out, but that was out of necessity. The consoles of the past had to be simple because the technology was limiting in its nascent stages of development. Nowadays the factors of "ease of use" and "interactivity" are crucial not for how much they limit gameplay, but how much they can further it. Ten buttons on a controller used to be better than four because you could accomplish more actions. However, that perception has evolved to a point where consoles are seeking to accomplish all of the functionality they used to have, with less complicated input necessary from the user.

After I had established all of this, the subsequent plots are my approximations of where each of the three systems might fall on the strategy canvas. Playstation 3 shoots for the high-end price range with cutting edge graphics, extensive memory and in depth gameplay. X-Box 360 seems to be in the mid-to-upper price range, focusing on the best internet community with good graphics and an extensive range of games. Nintendo Wii, on the other hand, comes in at the lower end of the price range with OK graphics and cartoon, family based games. The Wii focuses on interactivity and basic games that require physical motion on the part of the player. The resulting visual should paint a relatively good picture of how each firm is trying to compete in the current market. Their subsequent plots are indicative of the business model they are using to target their consumer base.

In the past, most of the new game console releases focused on what Playstation 3 currently focuses on; better graphics, more capabilities and more in depth gameplay. Most of the major players mirrored each other in what they were competing on. In fact, there was good reason for this. Gamers traditionally wanted better graphics, more capabilities and in-depth gameplay. The technology was not yet good enough to meet the wants of the consumers in the market, so they kept pushing these features. For many years the major video game console producers were trying to best each other at the same business model. They were trying to push the envelope and "wow" gamers while trying to maintain profitability. The important thing to note is that, if you had put them on a strategy canvas as Kim and Mauborgne suggest, they would have looked nearly identical. Their business models were the same and they were all striving for the same goals. In fact, looking at the graph, Playstation 3 and X-Box 360 still have very similar business models for competing in the industry. The reason I used this example is because, with the most recent product offerings from these firms, Nintendo changed all that. The Nintendo Wii sought to depart from the business model of the past and the one that Sony and Microsoft still compete on. Nintendo decided to create something uniquely their own.

In the latest releases, Nintendo illustrates my point about changing the bases of competition. Nintendo could have spent the past 5 years researching the next implication of cutting-edge technology and how far they could push the envelope to profitably include it in their next system release. They could have been working on besting Microsoft at online multiplayer communities or catching up with Playstation in developing in-depth games. But instead of heading into that bloody battle for market share, Nintendo went in a completely different direction. They chose to change the bases on which they would compete and pursued a business model that departed from the industry norm. Instead of competing on graphics and game depth, Nintendo decided to keep the graphics modest and push the system in its interactivity and ease of use. The Wii sought to bring a new level of intuitiveness to the gameplay. In a tribute to the days of Duck Hunt, Nintendo decided to get the gamer physically involved. Games such as bowling, baseball, golf and boxing have the gamer physically moving around a wireless, motion-sensing controller. The result is that the characters of the game replicate the movements and actions of the gamer in real life. The result is simplified, intuitive controls. Instead of having 10 buttons to accomplish all the necessary actions of the character in the game, you substitute it with physical motion. By doing this they are catering to the needs of a different type of consumer. When Nintendo altered their attack, they knew full well that they were giving up a certain consumer set that wants the best graphics and intense gaming. On the other hand, this approach has allowed them to attract less serious gamers and also people who might not have bought one of the new systems at all. They are pulling in parents, grandparents and all kinds of people who previously wouldn't play video games. They are getting people who might be intimidated by a controller with 15 buttons or a game that requires 50 hours of time to complete. Nintendo's business model now partially competes with the other two systems but also draws in a whole new crowd. Their new business model is a departure from the industry norm and a great example of changing the bases of competition with a distinct purpose.

The key to the prior example is understanding why Nintendo saw an opportunity to depart from the old bases of competition. They knew what the players in the industry had competed on in the past. They had lived the history. However, they changed their approach to the business model because they recognized a need that was being underserved. Consider this; video games have always been pushed in the way of graphics and artificial intelligence in an effort to mirror reality. The standard way to do this was to increase the amount of controls and push technology to create more life-like graphics. However, Nintendo spun this idea with the Wii. Instead of pushing technology to replicate real life, they pushed technology to capture real life motion. While the graphics look nothing like real life, physically acting out the game and capturing that motion has changed the way the industry will understand interactivity. Nintendo recognized the needs of consumers and then framed them in a new light. By doing this they altered the strategy canvas. They reduced elements such as graphics and in-depth gameplay, then increased ease of use and interactivity above the other players. Their new business model reflects this approach and that is why their plot varies so much from the other two competitors.

Nintendo also departed from the old way of doing things because they recognized an underserved need in "would be" gamers. They recognized that there were people at the fringe of the market who chose not to play because of the complexity of games and the time outlay necessary to play them. By giving those fringe consumers intuitive controls and games that require much less time to play, they were able to turn non-consumers into consumers. They radically increased the levels of "ease of use" and "interactivity" over their competition to accomplish this. Now Nintendo has a subset of the population that Sony and Microsoft can't touch with their current products. By changing the bases of competition, Nintendo was able to capture a new consumer market. The result is that Nintendo is now in somewhat of a "blue ocean" of their own. They still compete with Playstation and X-Box to a degree, but not toe-to-toe. For doing this, they didn't just avoid extinction, they're system is sold out and it has paved the way for their future success.

This example illustrates all of the key ingredients that entrepreneurs need to understand to utilize this source. Now it is up to you to supplement this chapter with further reading and practice. There are plenty of opportunities in the marketplace to do what Nintendo did in the video game console industry. First, figure out what market you are going to target. Second, lay out a strategy canvas of the industry. Third, understand the solution the consumer is seeking. Finally, start theorizing ways to change the bases of competition based on the needs of consumers. By purposefully altering your approach to a market, you change the rules of how the game is played. Start thinking about what this means for your target market today. What implications could a new business model have in your target area? You have the knowledge to alter where industries head in the future. Your ideas can change the way things are done and provide you with the venture opportunity you have been searching for.

New Inputs and New Knowledge

Chapter 26:
New Knowledge

"There is nothing more difficult to take in hand, more perilous to conduct, or more uncertain in its success, than to take the lead in the introduction of a new order of things. For the reformer has enemies in all those who profit by the old order..."

- Niccolo Machiavelli

They say that humans underestimate the amount of new ideas, concepts and products that are left to be invented or discovered. The present accomplishments of our race only seem close to the pinnacle of innovative thought because we are not graced with the foresight to see the future. However, if you look at history, humans are very adept to finding new discoveries to change the way things are done and what is possible. One of the most intriguing sources of innovation, and the one that gets the most attention, is the application of completely new inputs and new knowledge. Think of the toiling inventor or theorist who works day in and day out to discover new thoughts, concepts and products. Think Albert Einstein, Alexander Graham Bell or Leonardo Da Vinci. All of these people created new inputs that revolutionized the way humans are able to do things and conceptualize the world around us. It is new inputs that take the old equations and throw them out the window. They change the rules of the game and often purge industries of the past. It is the most intriguing, rare and difficult form of innovation, but when it happens it has the capacity to completely change the ways things are done.

Sometimes creating something entirely new is purposeful, and sometimes it is by complete error. The introduction of new knowledge is the most interesting because it resets the equation. Instead of recombining within the group of inputs that are available, you now have a new input to work with; something people haven't seen before or worked with before. It is evolutionary and intrinsically entrepreneurial because it adds value without necessarily having to change other things in the equation. Noone knows what all the new implications will be. Who knows who could use it? There may be some obvious applications, but chances are there are many not so obvious applications. Take for instance the idea of radio frequency identification (RFID). The concept has been around for years, but we are just now getting to the point where some of its applications are

economically feasible. We know that Wal-Mart sees an application
for their logistics system. We know that some clothing retailers have
them in their higher end clothing. There are some basic applications,
but who knows where it could go beyond that. Your ideas for what
could be tagged and why are as good as anyone else's speculations.
Where is the future of RFID? The application of the technology is in
its infancy, but people are already speculating the various industries
that could be revolutionized if certain capabilities come to fruition.
That is the point of new knowledge. It is so powerful because all the
possibilities that it unleashes are unforeseen.

        The first thing that you need to determine is if you are indeed
in need of developing new knowledge. Developing new knowledge
means that you have identified a problem or decided to create an
industry. Hopefully, one of the sources in this book will have gotten
you this far. However, after determining an avenue to follow you
decide that the components for a solution do not exist. A common
mistake made by the inventor and the entrepreneur alike is that
they rush to solve the problems at hand. Einstein once said, "If I
were given 20 days to solve a problem, I would take the first 19 to
define it." This statement can't be emphasized enough. Many times
entrepreneurs believe they need to start solving right away. However,
in actuality, once you have located a problem, a substantial amount
of time should be devoted to figuring out what exactly the problem
is. The better defined the problem, the more you understand it and
the more successful you will most likely be in solving it. Framing
the problem correctly might be the single most important step in
eventually coming to a solution. On the same note, without proper
research, you may not realize that someone has already solved your
problem or at least partially solved it. So before you start throwing
time and money at a potential innovation, make sure you are actually
in need of employing new knowledge as a source to begin with.

        This area of innovation is one of the trickiest to describe in
words. You have your problem and you need an answer. This type
of innovation requires you to pull together thinking out of the blue.
It is about logic and intuition. It is about breaking down the problem
and being able to pull information from various disciplines. Think of
the problem of humans desiring to be able to fly. As far back as Da
Vinci we had people contemplating how we could go about this. We
associate the ability to fly with birds. So we study birds and gather
insights that way. It was not until hundreds of years later that we
discovered principles in nature that describe why a bird can fly. So

now you bring in engineering. The concepts of lift and thrust then become apparent to us. We know that the human body isn't made for the task, so how do we improvise? Well, we can build a structure that harnesses the power of lift and thrust that we can go inside. It is no coincidence that the structure we devised, the plane, looks exactly like a giant bird. But new knowledge tends to come together slowly and develop from areas that may not logically connect at first. There is no easy answer, but we can diminish the amount of irrelevant paths by properly researching the problem and understanding what is left to be uncovered.

So new knowledge has a lot to do with pulling existing knowledge from a variety of related disciplines. Once you have identified a problem or envisioned an industry you would like to create, it's time to start assessing whether the necessary elements exist in order for you to pull it off. Many of the innovative industries of the past and present are simply mash-ups of a variety of known or established industries. The search for "new knowledge" generally begins with a search for what components are in place and what components still need to be invented in order to pull off the vision of the entrepreneur. Existing knowledge and observations get us so far and then we have to break down the problem and understand what else needs to be harnessed to solve it. It may take years to discover that X factor.

Figuring out the X factor and what needs to make your vision a reality harkens back to the days of 3rd grade science. There is no easy answer for truly original thought. We all recall the days when we were introduced and asked to call upon the "scientific method." When confronted with a blank slate of possible things to try, it still may be the best answer to how to start down the path of innovating in new areas. The most alluring type of innovation turns out to be the hardest to pull off. Much of the efforts of the entrepreneur are left up to trial, error and perseverance. Once you have properly defined your problem or the industry you want to create, it is time to start theorizing how to get from point A to point B. There is no magic answer or commonalities for this one; it is about intuition and then developing theories. You have to take those theories and go through the steps of trial and error until the problem can be solved. It is a process of reasoning backwards and then extrapolating to a solution. And when it is done, it has the power to transform industry or leave you in ruins.

Unlike established industries, products and services,

entrepreneurs can have the upper hand when they are in possession of new knowledge. Even if established market players have access to it, many times they are limited by the businesses and systems that they are entrenched in. New knowledge and new inputs allow the nimble entrepreneur to topple huge industry players. Take voice over internet protocol (VOIP) for example. Think of companies such as Skype that were able to launch an assault on the established telecom industry. In the past, the proprietary systems and massive asset based companies were immovable. Now the millions of miles of cabling and telephone wire are a liability as a new way to communicate has been launched. VOIP is a new input. The internet has the ability to at least partially, if not fully, replace the old ways of doing things. Finding a new input that substitutes internet connections for landline connections has given entrepreneurs the ability to upend an industry. It creates value intrinsically because the substitution renders the cost of your average telephone call to a fraction of the price that it once cost asset based companies to charge.

Just think of new knowledge and its implications. The idea that sound waves could be transferred into electric signals and sent across wires was revolutionary. Think of all the products that new knowledge is capable of spawning. From the telegraph to the telephone to the cell phone and now voice over internet protocol. The new input of transmitting sound over a wire had the ability to create thousands of companies, thousands of products and thousands of jobs in industries that never existed prior. Unfortunately there is no magic answer to this one. Deciding that you actually need new knowledge is the first step. Focusing in and researching the problem narrows down the possibilities. From there you should revisit your third grade textbook. New knowledge is an exploration of the unknown and a matter of failing your way forward.

The most exciting thing about new knowledge is that it is such a mystery. If it is pulled off well, it has the capability to wow the mind. Some new knowledge may not be as profound as other new knowledge. At the same time, the more profound the knowledge, the more exciting, the more risk and the more chances to fail miserably or revolutionize the world. There is no "how-to" for new knowledge. It is about piecing together theories and practices from various disciplines to form a base. From there it is a matter of filling the gaps with theories, tests and extrapolating on what we know. New knowledge is as much about insight into ideas as it is aboutexperimenting and hard work.

Chapter 27:
Part-Time Entrepreneur

"No one gets out of the game of life alive. You either die in the bleachers, or on the field. So, you might as well play out on the field…"

- Les Brown

By now its chapter 28 and you understand the concepts and what I am saying, but none of the ideas you generate are resonating. That's OK. It is OK to not have an idea that you want to invest months or years of your life into right this second. It is NOT OK to quit and start a consulting firm or a day spa or a combination day spa consultant. Just do not quit and do not give up on an innovative concept. The most important element is that you have been exposed to the information within this book. It's like a good virus. It will have an effect on the way you think from here on out. Hopefully, consciously and subconsciously you will filter information through the ideas in this book. It is not an end in itself just to read information. It is the beginning of a new way of looking at things. But while that is taking place you should still be doing something. Instead of gladly schlepping back to work for the boss, start taking small steps towards owning your own venture. Commit to being at least a part-time entrepreneur. It is entirely possible to be entrepreneurial in the process of finding the idea that suits you for your full-time venture.

Being a part-time entrepreneur has a lot to do with capitalizing on the things that you have to do or enjoy doing in the first place. Your first entrepreneurial venture does not have to involve venture capitalists, millions of dollars or extensive experience. Part of the reason for focusing on your passions when thinking about ideas is that these things just come naturally. Whether you collect guitars, rebuild cars or enjoy investing in stocks, you should be looking at what you do in your spare time as your own small entrepreneurial venture. What would happen if you framed your hobbies or duties as a venture rather than just something to do? Why not get more aggressive with the things you are already doing? You can and you should. You can be entrepreneurial while you wait for an idea that you want to run with. Slight expansion of your passions might even lead to your actual venture, you never know. So this is actually a pretty interesting exercise. Figure out what it is that you enjoy doing during your free time. No really, get out a pen. Hobbies, chores, errands, whatever it may be that you do. You already have the time allotted for these things. Now try and think of a way to expand on these. Can you create a venture by expanding these areas? Is there a way that you could charge money for the things you already do? Turn the corner from amateur to professional? Tweak your spare time activities with one of the sources in this book? However you can put a spin on what you are already doing and turn it into an entrepreneurial experience; that is being a part-time entrepreneur. Start brainstorming.

Let's look briefly at a pretty common spare time activity. That activity is investing your money for the future. Take for instance the area of stocks. A decent percentage of the population does this or at least has someone to do it for them. The idea of investing in the stock market is basically buying part of a company. You are investing in a business opportunity on a small scale. You're like a mini Warren Buffett. Unfortunately most people are hands off when it comes to investing. Few take an active approach to choosing and trading their own stocks. But you do not have to be a financial analyst to be quasi entrepreneurial in the stock market. Beating the Street by Peter Lynch explains that there are plenty of basic investment tips that the everyday person can use to invest. If you haven't already, I suggest you read it. Many of the tips involve investing in the types of businesses that overlap your passions. It also includes common sense ideas such as investing in companies you frequent or that you recognize are poised for growth. Even if you do not have the means or the gumption to start the next Dell computer, there is no reason why you can't invest in the person who does. It is examples like this where you can take something you are already doing and expand it entrepreneurially. Instead of passively handing money over to a broker and cutting him a portion every time, take matters into your own hands. If you are so driven, start doing your homework. Figure out an industry. Start trying to expand your horizons and leverage the things you already do. From the New York Stock Exchange to over the counter penny stocks you can choose your level of risk. You can bet on a new technology coming from a Fortune 500 company, or you could bet a little on an obscure software company in Oklahoma. No matter what your life position is, you can still be edging towards taking the entrepreneurial plunge by doing things on the side. Part-time entrepreneurship is self-descriptive. These adventures will go at your pace.

The list goes on and on of the possible spare time activities we humans do that could be turned into profitable businesses. Your house could be a foray into real estate. Your collection of baseball cards could turn you into an eBay dealer. The night photography class you run could be put on the web in purchasable podcast format. Whatever it is that you do, expand it. Leverage it. Exploit it. Take the time to do your homework and put in a little extra effort to turn the corner on your spare time activities. In the book The Entrepreneur's Manual, Richard White refers to these side businesses as "mini-incomes." White, in 1977, commented that "there is no alibi for any qualified individual in America not to realize a minimum of $2,000 a month (or $20 an hour) from his[/her] non-prime hours (evenings and weekends)." That was 30 years ago. Even today $2000 extra dollars a month would be a substantial boost to most people's income. To generate this much, you may come up with five $400/ month streams. Any of these side businesses have the potential to fully develop into a new venture. So start expanding on what you are already doing. If it all works out you will have an income or at least some extra cash to fall back on when you do decide to take the plunge with your full-time venture.

All of the things that I mentioned are obviously not as easy as I can make them sound in one paragraph. This book is just a watered down version of what you need to think about to get your mind rolling in the right direction. But seriously, start to think of the things that you do for fun or have to do anyway in your spare time and frame it as an opportunity to make money or create value. It probably means that you will have to become more aggressive with your passions. Once you frame something as a business opportunity and not just a casual occurrence, you can be more aggressive. Maybe that means investing in high growth, high risk companies as opposed to a mutual fund. Maybe it means leveraging a real estate deal instead of settling for the price range you know you can afford. Maybe you will buy vintage guitars not because you love a certain sound, but because you know you could restore it and flip it for a profit. Whatever it is that you do in your spare time, start framing things as an opportunity to be entrepreneurial. Get more aggressive with your passions. Be entrepreneurial on your way to becoming the entrepreneur you envision yourself becoming in the future.

Chapter 28:
Pure Profit Plays and Being Trendy

"If you want to be one of the first into a new territory, you cannot wait for large amounts of evidence."

- Joel Barker

Buy low, sell high. Guaranteed wealth creators. Pure profit systems. These phrases and similar ones have been the mantra of many get rich quick schemes and late night infomercials. While the concepts and phrases get used and abused by hoaxsters, there is some truth to the idea of a pure profit play. A pure profit play is a simple concept. It is where a known demand exists and the product or service can be sold at a higher price than the entrepreneur can buy it for. It may seem idealistic but it happens quite often. Think about all of the trends that a human being encounters month to month, year to year and decade to decade. Everything changes; music preferences, movie preferences, art preferences, popular toys, popular fashions, et cetera. These trends have an adoption curve and many entrepreneurs find profit potential by being in front of it and subsequently riding out the wave. The pure profit play is about being keen to emerging trends. You only need to be aware of your environment and the concepts of supply and demand for most of the plays out there. The only thing that prevents you from capitalizing on such trends is a failure to act. Most "buy low, sell high" type opportunities are fleeting. In this chapter we are going to discuss how to identify pure profit opportunities and how entrepreneurs can exploit them to capitalize in the short term.

Pure profit plays are the trends that you hear about on the evening news or in the daily paper. However, by that time you are sitting down to read about the trend, it is probably too late for you to get in on the action. One of the most recent trends that comes to mind is the yellow wrist bands made popular by Lance Armstrong and his fundraising group.[69] The bands, which started as a cheap way of raising funds, became a nationwide hit among supporters and trend setting youth. The initial wave caught on quickly and subsequently spawned many imitators and spin-offs of the idea. The concept was simple. There was a known demand for these bands. They could be bought very cheaply and sold at a higher price. The

---

69 Influenced by class discussion, Entrepreneurship MHR 494, Professor Michael Camp

trend flooded the markets and disappeared almost as quickly. This is the idea of the pure profit play. Many early entrants or bulk buyers of these bands got in and out before most people realized what had happened. A classmate of mine was able to turn $3000 in profit in a few short months buying and selling the bands prior to the onslaught of competition. Albeit a simplified example, it serves the purpose to show that business plays do not have to be overly complex. In this case, all it took was a little economics knowledge, and the competency to see a low risk trend sweeping the nation, to turn a few quick bucks. Anywhere a gap exists between the price a product or service can be bought for and what it can be sold for, there exists the possibility of a pure profit play.

Most of you probably scoffed at hawking plastic bands over eBay or speculating on the next hot toy in the teenage marketplace. As I said above, the bands are a simple example to prove a point. There are more complex profit plays in the world of business. The lower the barriers to entry into a market, such as the bands, the quicker the competition can saturate the market and deplete the opportunity. A good example of a more difficult type of profit play can be seen in the currency exchange market. Day to day and month to month we trade them. We purchase the Yen or bet on the Dollar. Sometimes we trade between three currencies. If a gap exists between currency exchanges of any nation and another nation or two other nations, then that gap can temporarily be exploited for pure profit. Sharp buyers are able to buy a currency at a lower price and turn it around and sell it at a higher price. Like the plastic bands, these gaps are quickly closed and opportunity is afforded only to those who are on top of their game. The concept is as simple as the plastic band idea but the execution takes a bit more skill to recognize and a bit more prowess to pull off. Educating yourself at various levels of business puts you in a position to be ahead of curves no matter what markets you are targeting. Whatever level of knowledge you possess in the world of business, there are plenty of doors of opportunity to exploit pure profit plays on your level. Take the time to realize where they exist. Take the time to learn about new concepts and figure out where you can exploit supply and demand. If you are having a difficult time forming an entirely new venture for yourself, maybe speculating on some profit plays is just what you need to get your feet wet.

Pure profit plays are an ever changing thing. One minute too early or too late and you can find yourself with a lot of money tied up in the wrong place. Pure profit plays elicit the thrill of speculation and then it is on to the next trend. The great thing about trends is that they can be as small as selling a $.05 piece of rubber for a $1.00, or as large as multi-million dollar gambles on the next generation diet trend. Trends offer great opportunity for those people who are willing to stay ahead of the curve and have the tenacity to act when they see an opportunity. The unfortunate thing about pure profit plays is that they border with get rich quick schemes and scam artists. It almost goes without saying that you have to be very cautious if you are making big gambles in speculative areas.

I would like to close this chapter with some more tangible advice for spotting trends. Pure profit plays can be hard to be on top of, but there are some resources out there to help out. The internet has paved the way for trend information to be spread at the click of a mouse. Websites such as Trendspotting.com, Springwise.com and Trendhunter.com have made it easier for us to stay abreast of upcoming trends. The sites feature trend watchers around the globe who report back to the websites what they see emerging out in the marketplace. By reading and identifying sites such as these, the average consumer can be one step ahead of the competition. Also, key industry players and influencers are now spilling their opinions and insights on blogs on a daily basis. Reading what they have to say and considering their insights for the months and years ahead can be beneficial to plotting out when your next opportunity might arise. Finally, early adopters and first movers in an industry usually congregate months or years before the mainstream public is aware of upcoming trends. Whether it is a website, a blog or an online community, figure out where the trendsetters in your industry are congregating. These people can be a wealth of information about what is to come in the near future.

The key for someone looking for a pure profit play is to stay informed. People who are constantly reading and searching out knowledge tend to be much "luckier" than those who sit back and wait for the light to go on. Read books. Read Magazines. Be on the lookout for gaps to exploit. Figure out what knowledge or information you have that keeps you ahead of the curve in your target industries. Speculating on a pure profit play in the stock market, real estate market or something as simple as plastic wrist bands can be a good first foray into the world of business for many novice entrepreneurs. The barriers to entry are often low and you can limit your exposure to risk as you please. Pure profit plays are not meant to produce your income for the next 40 years. They are something you can do on the side and something to get your feet wet in the world of business. Use the ideas in this chapter to identify them, react quickly and get out. Stringing along a series of pure profit opportunities can produce a nice side income for those individuals willing to invest the time to stay ahead of the curve.

Chapter 29:
Base Hit Businesses

"Our originality shows itself most strikingly not in what we wholly originate but in what we do with that which we borrow from others."
- Eric Hoffer

The idea of entrepreneurship is often stereotyped to make it seem like it must involve ground breaking ideas, charismatic risk takers and access to millions of dollars in venture capital. However, most aspiring entrepreneurs have few or none of these at their disposal. So what about the rest of us? It wouldn't suffice to give up on our dreams of owning our own business. The idea of the "base hit business" plays to new and aspiring entrepreneurs as sort of an offshoot of entrepreneurship. It involves buying something that already exists and building on it. It is like a starter guitar or your first children's book. Before you can master Shakespeare or jam with Led Zeppelin, you take smaller steps. You learn gradually and you move on to bigger and better things. The base hit business is an interesting take on how a person can achieve self employment without necessarily starting from scratch. It was brought to my attention by my entrepreneurship professor Michael Camp. If you are a new entrepreneur your skill set is limited. You have a working knowledge of only a few specific industries. You may not be ready to or have the requisite skills to identify, build and exploit opportunities from the ground up. It might also be the case that you just do not want to. The base hit business is about purchasing the start-up process. This type of new venture creation is based on the idea that your first business might not be a Bill Gates smash into left field, but about purchasing and building an established business to get warmed up for your next time around.

The base hit business is an extreme form of hiring people who are strong where you are weak. In this case you are weak in the ability to start your own ground-up venture, for whatever reason. In essence, base hit businesses are about hiring a whole company. You are buying the start-up process, a revenue stream, established relationships, et cetera. You purchase a company to gain your first steps into self employment. Sure, it's not as glamorous as having your face plastered across Forbes Magazine as a pioneer, but at the same time it is not as risky as the majority of start-ups that take a nose dive each year. You are talented enough to run your own

organization. You know you have the ability. Some of us are just
not prepared or yet skilled enough to start everything from ground
zero. Your background has only prepared you for handling certain
aspects of the business as opposed to the whole. If you have minimal
experience or minimal funds to build an entirely new infrastructure,
this could be a good way to get out of the gates. You buy a base
hit. It's not the home run that you will eventually get to but it's
something. It's autonomy and it's self employment. It's you calling
the shots and gaining the necessary skills that will allow you to
succeed on larger levels down the road.

Every day in the United States businesses are going up for
sale. For whatever reason, business owners are exiting. Whether
it be for retirement, failing finances or just an exit strategy, owners
are looking to sell. You can see hundreds of them at sites such as
Mergernetwork.com. There are more than you would ever realize in
your local region and state. If we use the idea of the base hit business,
we can gain a new perspective on how people can start down the path
of entrepreneurship by purchasing their autonomy.

What the base hit business does for you is that it allows you
to build off of something that is established. It is an eerie thought to
go deep in debt and risk financial trouble knowing full well that it
may be years before you turn a profit when you start from scratch.
Whether you change the business that you purchase completely or
not at all, you are buying the start-up process. It is already in place.
This type of business can be beneficial because you can buy what
you do not know. Variables such as your competive advantage,
customers and manufacturing processes are well defined. You also
have the benefit of known inputs and a history of their outputs. If
the business has a revenue stream then you are buying that revenue
stream. The nice thing about a revenue stream is that you know
what you have available to spend on yourself, your employees and
expanding the business. When you look at something that is proven
and has a track record, banks, investors and you yourself are more
confident in pumping more money into the business. You can use it
as leverage to expand the firm. You have a tangible, proven stream
to which to secure more financing. Buying all of these tangible and
intangible assets gives you an advantage with things that start-ups are
not privy to. With that being said, your first step is to start identifying
opportunities, starting as usual with the businesses you are passionate
about in life.

When you figure out what type of businesses you might be

interested in, then you have your starting point. As with purchasing anything else in life, you then need to figure out what you can afford and what type of risk level you are open to. With base hit businesses you still have many of the strategic options to consider. You could purchase a thriving business that is expensive but a safe bet. On the other hand you could also purchase a business that is in shambles and revive it. The market is similar to the real estate industry. Are you going to purchase a revamped rental house that will take years to pay back or will you purchase the condemned house with an ideal location on the cheap and flip it?

One of the best opportunities in the world of base hit businesses is the ability to insert knowledge. Thousands upon thousands of small time firms are doing business the same way they did 20 years ago just because it works. Many of them are outdated and lost a sense of purpose and direction long ago. That is where you can come in. For instance, the mom and pop coffee store down the street may have never heard of the word logistics, supply chain or marketing. They just had a business. It may have had the same owners for 40 years who rarely kept inventory and never thought about competitive advantage. Often times you see businesses that might have been someone's hobby, made enough money to let them live comfortably, but that was completely a mess by today's standards. They had a loyal following but outdated organization methods, little concept of branding and no way of forecasting sales. Someone who knew even base line ideas of what it takes to manage inventories, supply chains and forecast demand could turn a slow bleeder into a decent income. With the onslaught of retiring baby boomers, there are going to be thousands upon thousands of businesses for sale in the coming years. Many of them are local, marginally profitable and outdated in their methods. You have the opportunity to identify these types of businesses and employ up to date knowledge and tactics to turn them around or expand them. Having a specialty or working knowledge of an industry allows you to see businesses that are in need of your expertise. It is about locating and taking the first steps to acquiring those assets. It is recognizing that 80% of companies are in their maturity stages and due for an overhaul.

Another use of the base hit business is to enter markets you see expanding elsewhere in the nation. If you recognize a particular type of business doing well and rapidly expanding in one part of the country you can emulate their success in your area. Say for instance that you saw Chipotle having wild success peddling burritos in the Southwest, then maybe you look to buy a small chain of marginally profitable burrito joints in your area. You emulate Chipotle, change things up, turn things around and start an expansion plan. It is going to take a long time for the original innovators to reach your area. By that time you will be firmly planted in the marketplace. At worst you set yourself up to be bought out. At best you can be a competitor or maybe even more successful than the original place you were emulating. Base hit businesses are the easy way to get started. They give you the advantage of knowing what you are walking into. You know their strengths and weaknesses. You know if they lack the skills that you could bring to the table. You know what type of position they are in for expansion. They offer a level of security while maintaining the flexibility to behave like start-ups. I do not think that this idea is too complex, so I don't feel the need to further explain it. Make the effort now to start looking and researching opportunities. Your first business may only be a few mouse clicks away.

Looking back at the quote at the beginning of this chapter, I think it is important to emphasize Hoffer's idea that it is not always about the ideas that we come up with from scratch that are important. Entrepreneurship and originality are often about how we build on what is available to us. We can create entirely new ventures and concepts by putting a spin on firms that already exist. While base hit businesses might not be what we traditionally think of as entrepreneurial ventures, it doesn't matter. It is about what we do with the opportunities available to us and how we can build on them. It is about gaining autonomy and building our skill set as entrepreneurs. I will leave you with one last quote that almost made the beginning of the chapter and I think it sums things up nicely. William Ralphe Inge put it quite succinctly by saying; "What is originality?... Undetected Plagiarism."

Chapter 30:
Copy Cats

"Out in the sun, some painters are lined up. The first is copying nature, the second is copying the first, the third is copying the second... You see the sequence."

- Paul Gauguin

If you've ever sat through a basic economics course then the idea of the copy cat should make a lot of sense to you. This is not the most glamorous form of entrepreneurship, but none the less it can be rewarding and highly profitable. The idea is simple. A market is created by the original entrepreneur by introducing a product, service or a mix of the two. Once the idea is out there and people are consuming the product, this invites competition. The first mover position that the original entrepreneur held is now going to be challenged by rival firms. This competition should drive down the price, eliminate waste and overall create a more competitive atmosphere. This is normal and good because it ensures that a monopoly will not exist. It should also ensure that the consumer will benefit from this competition. Rivals come in to trim out costs of the business model and innovate ways to improve the product. Theoretically, consumers will be receiving more value with multiple competitors than they would have otherwise. The element of introducing competition is where you could come in. Being a copy cat can be a launching pad for your next big idea.

If you are struggling to think of that original idea, if you have yet to be blindsided by a bolt of genius, this area of entrepreneurship may be right for you. The concept is basic. You are copying a successful business idea and becoming a competitor. If you are passionate about an idea that already exists, there is no reason why you cannot use the idea to create your own venture. This is especially true if you think you could improve on the idea. The competitor firm that you create will not be a carbon copy. Each person that undertakes a venture will put their own spin on an idea and shape it differently than his or her predecessors. You are taking the same set of inputs and rearranging them in new ways. Maybe it is only a slightly new entity but that is not the point. Whatever you create will be shaped over time by your own deviations from the original idea and the deviations that the market requires you take. The real aim is not simply to copy an idea verbatim and does not have to be plagiaristic. Each competitor that enters a market will have to have their own solutions to suit customers' needs. The aim of copying is to create a catalyst to starting your own entrepreneurial career. In many cases you will be smarter than the people who run the original firm anyway. You won't be watching them to see what the next move is, you will be creating the next move. Your entrance as a competitor will enhance the competitiveness of the industry and push everyone to figure out how to best suit the target consumers.

The idea of being a copy cat often has a bad connotation in our society. Ripping off something exactly the same as the original probably should. However, using an idea as a launching pad should not. Throughout history man has copied from nature and other men to bring about original inventions. As Gauguin points out in the quote at the beginning of this chapter, the first original ideas were copied from nature. Ever since then man has been copying from other men to get to the point where we are today. Copying teaches the individual and is essential in most things that we learn to do in life. It is after you are successful at imitating that you can start applying your own original ideas to the base you have formed. In any event you are not here to please the idealists or the academic world. You are here to create a living for yourself and a living that you have been looking forward to for a long time. In that respect you can't be worried about doing what you've always wanted to do just because someone else enjoys it as well. If the market demands more supply of a product or service than the current suppliers can provide, then there is a demand for people like you to start a venture. If existing organizations aren't living up to consumer expectations, then there is room for your innovation. Not everyone can be the first to do something. Even if someone is first, it usually doesn't mean that they are the best. We would not have artists around today if Leonardo and Michelangelo could satisfy every art enthusiast's needs and desires. And yet most every art student has copied, learned from or been influenced in some way by their works.

The idea of being a competitor to something that already exists can be equally as profitable and rewarding as launching something you dreamed up on your own. Think of Sam Walton. Sam Walton wasn't the first retailer. He wasn't the first person to realize the value of low prices. Wal-Mart was started decades after many other leading grocery chains and department stores. Sam Walton simply did what he loved to do. The key is that Sam Walton did it better.

He improved upon the idea of retailing. He spent hours upon hours dissecting the industry and copying from competitors who did certain aspects of retailing better than Walton could have ever dreamed up on his own. There are very few industries, if any, where there is only one competitor. There are even fewer industries where the original innovator is still at the top of their industry. Many great entrepreneurs have come from taking a base concept and improving upon it. Many great entrepreneurs have made a lot of money doing this. This style of new venture creation is common. It can still be entrepreneurial because you are innovating and building on concepts. You are still taking on the risk associated with a new business and rearranging inputs. It is said that the key to entrepreneurship is adding value. Could you be a carbon copy of an organization and be profitable? Yes. Would I call it entrepreneurial? Not necessarily. However, any improvements and any rearranging of inputs to produce a better outcome and a better end product is absolutely entrepreneurial. It may not be as glamorous, but you may not be the fallen first mover either.

We don't have to dive very deep into how you are going to start using this source. It is as self explanatory as it gets. Find some job or market that you are passionate about, become a competitor and improve on the value proposition. Seriously. It's that basic. You've been waiting around all your life for a big AHA! moment. Well, what if in the mean time you start something just because it is what you want to do with your life. Chances are most of you are in a job that provides you with income but not satisfaction. Most of you are ready to risk the entrepreneurial plunge but do not know where to start. Nothing is stopping you from taking it except yourself. You are probably driven by the security of your job or the lack of risk you have by being an employee. If you can't get over that hump now, how will you do it in the future? If you cannot risk to do something that you are passionate about and good at, how will you react when your AHA! presents itself with some wild business idea? You'll dismiss that opportunity as easily as you have dismissed this one. Think about it for just a second. You know you are more talented than other people who are doing what you dream of. You know you have the passion. You know you have the drive. As Seth Godin put it, "Actually, you don't have to quit right now. You could just decide to quit right now." By this I believe he means that you will quit when your venture is planned and ready to launch. Decide to quit now. Start building a business plan. Decide to copy an idea of something you have always wanted to do and run with it.

You do not have to be a genius to recognize profitable markets and great ideas. Every day you encounter businesses that you know are winners. Every day you see industries and companies in the nascent stages of markets that excite you. Every day you see people innovating and participating in industries that you would rather be a part of than the one you are in. If you are struggling to find your gold mine idea, why not start something you enjoy in the mean time? Until you find it, you have to do something. You can either be an employee in an industry in which you are bored, or you can take the initiative to do something you enjoy until you figure out how to change the world. The possibilities of copying ideas for a launching pad are endless. Figure out your passions. Decide to make a change. Identify a business and use their idea as a launching pad to your own personal success.

Recurring Techniques

Chapter 31:
Asking Questions

"It is important that students bring a certain ragamuffin barefoot irreverence to their studies; they are not here to worship what is known, but to question it."

- Jacob Bronowski

Entrepreneurs are often viewed as agents of change in the business world. The ideas they employ break down industry standards and establish new ways of satisfying consumer needs. The only way the entrepreneur can do this is to question the fundamental reasons why things are done the way they are in the first place. Albert Einstein was once quoted as saying, "I have no special gift. I am only passionately curious." This quote is indicative of the mindset that an entrepreneur must have. In order for innovation to be an active pursuit in your daily life you need to have a passionate curiosity about the world around you. You need to constantly be questioning the realm of established thought and practice. Asking questions begins to form the causal chain of how things operate in the business world. You start to answer the "whys" and the "hows" of business. Only once you understand it will you have the ability to change it. People fail to become innovators in their lifetime because they fail to question the legitimacy of the way things currently get done. They are consumed by established thought. Asking questions is a way to break free of that mindset. Constantly questioning the world around you introduces catalysts for ideas day in and day out. Asking questions is just another piece of the mindset to take innovation from an AHA! moment to a process of daily active pursuit.

Think for a moment about the child who asks the question "why" numerous times in a row. What does this accomplish? For the child, asking the same question over and over again brings out slightly more information each time they ask it. After the nth time, they start to understand. They have gotten closer to the core of the issue and to satisfying their curiosity. Posing questions about business and the business world works in much the same way. If you never question the solutions that exist, why would you ever be inclined to change them? On the surface of things, all of the markets of the world are solving their problems in one capacity or another. If people fail to question these solutions our insight ceases to advance. New ideas would become obsolete. If the perception is that there is no need to change, then things will not change. Luckily, we do have entrepreneurs like you. We do have people who are willing to question the world. The key here is getting you over the hump to entrepreneurship. Most of you are still hoping to become entrepreneurs and have not actually taken the plunge. You are still lumped with the majority of followers even if your mind is entrepreneurially leaning. Part of finding your great idea has to be a dedication to changing the way you think about innovating. Your old mindset didn't get you over the hump. You bought this book because you were looking for a new solution to the current state of your entrepreneurial career. One of the key elements has to do with what Einstein was referring to. You have to be "passionately curious." You have to believe that the passive approach to entrepreneurship rarely works. You have to believe that it doesn't take special talent to change the world, it just takes dedication. Dedication to furthering your entrepreneurial mind. Dedication to actively search for innovative ideas. Dedication to actively questioning the world around you each and every day. Doing so will lead you to new understandings, new ideas and new theories for change. Accept nothing as permanent, question everything.

Much like anything else I talk about in this book, asking questions is not just a random act. Asking questions should be a focused task. You should take the sources from this book, or maybe some you have in your own mind, and pose them as questions on industries that you encounter or interact with on a daily basis. For instance; Where is there "waste" in my industry? Why does it occur? Could we reduce the waste? Could we profit from the waste? What other industry could use our by-products? You could also look at it from an outsider's perspective looking in. An advertising man might realize that he can be very profitable using other industries captive audiences, or their "waste." Understanding that a captive audience could make him money, he might ask: What industries have captive audiences? How could I benefit from their boredom? What do people do in a captive situation? What can I do to entertain them while profiting? Is there a service that I could do to reduce the waste created? What other industries are exploiting captive audiences and how? Anyway, you get the point. Constant questioning helps you to understand where the opportunities lie or where they can be created. At the very least, it gets your mind going about business and creating opportunities. You are much more likely to generate novel solutions to problems if you are actively seeking out where they lie and how things operate. Do not sit and wait to have an AHA! Do not simply hope that an opportunity will come across your desk. Go out and pose the questions. Try to find answers. Try to uncover where opportunities exist. Try to figure out how opportunities can be created. Question everything and the worst that can happen is that you will have a much better grasp on how business is transacted.

So from here on out, if you really want to be an entrepreneur, use constant questioning as a method to transform your approach to entrepreneurship from a passive desire into an active pursuit. Asking questions and posing thoughts about industry is one way to keep your creative mind going. Even if your answers to the questions turn out to be wildly absurd, you can at least work backwards to solutions that you might be able to enact today as a partial solution. Asking questions is about forming the causal chain in your head. Much like the child who asks "why" thirty times, you begin to really narrow down how businesses operate, how each party profits and how the industry is structured. Then if you question why it has to be that way and what other alternative solutions exist, you begin to get innovative answers. Question everything and question it often. Do this in an active pursuit of your opportunity.

Chapter 32:
Mix and Match

"One of the advantages to being disorderly is that one is constantly making exciting discoveries."[70]

- A.A. Milne

One of the beautiful things about business and entrepreneurship is that there isn't a rule book. Beyond operating within the confines of what is legal, a process to creating successful ventures and creating wealth does not exist. If such a process existed then everyone would do it and it would no longer work. It would be the next innovator to branch out and redefine the rules of the process who would actually become wealthy. So in the spirit of redefining things, you should take the same approach to this book. I've mentioned some sources and probably left a lot out. Like the title suggests, this is only a starting point. There will never be a definite road to creating viable business ideas, but you can lay the foundation. You can loosely define where you are going. You have been exposed to some new stimuli and you have brought some of your own to the table. There are no rules. Maybe the magic formula for your future successful venture is going to be a gob of chapter 5, a pinch of chapter 8 and then that article you read today in the paper that sort of sounds like an idea you had when you were in the shower. That's the beauty of it, everyone's formula and everyone's process is going to be different. Mix, match and blend your ideas and theories. The crucial part is that you make a conscious effort to actively pursue innovation.

---

70 Thank you to www.creatingminds.org for their database of excellent quotations, from which I have found many of the quotes for the openings of my chapters

Chapter 33:
Projection

"I don't want people to copy Matisse or Picasso, although it is entirely proper to admit their influence."
- Stuart Davis

Take a visit to a bookstore and look around at all of the books that are written to teach you how to be successful in one area of your life or another. You can learn the habits of highly successful investors, CEOs, religious figures and the like. You can learn to draw, play an instrument or cook. Successful people are trying to help others and teach them how to use a system for success. Much like a franchise that creates a system for business success, how-to books are written so that the average person can emulate certain accomplishments in their life. Utilizing the tactics of successful people is a way of "projecting" that system on your life or business. Much in the same way that a how-to book works, creating innovative ideas has a lot to do with projecting ideas, stimuli, concepts and theories from some walk of business onto other segments of the business world. Projecting is a tactic that replicates successful systems from various influences onto your own industry of choice. Projecting a source of innovation, a business model or any stimuli onto a new area in life can have profound effects on your thought process. Projection begs the question, why not? If this concept or stimuli worked in one industry, why not this one over here? Entrepreneurs who take the opportunity to project success in one area onto another have the chance to see how to employ entirely unique successes elsewhere in business.

Look around the business world and you will begin to realize how often concepts are projected, copied and ripped off from other areas of thought. Take for instance the low-cost, no-frills approach to a business model. Aldi's is a low-cost, no-frills grocery chain. Southwest is a low-cost, no-frills airline. Easy Cruise is a low-cost, no-frills cruise line. The examples abound and in entirely unique industries. Low-cost, no-frills is a concept that has proven to be very successful in many different industries. That is what is at the heart of projecting. You can take any idea source that you come across and start projecting the concept, theory or stimuli onto other areas of life and other industries. It doesn't have to be strictly business models either. Designers are constantly borrowing from nature or anatomy to influence their product designs. Marketers are constantly projecting tactics of successful PR and advertising onto their own situations. Entrepreneurs are constantly transplanting the technology of one industry into use in completely unique industries. Throughout business, people are using stimuli from other places to affect and change their own industries. You are not simply copying or stealing ideas, you are being influenced by ideas. Any time that you emulate a concept, you will build on the concept or stimuli and morph it into something that is completely your own. That is what this tactic is all about, projecting successful influences into completely new and unique areas of business.

Using projection as a source of innovation is first and foremost about feeding your mind with relevant stimuli. We have talked about this before, but if you have forgotten, refer back to the chapter called "flash-in-the-pan innovation." Chances are you will not innovate if you never step beyond your current state of mind or thinking. It is about bringing the catalysts of change to the mind. It is about inundating your business brain with useful new stimuli so that you have an arsenal of sources to project.

The second step to using projection as a source of innovation is keeping with the mindset that innovation can be an active pursuit. When you are submitting yourself to relevant stimuli and even when you are processing random stimuli, you have to be consciously aware of what is going on in your mind. Every day you should be considering how the stimuli you are collecting fit into the overall picture. The passive mind will read but not consider the implications. The passive mind will take in randomness but not wonder about its usefulness. It is one thing to recognize stimuli as unique, new or interesting and to keep going about your daily life. It is an entirely different process to capture those moments when you find something unique, new or useful. You need to develop the discipline to step back and analyze when the sparks are flying around in your head. Instead of identifying something as cool and proceeding with your day, you should write it down. You should step back and consider the implications that new idea brings. You should be questioning what makes it new, unique or interesting and where else it applies in the world. The moments when your brain starts going a million miles a minute are the times you need to capture and register those thoughts for future use.

The third step in using projection as a source is doing the footwork on the ideas you have captured. Like I said above, it is not

enough to simply recognize interesting stimuli. You should hold on
to these thoughts and analyze them. The successful entrepreneurs
will then begin the real work of submitting the new stimuli to
scrutiny. Where would this be useful? What implications does it
have for this or that industry? Which of the sources of innovation
could I use to exploit this? What are the implications for the future?
Too often we view the innovation process as being a lightning bolt of
genius. In actuality, many innovations and inventions took years of
thinking and gestation until they came to be useful. In those moments
that you were able to capture a unique stimulus, you only started the
process of innovation. From there on out it is about developing the
idea. It is about considering the implications and figuring out how
to exploit those implications. Entrepreneurs who can capture the
moments when new stimuli are rearranging their views of the world
have the ability to exploit the stimuli that caused it and possibly
change the world.

A final thought on projection that I have, is that while new
stimuli are a great catalyst, you can create your own catalyst when
stimuli are in short supply. Going along with the last chapter,
questioning can lead you to become successful at projecting. A
great way to get your brain going is to start questioning the things
you believe to be true. It doesn't even have to go that deep. Start
questioning why things are done the way they are in the world
around you. Start questioning why certain businesses are successful.
What makes them successful? What business approach are they
using? What makes them unique? Not only will that allow you to
see new solutions in current markets but it will also allow you to
further understand where else insights from other firms can have
implications. Questioning and trying to understand industries
around you allow you to see similarities across industries that will
lead you to projecting successful methods in new areas.

People emulate other successful people. Businesses emulate
other successful businesses. Entrepreneurs can emulate success in
completely new areas and create something entirely unique. Just
think of all the businesses that are touted as the next Southwest of
an industry, or the next Net-Jets of whatever. It's no different than
a band being touted as the next Beatles. People are already prone to
project. For one, it is easier to copy success than invent it. Secondly,
along with the chapter on combining alternatives, projecting is a
way to take two concepts that are not foreign or completely new and
merge them into something that is. Projecting business concepts

and other stimuli is no different than copying your favorite author's writing style or your favorite painter's painting style, but offering up content of your own. You take a concept, you project it onto your own situation (or one that you are imagining) and you morph and build upon it until you have something that is your own unique solution.

Projecting is a simple concept. You can use it daily whenever you have idle time. Doing little things like projecting stimuli when you have idle time is one way of taking innovation from a passive thought to an active pursuit. It can be fun and it will undoubtedly expand your business mind. The main point of the chapter is developing a mindset that will allow you to utilize the idea of projection. So when you are going about your daily routine digesting stimuli, be aware of what it is that is running through your mind. Capture the unique thoughts and begin to consider what it is that the stimuli entail. If you understand the task that is being accomplished by a product, service or stimuli, you can extrapolate outward to think through other industries that have a similar task to be done. Consider projection daily and valuable insights will ensue.

Chapter 34:
What We "Know"

"Confusion is a word we have invented for an order which is not yet invented."

- Henry Miller

To get to the point where I feel I could articulate what we "know" about generating business ideas and the sources of innovation, I have had to sift through a plethora of sources. From Schumpeter and Drucker to Clayton Christensen and the Blue Ocean Strategy, each person along the way has added something new to the mix. In the process of adding something new, each person organized and presented their ideas in the way that made sense to them. Not only did their own categories and ideas overlap themselves in many cases, they also overlapped the ideas of the people who came before them. The resulting body of knowledge, albeit helpful, complicates the problem of innovation because each person expanded on the nuances of the topic in their own way. For the person trying to figure out a logical whole of what innovation is and how to capture it, it makes the task that much trickier. What I would like to do in this chapter is look at where we have been and what we know from the people who first started to articulate innovation and its sources. In the process I would like to fit together the pieces. I want to consolidate the fragmented information into something that comes closer to a logical whole. The idea behind this is to give innovation practitioners a common starting point and basis of understanding to help wrap our minds around this tricky topic.

What I want you to realize in this chapter is how innovation thinking has evolved over the course of time. It is not that the art of creating a business idea has changed that much over the years. People still create firms today for many of the same reasons they created firms in years past. What has changed is how we understand the process and our ideas on how innovation can be replicated. While the list of innovative thinkers I am going to use as examples is nowhere near exhaustive, I believe their thinking marked some of the major advances in the understanding of innovation. What I want you to see is the progression from a vague level of understanding in the past to a more specific level that we are approaching in the present day. Then, with the addition of the information in this book, I want you to understand where I believe innovation thinking is going in the future. What we "know" is constantly changing and being added to every day. Entrepreneurs who are ahead of the curve in understanding where we are headed for the future are going to be the ones who are empowered with ideas for getting us there.

Before anyone started researching innovation and writing about it, people were creating businesses all the time. We hadn't established a plethora of theories on the topic or methods for innovation, we just had instinctive ideas about how to make money. The easiest way to do that was to create ideas and create businesses based on the needs that other humans were willing to pay us to fulfill. We observed them in our daily activities, and we observed them in the daily activities of others. People were essentially locating unmet consumer needs to fill and consumer problems to solve. Locating business opportunities via these sources in the past explains a lot of the reason that the idea of locating problems is still such a prevalent notion today. This tactic predates any other method that people talk about. It was what we did instinctively, even if it didn't have a title at the time. In my opinion, that is how our understanding of creating business ideas began. We recognized where we could get paid for fulfilling the needs of others. It was and still is the most basic and relevant way to think about finding ideas for businesses. However, even with its relevance to the present day, the idea of locating "unmet needs" of consumers is no less vague than it used to be. Understanding the concept of uncovering consumer problems doesn't get you much closer to actually creating a business idea. It is from the vagueness of "unmet needs" and consumer "problems" that I believe the rest of innovation thinking has evolved. What are the problems? What are the needs? What are the inspirations? How do we uncover them?

When business minds finally did start exploring the topic of innovation, we began to take this vague concept of "unmet needs" a little further. We started looking to understand and categorize the things happening in the world of innovation. I think that the work of Joseph Schumpeter well represents where innovation thinking headed next. What Schumpeter did was to begin to describe the end products of innovative ideas. He showed us the end products that are created when people establish firms around the needs of humans. Schumpeter said that innovation produced the following; new processes, new products, new knowledge, new markets and new business models.71, 72 His work didn't describe "how-to" create these end products, but at least now we had a beginning and an end to work with. In doing this he gave the rest of us the chance to extrapolate on what was happening in the middle. Once we are able to identify the results of ideas and innovation, we can then trace back the "how" and "what" that occurred so that we can replicate it. We can see the methods and the ideas employed by entrepreneurs and gain a sense of what type of business moves it takes to create innovative products and services. Schumpeter was one of the first people to start to lay the groundwork for the current thinking on the topic of entrepreneurship and innovation. He was one of the first thinkers to take us a step beyond creating businesses just on our observations of what other humans need.

So after we understood the vague beginnings of entrepreneurship, and the vague end products of entrepreneurship, the next logical step was to start filling in the gaps between the two. Again, while there were many great thinkers between Schumpeter and the author I am about to mention, I think his work is a good summarization of where the topic of innovation went next. That man was Peter Drucker. Drucker's main contribution to the topic of innovation, from his famous book Innovation and Entrepreneurship, is that the sources of innovation could be systematically identified and managed for. Instead of just recognizing the end results of innovation and classifying them, he thought that you could actively identify the sources that create these end products and search them out. He thought that you could actively manage for them and recognize them. It was an effort to try and fill in the gap left open by Schumpter. Drucker said the sources of innovation are; the unexpected (random occurrences), incongruities (problems), process needs, industry and market structure needs, changes in demographics, changes in perception and new knowledge.73 While some of Drucker's sources echo Schumpeter's, the interesting part is how he spins them to show us how to use them and not just categorize them. The "how" that Drucker seems to hit on is about exploiting change. In the book he talks about recognizing changing perceptions, changing

71 Schumpeter, Joseph. The Theory of Economic Development. Cambridge, MA: Harvard Business School Press, 1934.

72 Class Discussion on: Baretto, H., "The Entrepreneur Throughout the History of Economic Thought," pp. 4-44

73 Drucker, Peter. Innovation and Entrepreneurship. New York, NY: HarperCollins Publishers Inc., 1993 pp.35.

demographics, changing market structure, changing processes, et cetera. By understanding where change was occurring out in the marketplace, we can see where we also had to change our solutions to adapt. By instructing us to look for change and where to look for it, Drucker established some powerful ideas about how we think about innovation. He showed us there are identifiable sources of innovation that people use to create innovative ideas and businesses. This idea was a major shift from where we had been before his work. Drucker's ideas were influential in the evolution of innovation thinking by starting to show us how to replicate business idea inspiration.

While I thought that Drucker's work was interesting and pioneering, it left me wanting more, and his ideas about innovation still felt too vague for practical application. In my mind, it wasn't until very recently that innovation thinking finally took the turn towards a level of detailed analysis that is practical for everyday use. The next person I want to talk about, Clayton Christensen, was the first person whom I felt approached a level of detail fit for applying the sources of innovation to the real world. Christensen said to find sources of opportunity you target; non-consumers, low end and least desirable consumers, markets the competition is likely to ignore, the bases of competition and the places money will be in the future.[74] Christensen added new layers of detail to some of the sources Drucker and Schumpeter presented. He also started breaking down the categories into specific subcategories of focus. I think the most important thing to note is the elimination of the vagueness involved with his ideas. Christensen could have said that in order to innovate you use "demographics" and "changes in demographics" as a source. Instead, he dives into the specifics that underlie innovation within demographics. Here is where to look, demographics. These are the specific customer bases to analyze, non-consumers and least desirable consumers. Then in his series of books on innovators, he goes on to detail why you should focus on these specific segments. He looks at daily motivations, barriers to consumption, attitudes, et cetera. While I cannot replicate how he accomplished all of this in one paragraph, the point I want to make is that Christensen showed us why his specific sources of innovation work. His thoughts are a turning point to what I think any innovator wants to understand. We don't just want categories and vague notions about the topic. We want to know where to look, how to exploit it and why it works. I think Christensen

---

74 Generalized from across Clayton Christensen's three books: The Innovator's Dilemma, The Innovator's Solution, and Seeing What's Next

was one of the first people to approach this level of analysis. The more we can grasp how and why something works, the closer we get to a "systematic" approach that Drucker described. Clayton Christensen set the stage for where we should continue heading with the level of detail on the topic, but he only offered it in a few areas. What I think is coming is generating the same level of detail across all of the sources of innovation. Understanding the intricacies of each area of innovation is key to mastering them. Christensen's style is indicative of what we need to know to truly grasp this difficult topic.

The final major shift in innovation thinking that I believe has occurred brings us to the present day. The recent work by W. Chan Kim and Renee Mauborgne titled the <u>Blue Ocean Strategy</u> is a great example of what I am going to talk about. You see, when we first started thinking about innovation, people like Schumpeter were interested in categorizing it. Then, with the work done by Drucker, we shifted to recognizing opportunities and uncovering opportunities. However, what I think most entrepreneurship programs are teaching and what the <u>Blue Ocean Strategy</u> talks about, is a shift away from recognizing and uncovering ideas to actually using sources of innovation to *create* ideas. Instead of believing that there are a finite number of opportunities for businesses out there for us to uncover, the focus of current innovation thinking is that we can use the sources of innovation to create an infinite number of opportunities. Instead of racking your brain to uncover hidden ideas or researching markets to death looking for opportunities, the focus is put on the individual to use their creative skills to create beyond what exists. By creating beyond what currently exists, we invent entirely new markets. I recommend reading the <u>Blue Ocean Strategy</u> to truly understand the point but, as a preview, here are some of the areas Kim and Mauborgne suggest targeting as sources; look across alternative industries, look across strategic consumer groups, look across the buyer chain, look across complementary products and services, look across functional and emotional consumer groups and look across time.75 The <u>Blue Ocean Strategy</u> did exactly what Christensen did by adding new levels of sub-category detail to Shumpeter and Drucker's sources. However, and more importantly, they put their focus on creating ideas, not just uncovering them. The key words you will notice in their sources are "looking across"

---

75 Kim, W. Chan and Renee Mauborgne. <u>Blue Ocean Strategy</u>. "How to create uncontested market space and make the competition irrelevant." Boston, MA: Harvard Business School Press, 2005, pp. 49-79.

categories instead of "looking within" them. When you look to uncover opportunities within a specific demographic or consumer group, you are trying to look for ideas within the framework of what already exists. By looking across consumer groups, you start to see what is possible beyond what exists. By framing the issue of innovation in this manner you can see a whole new way to look at the topic. This idea is one of the more recent additions to the topic and one that I feel will propel our thoughts on innovation into the future.

So now that you've had your innovation history lesson, I would like to tell you what I feel my book has added to all of this, and then I will finish out the chapter with where we go for the future. The first thing I want to point out is the "point of view" I have presented throughout the book. While I was studying innovation and sifting through all of the material on the topic, I realized that few people framed their ideas in a way that was specifically catered to entrepreneurs starting from scratch. Schumpeter shaped his idea in terms of economics. Drucker was a management writer. Christensen was showing established companies how not to get beat by disruptive ideas. With the exception of the <u>Blue Ocean Strategy</u>, I don't think any of the aforementioned thinkers had individual entrepreneurs at the heart of their focus. With this book I sought to change that. I believe that each chapter is specifically catered to show you how the sources of innovation are relevant to you, the entrepreneur, and not some existing company. I think that I have created something that entrepreneurs can specifically reference and think through as opposed to trying to decipher relevance out of advice to established firms.

Secondly, as I pointed out, it wasn't until Clayton Christensen and the <u>Blue Ocean Strategy</u> came along that I felt innovation thinking had reached a point of practical application. While these two sources were invaluable in their own right, they only touched on a few of the categories of innovation sources that Drucker and Schumpeter showed us. With this book I feel that I have incorporated their thoughts, but also expanded into areas that have been left untouched. I tried to replicate the depth of understanding and detail across all of the sources of innovation, not just one or two. What I believe I have accomplished is a more complete picture. I hope to have provided you with the level of detail you need across all of the sources of innovation to start applying the ideas today.

Finally, I think I have accomplished consolidation. The innovation thinkers I mentioned in this chapter are some of the highlights of the sources I have sifted through over the years in order to wrap my mind around innovation. While you could have amassed the same sources over time, I am glad you did not have to. First, it took an awful lot of time to sift through it. Secondly, with all of the highlights I have extracted, there was a lot of extra information. What I was really seeking over the years was the where, how and why of innovation. While I did manage to find it, most of it was buried. Most of the above highlights were buried in books that focused on managers or economics. In any given book I might have found 6 pages of extremely valuable insights, but I had to sift through the other 290 pages to get it. To complicate matters, most of the ways the sources were presented were in different contexts. A lot of times it was about spinning ideas and extracting observations of value to entrepreneurs, who were not the original intended audience. Finally, I am glad you didn't have to amass this on your own because of the extensive amount of overlap. As I mentioned before, there are enough nuances and overlap in the world of innovation as it is to try and wrap your mind around it. While sorting through these sources gives you many insights, at the same time it complicates things. Each individual who writes on the topic presents their own categorizations, their own nuances and their own ideas of how to make sense of it all. While these categorizations made sense individually for each book, the overall picture only became more cloudy.

The last thing I want to do is to give you the snapshot of where I believe we are with innovation. The goal here is to provide you with an overall picture of the topic and point out some of the key people who have contributed to the topic. To do this I have created a chart that shows the evolution of innovation thinking from its vague beginnings to where we are at in the present day. The chart is broken down into all the areas that are responsible for innovation and how we came to know about them. Here is how I believe the current picture shakes out:

The Evolution of Innovation Thinking from Vague to Specific

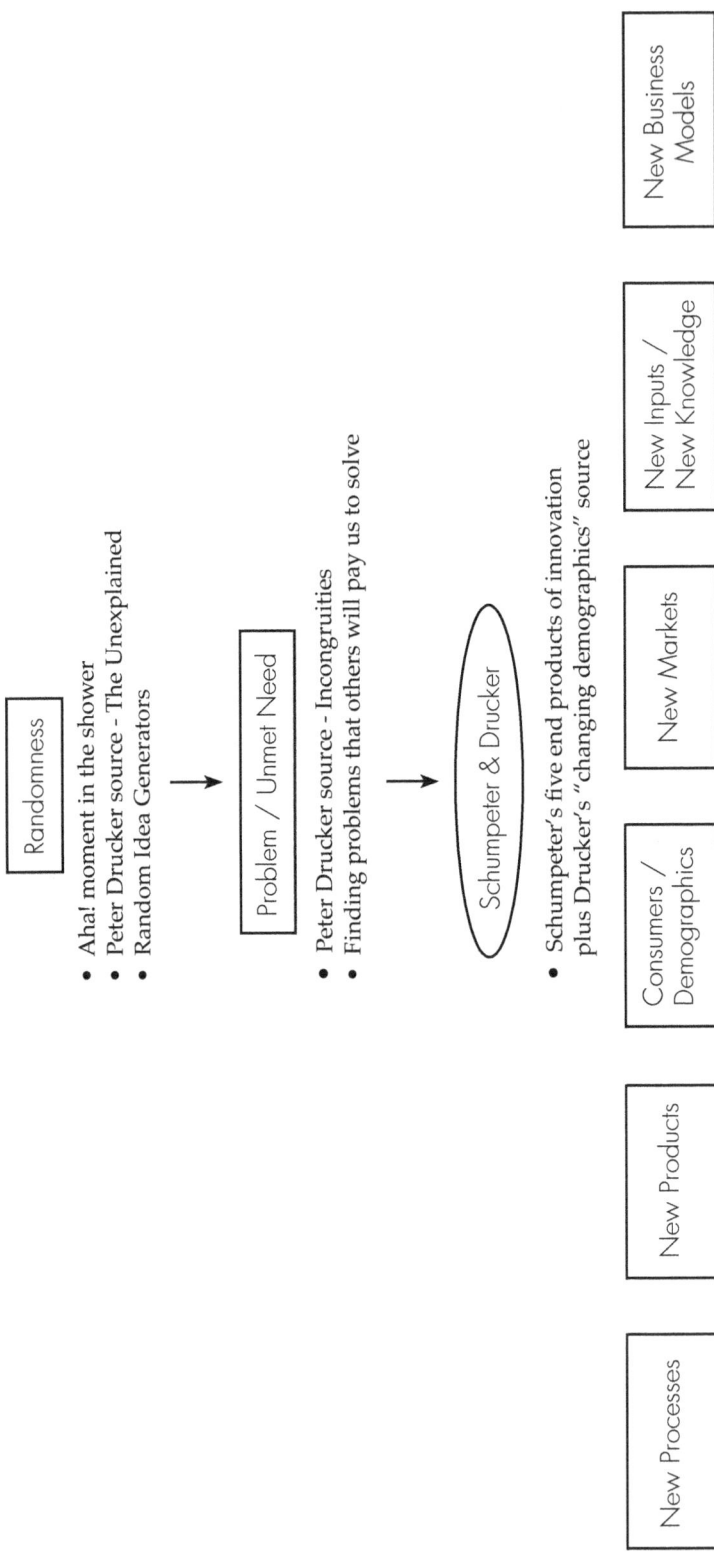

Randomness

- Aha! moment in the shower
- Peter Drucker source - The Unexplained
- Random Idea Generators

Problem / Unmet Need

- Peter Drucker source - Incongruities
- Finding problems that others will pay us to solve

Schumpeter & Drucker

- Schumpeter's five end products of innovation plus Drucker's "changing demographics" source

| New Processes | New Products | Consumers / Demographics | New Markets | New Inputs / New Knowledge | New Business Models |

Clayton Christensen

- Articulated actionable frameworks for how to identify and exploit opportunities in:

Consumers / Demographics

- Compete against non-consumption
- Go after low-end, least attractive consumers

New Markets

- Markets the competition ignores
- Change the bases of competition
- Go to where money will be in the future

Blue Ocean Strategy

- Authors W. Chan Kim and Renee Mauborgne
- Focus on specific strategies for:

New Products

- Look across complementary products
- Look at functional and emotional appeal

Consumers / Demographics

- Look across strategic consumer groups
- Look across the buyer chain

New Markets

- Look across alternative industries

As you can see with the above charts, the overall picture of innovation is starting to take shape. We began with problems and random inspiration, progressed to the categories of end products and finally are getting into the specifics of how innovation works. However, the chart is not complete. As you can see, there are still some categories that have not been explored. Pieces of the puzzle are missing. My hope is that the information in this book has added to the overall picture and brought us a step closer to a full picture. While the chart will never be void of the forces of randomness and unexplained creative injection, the more we know about innovation, the closer we can come to understanding it. Below is the next layer of the chart as I envision it after this book, in addition to what has already been laid out for us.

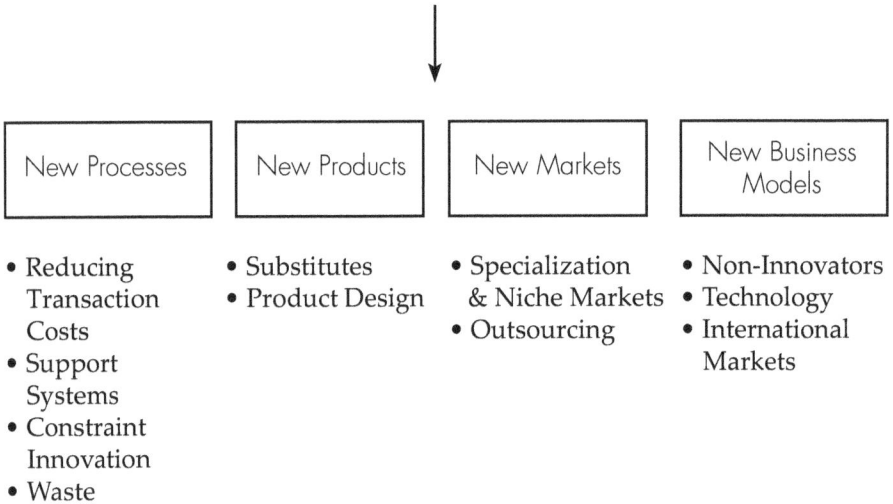

New Processes	New Products	New Markets	New Business Models
• Reducing Transaction Costs • Support Systems • Constraint Innovation • Waste	• Substitutes • Product Design	• Specialization & Niche Markets • Outsourcing	• Non-Innovators • Technology • International Markets

As we move into the future of innovation thinking, I think you will continue to see the level of detail increase in our theories and methods. I believe that it will become increasingly important to get more specific about where to look for ideas, how to exploit ideas and to describe exactly why each source works. Likewise, I believe the shift from "recognizing" opportunity to "creating" opportunity will continue to play a key role in our development on the topic. By continuing to tighten our grasp on the subject we will continue to evolve from a "fuzzy art" that we discussed at the beginning of the book. Ideally, we will turn the corner to where innovation is closer to a science than an art form. Finally, I know full well that I have overlooked some sources and probably incorrectly dealt with a few others by your understanding. For that reason I hope that you will turn around and add to what I have laid out in this book. By continuing the discussion and constantly re-evaluating what we "know," we will continue to progress with our understanding of this difficult topic.

Chapter 35:
Motivation

"I must create a system, or be enslav'd by another man's."
- William Blake

There are many cliché, go-get-em quotes that I could have chosen to kick off this chapter on motivation. However, I chose a quote that is much more simplistic in its ways. Not a threat and not an adrenaline pumping speech to end all speeches. I chose this quote because it is straightforward and cuts to the chase. You have two options in our society; start living your dreams or be controlled by someone else's. Whether you achieve your dreams as a business owner, or as an employee, you only have one shot at it, one life, one chance. The chance to live out your desires is fleeting. It's that simple.

As you look at the current state of the global economy, it is hard to make a case to be anything but your own boss. Labor is being outsourced to the third world, layoffs abound and technology consistently absolves the need for actual people. What you should come to realize, if you haven't already, is that the United States is a knowledge based economy. There's no turning back. People in our society are going to have to learn to accept that this is the case. Our prosperity for the future is dependent on the quality of our ideas and the quality of our innovations. The question will then become whether you are motivated enough by this knowledge to do something about it. The people who prosper in the future are going to be the people with ideas.

If you have read the book through to this point, I am going to make the assumption that you do indeed fashion yourself an "idea person." I am also going to assume that the bulk of you would not want your life to be defined by the tasks you completed working for someone else. But the truth is that few people ever accomplish the visions of entrepreneurial greatness that they have for themselves. Had you told me five years ago that after college I would move to another city in Ohio, become an average sales man at a freight brokerage and settle into relative obscurity, I would have laughed at you. However, that is where I found myself after college. If my career epitaph read; Dan – "the finest freight broker in Cincinnati," I would be extremely disappointed. Yet few people take action to break out of a similar fate. All of the things that we aspire to become and all the dreams we have for a legacy are rarely manifested in our daily lives. That is why the time is now to take stock of your aspirations. Understand the direction you want to start heading with your career and how you want to be remembered. The time is now to start striving for those things every day.

So the question you have to ask yourself is; what are you currently doing to get over the hump to being an entrepreneur? If you are reading this in hopes that it will miraculously bring you great new ideas and riches without hard work or dedication, I think you will be extremely disappointed. When you get home after work or after school, what are you doing? Are you choosing to unwind in front of the TV or are you digesting business books? Are you mindlessly surfing the internet or are you generating ideas for new ventures? I'm not trying to push the idea of working around the clock or guilt you into doing work. Innovation is the same as any other avenue of work. You get out of it what you put in. It is just something to consider. How bad do you want the benefits of becoming your own boss? I do not even consider myself to be in a position to judge your efforts. Writing a book as an act of entrepreneurship is not even close to what I envision for my future undertakings. However, I now know what it means to dedicate myself to something on top of my career obligations. I wrote this book partially while I was a full-time college student and partially while I was working ten to eleven hour days as an entry-level account executive. It meant taking two to three hours of free time that I had at night and dedicating it to writing. It is about sacrificing some free time now in hopes that it will multiply my free time and money for the future. Noone will judge you if you do nothing. No boss will come down on you for not setting aside the time. The question is how bad do you want it? How much are you willing to invest now for a lifestyle change tomorrow?

It is imperative to start translating your passive desires into action. I have consumed many hours over the past three years trying to find time to write this book. I found my passion; something that drives me. Each day that I wake up and go to a job that I am not passionate about, I get a pit in my stomach. Knowing that I have to go to work to strive for someone else's dream for ten hours of my day drives me insane. I am driven to get out of the rat race. I am driven by the chance to do what I love. I am driven by entrepreneurship and ideas. The questions you have to ask yourself as you wrap up this book are; Am I driven enough to go down the road of entrepreneurship? Does the desire eat at me each and every day?

The majority of people who read this book will put off becoming an entrepreneur, secretly happy not to face the risk that comes with the territory. It might be you, sitting back reading, telling yourself that you could do it, but just not today. While you may think it is outright fear or monetary loss that motivates people not to start something, that isn't entirely true. That is probably not what is holding you back. Seth Godin said it well, "We don't choose to be remarkable because we're worried about criticism. We hesitate to create innovative movies, launch new human-resource initiatives, design a menu that makes diners take notice, or give an audacious sermon because we're worried, deep down, that someone will hate it and call us on it." Many aspiring entrepreneurs can deal with the fear element of independence. Innumerable people have braved financial disaster, yet that doesn't seem to be the thing that really scares them. The true test is whether you can get over the fear of a bruised ego. It is a difficult thing to face the critics out there and find out that the vision of yourself is not quite what you thought it was. Will you put off your dreams, or will you take action today?

Forty hours a week, forty years a career, the latent potential in so many people is wasted. When it's all said and done, if you choose to stay in a job that you are not passionate about, approximately 80,000 hours of your life will be spent chasing someone else's dreams. The amount of time you could end up wasting working for the goals of others is staggering. Many people cannot understand my dissatisfaction for life as an employee. They don't get it. They like the security, they are satisfied with a consistent paycheck. The thing that bugs me is the unused potential. It is time to realize that you have what it takes to launch a venture. You have the skills, you have the abilities. With this book, hopefully now you have the tools to uncover an idea worth pursuing. It is my sincere hope that each of you will exploit this knowledge to pursue your dreams. Thank you for picking up the book, good luck, start now...

Acknowledgments

Thank you to my father, Ron Roberts, whose grammatical knowledge far exceeds my own, and who made time to read, reread and correct each chapter in this book. He was my go-to editor for this project and for that, I am extremely grateful.

Thank you to my wife, Ali Roberts, who has been a source of encouragement from day one of this project and is completely understanding when I stay up until 4 a.m. writing.

Thank you to Judy Halverstadt who took the time to proofread the chapters of this book and whose objective insights helped strengthen the final product.

Thank you to Roger Blackwell who has been an inspiration to me as a professor and who took the time to read the book when so many people said "no."

Thank you to my mother, Terri Roberts, and my grandma, Evelyn Stacey, who took it upon themselves to read the book and for subsequently giving me the best reviews to date.

Thank you to Scott Berkun, author of the <u>Myths of Innovation</u>, who took the time to respond to all of my e-mails and helped guide me through the publishing process. Check out all of his books at www.scottberkun.com, I highly recommend them.

Thank you to my brother, Ben Roberts, for catching the errors we missed in the initial editing rounds, and for helping me polish the final product. It is my hope that he won't be able to find any errors in his own acknowledgment blurb.

Index

About the Author

About Dan Roberts

Dan received a BSBA from the Ohio State University with a dual degree in Marketing and Logistics. After working in sales, and having worked at multiple start-ups, Dan set out to start a venture of his own. He is currently working on a new e-book platform for backlit displays, while pursuing his masters degree. Dan is enrolled in the Masters of Design program at the Illinois Institute of Technology, Institute of Design, where he continues to immerse himself in understanding innovation and new venture creation. Dan lives in Chicago with his wife, Ali, and their Great Dane, Roxi.

Visit www.innovatorssourcebook.com for the most up to date information on Dan and this book.

www.ingramcontent.com/pod-product-compliance
Lightning Source LLC
Chambersburg PA
CBHW022054210326
41519CB00054B/383